Expert Oracle GoldenGate

Ben Prusinski
Steve Phillips
Richard Chung

Expert Oracle GoldenGate

ISBN-13 (pbk): 978-1-4302-3566-8

ISBN-13 (electronic): 978-1-4302-3567-5

Distributed to the book trade worldwide by Springer Science+Business Media, LLC., 233 Spring Street, 6th Floor, New York, NY 10013. Phone 1-800-SPRINGER, fax (201) 348-4505, e-mail orders-ny@springer-sbm.com, or visit www.springeronline.com.

For information on translations, please e-mail rights@apress.com, or visit www.apress.com.

Apress and friends of ED books may be purchased in bulk for academic, corporate, or promotional use. eBook versions and licenses are also available for most titles. For more information, reference our Special Bulk Sales–eBook Licensing web page at www.apress.com/bulk-sales.

The source code for this book is available to readers at www.apress.com. You will need to answer questions pertaining to this book in order to successfully download the code.

Contents at a Glance

Contents

About the Authors

■Ben Prusinski is an Oracle Certified Professional (OCP) and database architect with more than 14 years of experience with Oracle data warehouse and Oracle E-Business applications. As a corporate database consultant, Ben has provided services to dozens of Fortune 500 clients. He is an internationally recognized expert in Oracle high availability, performance tuning, database security, and ERP implementations. As a top Oracle expert, Ben received the prestigious Oracle ACE award in 2009 in recognition of his contributions to the Oracle community. As an Oracle GoldenGate Certified Associate, Ben is a popular speaker at major conferences such as Oracle OpenWorld, Chilean Oracle User Group (CLOUG) in Latin America, the Independent Oracle Users Group (IOUG), and Oracle Collaborate OAUG (Oracle Applications User Group). In addition to Oracle consulting for clients, Ben regularly updates his Oracle blog at http://oracle-magician.blogspot.com with the latest database technology tips and information to share with the Oracle community. Ben is also a polyglot, being fluent in Spanish, French, Korean, and English, and he enjoys traveling to exotic places. In his free time, Ben enjoys racing in autocross events, golf, martial arts, reading, and cooking.

■Steve Phillips is an Information Systems Architect with Hewlett-Packard Enterprise Services and has been working with computer databases for over twenty-five years. Steve is an Oracle Certified Professional and a past presenter at Oracle Openworld and IOUG. Steve holds a master's degree in Information Systems from the University of Texas at Dallas and currently lives in Plano, Texas. In his spare time Steve enjoys playing tennis, coaching baseball, and watching sports.

■Richard Chung has 19 years of hands-on experiences in all aspect of IT environments. His recent focus is in the Business Intelligence area, such as Reporting, ETL, and Data architecture. Richard is Principal of BI and System Architect at Starwood Hotels and Resorts, where he built the current data warehouse and reporting applications; he also wrote highly sophisticated search engines and designed the ETL to populate the active data warehouse with near real-time data. Golden Gate is used to synchronize the critical business data around different cities in the US. Before Starwood, he worked at a startup dot.com, JP Morgan Chase, and Ernst & Young.

About the Technical Reviewer

Arup Nanda (arup@proligence.com) has been an Oracle DBA for over 16 years, working on all aspects of Oracle database management from modeling to performance tuning. He has co-authored four books, published 300 articles, and presented over 150 sessions at various technology conferences; he also received DBA of the Year in 2003 from Oracle. He is an Oracle ACE Director, a frequent blogger (arup.blogspot.com), and a member of the Oak Table Network and the SELECT Journal Editorial Board. He lives in Danbury, CT.

Acknowledgments

I would like to thank my co-authors, Steve and Richard, for collaborating with me on this book. Without their help, this book would not have been possible. I also would like to thank our technical reviewer, Arup Nanda, for his insight and time reviewing our book to ensure technical accuracy and quality. In addition, my thanks go out to the team at Apress including Jonathan and Anita for their support and insight. Last but not least, I want to dedicate this book to all fellow Oracle professionals who work hard in the trenches to support mission critical systems running Oracle and GoldenGate. My appreciation extends to my parents for motivating me to become a writer in addition to many pursuits recommended.

Ben Prusinski

I would like to thank my wife Kathy and sons Ryan and Jacob for their support, encouragement, and understanding while I took time away to write this book.

I'd also like to thank Jonathan Gennick, Anita Castro, Douglas Pundick, and everyone at Apress for their help and advice in writing the book. Also thanks to my colleague Sherri Trojan for her kind support and encouragement.

Finally, thanks to my friend Chris Giametta who got me started on this adventure.

Steve Phillips

My thanks to the technical review team, especially Arup Nanda, who gave me the opportunity to write this book and provided many good suggestions and comments in his technical review.

Also, thanks to the team at Apress for continuously working with me to improve this book.

Richard Chung

CHAPTER 1

Introduction

Oracle Corporation acquired GoldenGate in 2009 as part of future strategy to implement advanced replication technologies within the product suite of data warehousing and real-time transaction management. Before the advent of Oracle GoldenGate technology, data replication was performed using Oracle Streams and third-party replication solutions such as Quest SharePlex. This chapter discusses various types of database replication methods along with the techniques used by each method, to illustrate how Oracle GoldenGate came to be the logical conclusion for the current and future real-time-based data-transaction replication technology with Oracle database systems.

Before the chapter discusses the foundations of Oracle GoldenGate software, a brief history of time is warranted for how database replication technologies came into existence. Before GoldenGate software, data transactions were replicated across networks with simple file transfers via the File Transfer Protocol (FTP) for nonrelational databases. With the popularity of the UNIX operating system and the advent of client-server computing, data replication was implemented with Oracle basic and advanced replication software in version 8 of Oracle database software.

Distributed Processing and Replication

Oracle release 5 introduced distributed processing queries in the form of database links. Database links provided the ability to issue SQL queries across networks and were the first real attempt to achieve a replication solution. Figure 1-1 shows how connectivity is established between the source and target database environments via database links.

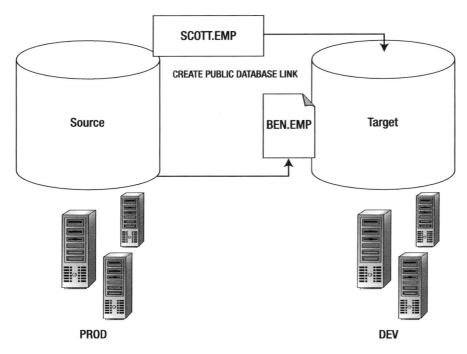

Figure 1-1. Database links for distributed systems

The next step in the march of data replication came into existence with Oracle release 8, which enabled database professionals to set up log-based and trigger-based replication solutions.

Oracle Basic Replication

Oracle basic replication existed in two flavors: log-based and trigger-based. With log-based replication, you had to set up snapshot schemas and database links between the source and target database environments. Data was mined from the online redo logs in Oracle to capture the changes and propagate them across the network to send data transactions from the source database (a.k.a. master) to the target database. The schemas had be configured on both the source and target databases as well. In addition, refresh groups had to be configured in order to keep the target environments in sync with the primary master database on the source system. As you can imagine, the design was crude and prone to errors in terms of establishing a successful conflict-resolution system of checks and balances.

Oracle Advanced Replication

Oracle advanced replication added more robust features to allow for multimaster replication with multiple environments, as well as trigger-based methods to establish conflict-resolution rulesets to improve data reliability and to maintain accurate data synchronization between source and target systems. Nonetheless, advanced replication had its shortcomings and flaws, particularly the lack of support for certain data types and failures that occurred with trigger-based conflict handling. Also, latency was an issue in terms of keeping the target systems in sync with source master systems.

Figure 1-2 shows how conflict resolution was set up for basic and advanced replication in Oracle environments.

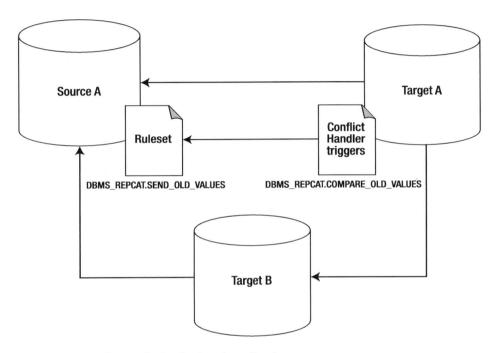

Figure 1-2. Conflict resolution for Oracle replication

Oracle Streams Replication

Oracle introduced the Streams replication solution in release 9.2. Streams resolved the deficiencies that plagued the older replication methods in previous releases. It established a log-based replication solution that mined the online redo logs for committed transactions on the source to move the data to downstream target systems. In addition, Streams introduced new background processes to maintain the communication and operations of replication activities within the Oracle ecosystem.

Streams further enhanced previous Oracle replication technologies by using advanced queuing technology to boost replication performance. *Oracle Advanced Queuing* (AQ) is a technology designed with Streams and other Oracle technologies including Oracle Data Guard logical databases. AQ provides a system of enqueues and dequeues based on the subscriber and publisher model for database communication. It allows for robust messaging and processing of data transactions between source and target environments and lies at the heart of Oracle Streams processing.

Further details on how to set up and manage AQ are available online in the Oracle reference documentation at `http://tahiti.oracle.com`.

Evolution and Oracle GoldenGate

With the advent of true log-based replication technology from Oracle and Quest SharePlex, advances made it possible to finally perform real-time-based replication. Out of the mainframe and midsize systems world arose a shining star in the development of real-time transaction-based replication techniques. In the late 1980s, a small software company called GoldenGate came up with a different method of replicating data between database platforms. Until GoldenGate, replication of data across platforms and vendors was problematic at best. For example, complex software development was required to harness the power of Oracle to non-Oracle database environments via the Pro-C and software development APIs to allow transactions to be moved between environments.

GoldenGate invented a powerful and novel way to replicate data while achieving high performance with accuracy. Instead of using different formats, GoldenGate implements a uniform format to perform data replication operations by using a command prompt interface called GoldenGate Software Command Interface (GGSCI). GGSCI commands are used to create new GoldenGate replication configurations as well as to perform administration tasks. Committed transactions are stored in flat files called *trail files* on the filesystem for both the source and target systems. In addition, GoldenGate provides a seamless and transparent method to perform real-time data replication with guaranteed transaction consistency between heterogeneous environments without the need to develop complex routines or code.

Summary

This introduction has provided a history lesson on how database replication technologies evolved into the robust Oracle GoldenGate technologies. The next chapter shows you how to install the Oracle GoldenGate product suite.

CHAPTER 2

Installation

The installation process for Oracle GoldenGate is simple compared to most of the other product suites available from the Oracle Fusion Middleware family, of which GoldenGate is a part. In this chapter, we will provide you with details on how to prepare for and perform a complete installation of the following Oracle GoldenGate products:

- Oracle GoldenGate 11g
- Oracle GoldenGate Director 11g
- Oracle GoldenGate Veridata 11g

Downloading the Software

For Oracle GoldenGate 11g, the first step is to obtain the software either online or from DVD media. Depending on the bandwidth of your Internet connection, we recommend that current Oracle customers download the Oracle GoldenGate software from Oracle E-Delivery at http://edelivery. oracle.com. For educational and non-business learning purposes, Oracle provides the software free for download from the Oracle Technology Network (OTN) at http://otn.oracle.com. In this chapter, we will download the Oracle GoldenGate software from http://edelivery.oracle.com.

We recommend that you register for a free account at the OTN site to receive access to free software for trial purposes, white papers, and webcasts from Oracle. We also advise that you review the documentation for Oracle GoldenGate online at http://download.oracle.com/docs/cd/E18101_01/ index.htm to become familiar with the particular release notes for your database and operating system platform. While the primary focus of this chapter will concentrate on Oracle database platform with GoldenGate, we will provide coverage for additional RDBMS platforms such as MySQL and Teradata in terms of the installation requirements and guidelines for Oracle GoldenGate.

Downloading from Oracle E-Delivery

Let's get started and download the Oracle GoldenGate software from edelivery.oracle.com. If you prefer to download from OTN, then skip ahead to the next section where we show the use of http://otn.oracle.com.

Figure 2-1 shows the results from a media search. Choose the platform and version for your operating system to obtain the Oracle GoldenGate software as shown in the figure. Choose Oracle Fusion Middleware as your platform. Then specify your operating system.

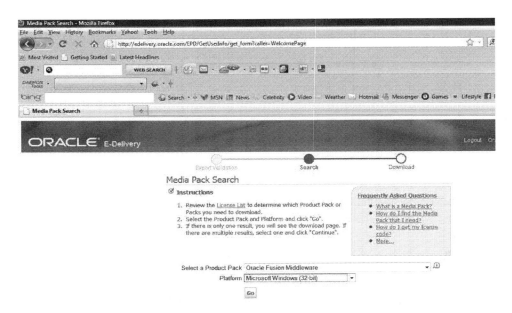

Figure 2-1. E-Delivery website for obtaining Oracle Goldengate software

Once you have chosen the correct platform, you will see choices for the Oracle GoldenGate software to download, as shown in Figure 2-2.

Results

Select	Description	Release ▽	Part Number	Updated	# Parts / Size
○	Oracle Fusion Middleware 11g Media Pack for Microsoft Windows (32-bit)	11.1.1.3.0	B55383-24	DEC-17-2010	102 / 57G
○	Oracle GoldenGate Application Adapters 11.1.1.0.0 for JMS and Flat File Media Pack	11.1.1.0.0	B59968-01	AUG-12-2010	16 / 433M
◉	Oracle GoldenGate on Oracle v11.1.1.0.0 Media Pack for Microsoft Windows (32-bit)	11.1.1.0.0	B59978-01	AUG-12-2010	2 / 20M
○	Oracle GoldenGate for Non Oracle Database v11.1.1.0.0 Media Pack for Microsoft Windows (32-bit)	11.1.1.0.0	B60580-02	NOV-04-2010	6 / 62M
○	Management Pack for Oracle GoldenGate 11.1.1.0.0 Media Pack	11.1.1.0.0	B60816-01	OCT-21-2010	4 / 583M
○	Oracle GoldenGate for Non Oracle Database (10.4.0) Media Pack for Microsoft Windows (32-bit)	10.4.0.0.0	B57525-04	JUL-15-2010	5 / 43M
○	Oracle® Application Server 10g Release 3 (10.1.3) Media Pack for Microsoft Windows	10.1.3.0.0	B36235-45	NOV-01-2010	155 / 55G

Figure 2-2. Downloading Oracle Goldengate software from E-Delivery

Once you have chosen the correct Oracle Goldengate software—which, in our example, is for the Windows platform—you will be taken to the download screen shown in Figure 2-3.

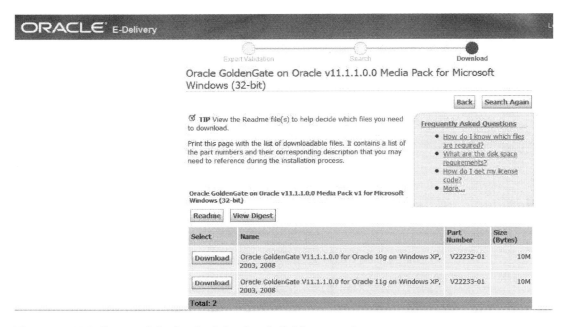

Figure 2-3. E-Delivery website for obtaining Oracle Goldengate software

At this point, we recommend that you review the readme file and release notes to best prepare for the installation process. By investing a couple of hours, you will avoid most errors during the installation and configuration phase .

Since we will use Oracle 11g with Goldengate, we will choose the Oracle GoldenGate 11.1.1.0.0 for Oracle 11g on Windows XP software to download.

▪ **Note** If you plan to use Oracle GoldenGate with Linux, you will also need to download the Oracle GoldenGate software for the Linux platform.

Figure 2-4 provides the readme instructions for the Oracle GoldenGate media pack.

Readme for Media Pack B59977-01

Print   Close

INSTRUCTIONS:

This table can help you determine what downloads are required to run your licenses. Additional Oracle product downloads for which you have not purchased a license may be used only on a trial basis. Please identify the license and options you would like to run and correspond them to the files that you have to download. For information on the licenses that you have ordered, please refer to your Oracle® Ordering Document. For information on trial license terms and conditions, please refer to the E-Delivery Trial License Agreement.

See Legend below on details regarding table notation.

X Required downloads in order to run the associated products and licenses

D Documentation

C Download the Client software if applicable.

O Optional download.

Oracle GoldenGate on Oracle v11.1.1.0.0 Media Pack for Microsoft Windows (32-bit)

zip files included in the Media Pack	Oracle Licenses and Options
	Oracle GoldenGate
Oracle GoldenGate V11.1.1.0.0 for Oracle 10g on Windows XP, 2003, 2008	O (select based on DB version and OS)
Oracle GoldenGate V11.1.1.0.0 for Oracle 11g on Windows XP, 2003, 2008	O (select based on DB version and OS)

LEGEND:

See Legend below on details regarding table notation.

X Required downloads in order to run the associated products and licenses

D Documentation

C Download the Client software if applicable.

O Optional download.

Figure 2-4. README instructions for Oracle Goldengate software installation

Downloading from OTN

For readers who want to set up a test demo environment to learn how to work with Oracle Goldengate software, we recommend that you download the software from OTN as shown below at http://otn.oracle.com. Oracle allows you to use the GoldenGate software for educational purposes without a purchased license. For use within a production environment, you would download the software from the E-Delivery site. Figure 2-5 shows the Oracle Technology Network (OTN) website.

Figure 2-5. OTN website

Since OTN is a massive site, it can be a little tricky to find where you actually obtain the Oracle Goldengate software. Never fear—when you scroll down the page you will find the list of documentation and software on the left side. Figure 2-6 shows the links to software downloads and documentation available for Oracle GoldenGate.

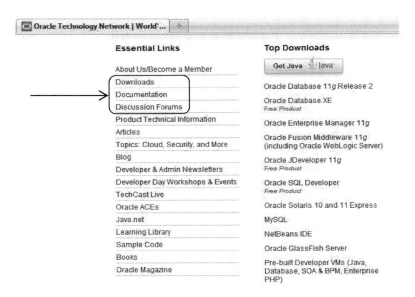

Figure 2-6. Download Oracle Goldengate from OTN website

Once you click the Downloads link from OTN, you will be shown the list of Oracle software for download shown in Figure 2-7.

Figure 2-7. Download Oracle Goldengate from OTN website

On the Software Downloads heading on the OTN website, you will need to accept the license agreement before downloading. Once you do so, you can download the Goldengate software for your platform to use on a trial educational and non-production basis. Be sure to navigate to the heading for Middleware software as shown in Figure 2-8 since Oracle classifies Goldengate as part of the Oracle Fusion Middleware product family.

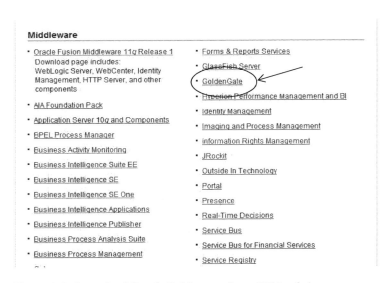

Figure 2-8. Download Oracle Goldengate from OTN website

Click the GoldenGate hyperlink and you can download all of the required software packages for Oracle Goldengate including Director and Veridata (Figure 2-9).

Figure 2-9. Download Oracle Goldengate from OTN website

Now that you understand how to obtain and download the Oracle Goldengate software and documentation, it's time for us to perform the installation and configuration for our test environments.

Understanding Your Environment

Before installing, you should have a good grasp of your target environment. For example, you may want to install both Linux and Windows for the Oracle 11g database environments. In Table 2-1, we show a test configuration that can be used for working with Oracle GoldenGate as a sandbox environment. We also recommend that you install the sample schemas included with Oracle 11g to have sample test data while working with GoldenGate. Our test platform will include the configuration in Table 2-1.

Table 2-1. Windows Test Environment for Oracle 11g GoldenGate for Homogeneous Replication

Environment	OS	Database	Software	Function
WIN11SRC	Windows XP	Oracle 11.2	Oracle 11g GoldenGate v11.1.1.0	Source System
WIN11TRG	Windows XP	Oracle 11.2	Oracle 11gGoldenGate v11.1.1.0	Target System
--	Windows XP	--	Oracle GoldenGate Director 11g	Oracle Goldengate Director Server and Client
--	Windows XP	--	Oracle 11g GoldenGate Veridata	Veridata

We will also use examples from the Linux platform in this book so you can follow along with either Windows, Linux, or both setups if you desire. Table 2-2 shows the test Linux configuration that will be used.

Table 2-2. Oracle Linux Test Environment for Oracle 11g GoldenGate

Environment	OS	Database	Software	Function
OL11SRC	Oracle Linux 5	Oracle 11.2	Oracle 11g GoldenGate v11.1.1.0	Source System
OL11TRG	Oracle Linux 5	Oracle 11.2	Oracle 11gGoldenGate v11.1.1.0	Target System
Director	Windows XP	--	Oracle GoldenGate Director 11g	Oracle Goldengate Director Server and Client
Veridata	Windows XP	--	Oracle 11g GoldenGate Veridata	Veridata

Table 2-3 shows the configuration that we'll use in our upcoming chapter on heterogeneous replication. The term "hetergenous" refers in this case to replication across database brands.

Table 2-3. Windows Test Environment for Oracle 11g GoldenGate for Homogeneous Replication

Environment	OS	Database	Software	Function
MYSQLS	Windows XP	MySQL 5.x	Oracle 11g GoldenGate v11.1.1.0	Source System (MySQL)
WIN11TRG	Windows XP	Oracle 11gR2	Oracle 11gGoldenGate v11.1.1.0	Target System (Oracle)
WIN11SRC	Windows XP	Oracle 11gR2	Oracle GoldenGate v11.1.1.0	Source System (Oracle)
MSSQL2K8	Windows XP	Microsoft SQL Server 2008	Oracle 11g GoldenGate v11.1.1.0	Target System (SQL Server)

We recommend that you download the Oracle Goldengate 11g software for MySQL and Microsoft SQL Server platforms from either OTN or Oracle E-Delivery in preparation for the exercises we have planned in Chapter 6 on heterogeneous replication with Goldengate.

If you need the MySQL database software, you can download it from `www.mysql.com/downloads/enterprise/`. Microsoft SQL Server 2008 Personal Express Edition database software is available from `www.microsoft.com/express/Database/` or, alternatively, you can use the trial license version of Microsoft SQL Server 2008 Enterprise Edition to perform the exercises in this book. You can download a 180-day license for the trial version from `www.microsoft.com/sqlserver/2008/en/us/trial-software.aspx`.

Now let's take a voyage into the system and database prerequisites that must be performed before installing Oracle Goldengate software.

Reviewing the Install Instructions

The Oracle GoldenGate documentation provides a multitude of installation and configuration guides that are available from OTN at `www.oracle.com/technetwork/middleware/goldengate/documentation/index.html`. Figure 2-10 shows a list of guides that explain the installation, configuration, and support procedures for Oracle Goldengate.

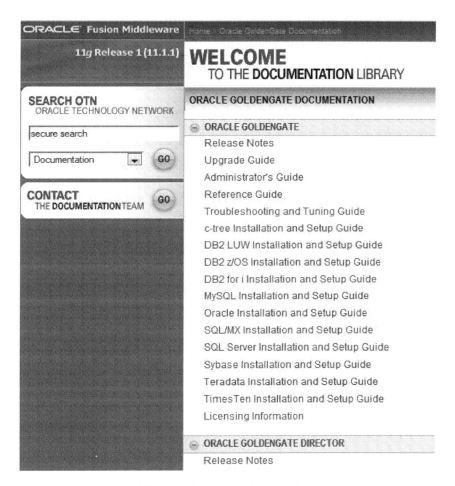

Figure 2-10. Oracle GoldenGate documentation repository

Based on your specific platform and infrastructure design, you will need to consult the appropriate guides shown above. As a first stop, we advise you to review all release notes to avoid potential issues in terms of errors before, during, and after the installation is completed. With each release for Oracle Goldengate software, new bugs are discovered and patches provided by the development team in time to address known issues.

▓ **Note** Always consult the Release Notes before you install Oracle Goldengate software.

Installing Goldengate

Before you install the Oracle Goldengate software for Windows and Linux platforms, be sure to verify that both the source and target Oracle database servers are online and available. This means that in addition to checking to ensure that these Oracle instances and databases are online, you need to also test network connectivity between both server hosts. If Goldengate cannot access the hosts via TCP/IP network connection, the software will not function correctly. You can use the ping network utility to check for network connectivity. In the event that a network timeout problem exists between the source and target environments, you will need to work with your network administrator to address this issue before installing the Oracle Goldengate software.

General System Requirements

The basic installation requirements using Oracle with Goldengate are standard across Windows, Linux, and UNIX platforms in terms of supported Oracle database versions, memory requirements, disk space allocation, network requirements, and operating-system support. We cover all of those areas in this section.

Database Server Versions

The following Oracle database versions are supported for Oracle 11g Goldengate:

- Oracle 9iR2 (9.2)

- Oracle 10gR1/R2 (10.1/10.2)

- Oracle 11gR1/R2 (11.1/11.2)

As of Oracle Goldengate 11g, both DML and DDL replication are supported for the above Oracle releases. Support for legacy versions of Oracle such as Oracle v7 and Oracle 8i is not provided. We recommend that you upgrade your database to Oracle 11g if you plan to implement Goldengate with your Oracle database environments.

Memory Requirements

At least between 25 and 55 Mb of RAM memory is required for each GoldenGate Replicat and Extract process. Oracle Goldengate supports up to 300 concurrent processes for Extract and Replicat per Goldengate instance.

As a rule of thumb, you will need to take into consideration that at least 1–2 Extract processes and multiple Replicat processes will be required in addition to manager processes for a basic Oracle Goldengate installation. The best way to assess total memory requirement is to run the GGSCI command to view the current report file and to examine the PROCESS AVAIL VM FROM OS (min) to determine if you have sufficient swap memory for your platform.

Next let's consider the disk requirements to install Oracle Goldengate.

Disk Space Requirements

Following are some things you should do to ensure having enough disk space to support your Goldengate replication needs:

- Allocate at least 50–150 MB of disk space for the Oracle GoldenGate software binaries.

- Allocate 40 MB of disk space per instance of Goldengate for working directories and files per server. For a basic configuration with Oracle Goldengate, you will need to allocate 40 MB on the source and 40 MB on the target system for a total requirement of 80 MB of disk space.

- Allocate sufficient disk space to temporary files to accommodate GoldenGate operations. By default, Goldengate stores temporary files in the dirtmp directory under the default installation directory. A good rule of thumb to use for temp file space is around 10 GB of disk space.

- Plan on at least 10 MB per trail file. As a rule of thumb, we recommend that you start with at least 1 GB of disk space allocated per system for trail files. Alternatively, use the following formula that Oracle provides to determine the amount of disk space to set aside:

  [log volume in one hour] x [number of hours downtime] x 0.4 = trail disk space.

  One way to calculate the total amount required for trail file space is by querying the V$ARCHIVED_LOG view from within the source Oracle database. The following query shows you how to do so:

  ```
  select trunc(COMPLETION_TIME),count(*)*100 size_in_MB
  from v$archived_log
  group by  trunc(COMPLETION_TIME);
  TRUNC(COM SIZE_IN_MB
  --------- ----------
  15-MAY-11        500
  ```

  Run tests after installing Goldengate to measure your specific transaction mix and load, and to gauge the total disk space required for trail files.

Network Requirements

Since Oracle Goldengate software operates between source and target systems over networks, you must configure TCP/IP networking to accommodate all hosts within DNS to include host names that will be included in the Oracle Goldengate infrastructure deployed. In the event of firewalls, hosts must be allowed to send and receive data for open ports that the manager, Extract, and Replicat processes require access to in order to send and receive data. This range of ports must be allocated for the Goldengate environments.

Also allocate ports for Goldengate manager, Extract, and Replicat processes. By default, manager uses port 7840. We recommend that you keep this port available. In addition, keep a record of ports allocated to Goldengate processes to avoid port conflicts.

Operating System Requirements

Following are some requirements when running under Windows:

- You must use the Administrator account to install the Oracle Goldengate software.

- You must Install the Microsoft Visual C ++ 2005 SP1 Redistributable Package. You must use SP1 for these libraries. You can obtain the correct version for your specific Windows platform at www.microsoft.com.

Under Linux or UNIX, you should do the following:

- Grant read and write privileges for the operating system (OS) account used to install the Oracle Goldengate software.

- Place the Oracle Goldengate software on a shared disk in a clustered environment, or on a shared clustered filesystem that all cluster nodes have access to.

- Install from an operating and database system account that has read/write access to Oracle database software, as well as to the Oracle online redo log files.

▓ **Note**   For Itanium you must install the vcredist_IA64.exe runtime library package which provides the mandatory Visual Studio DLL libraries required for running Oracle Goldengate on the Windows Itanium platform.

Requirements for Microsoft Windows Clustered Environments

Goldengate has some unique requirements that apply to Windows environments using Microsoft Clusters. Execute the following steps before performing your install:

1. As administrator privileged account, log on to one of the cluster nodes.

2. Select a drive that has resource membership within the same Microsoft Windows Cluster group.

3. Make sure that the disk group has cluster node ownership.

4. Place the Oracle Goldengate software on a shared drive accessible by all nodes in the cluster.

Installing Goldengate on Windows

Following is a complete run-through of a Goldengate install onto a Windows system. The process begins with downloading the software, continues through uncompressing the download file, and then moves into the install proper.

1. Download the Oracle 11g Goldengate software for Windows x86 platform.

2. Download and install the Microsoft Visual C++ 2005 SP1 Redistributable Package from http://microsoft.com as shown in Figure 2-11.

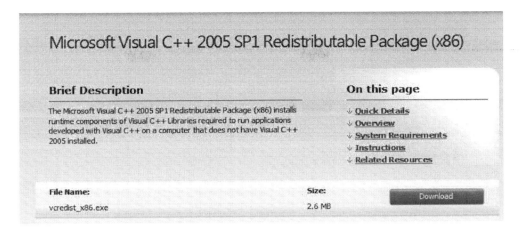

Figure 2-11. Microsoft Visual C++ package for Oracle GoldenGate installation on Windows platform

After you have downloaded the Microsoft Visual C++ package, save the file and then click the vcredist_x86.exe file, as shown in Figure 2-12.

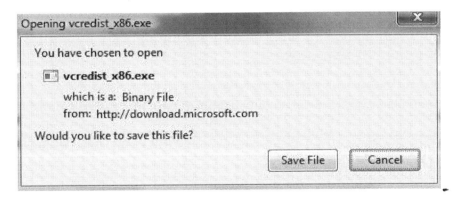

Figure 2-12. Installing the Microsoft Visuall C++ libraries

3. Create two new directories for the Oracle Goldengate software, one to be the source directory, and the other to be the target:

```
mkdir ggs_src
mkdir ggs_trgt
```

4. Using Winzip or your favorite extraction utility, extract the Oracle 11g Goldengate software to the C:\ggs_src directory on the source database server and to the C:\ggs_trgt directory to the target database server.

5. Execute the command `ggsci` on source and target:

    ```
    ggsci
    ```

6. Execute the command `CREATE SUBDIRS` on source and target:

    ```
    create subdirs
    ```

7. Finally, give the command `EXIT` to leave the ggsci environment to complete the installation process. Do this on both the source and the target lmachines.

Installing GoldenGate 11g on Linux and UNIX

We recommend that you have a basic understanding of Linux and UNIX commands before you undertake an installation for Oracle Goldengate on Linux and UNIX platforms. Basic syntax and knowledge of copy and archive commands such as `cp`, `mv`, `tar`, and `mkdir` are essential to function within this environment. Oracle ACE Director Arup Nanda has written an excellent tutorial series on Oracle Linux command mastery available online from OTN for Linux and UNIX novices and newbies at **www.oracle.com/technetwork/articles/linux/index.html**.

▓ **Note** Make sure that all system, network, and database requirements have been completed.

You will need to unzip the files for Linux and UNIX platforms by using the `tar` command. Once you have unzipped the files, run the `ggsci` command `CREATE SUBDIRS` as we performed previously for Windows.

Environment Settings for Oracle and Goldengate on Linux and UNIX

Since Linux and UNIX platforms use environment variables to configure software, you must set the ORACLE_HOME and ORACLE_SID environment variables. For multiple process groups with Extract and Replicat, you will need to configure the parameter files by adding `SETENV` as shown in the following syntax for the extract and replicat parameter files.

```
SETENV (ORACLE_HOME="<ORACLE_HOME directory path>")
SETENV (ORACLE_SID="<ORACLE_SID>")
```

If you have more than one Oracle database instance on a system with Extract and Replicat processes, you will need to issue a SETENV statement in the parameter file for each Extract and Replicat process group.

Following is a sample Extract parameter file:

```
EXTRACT ext1
SETENV (ORACLE_HOME="/oracle/ora11g/product")
SETENV (ORACLE_SID="ora11src")
```

```
USERID ggs, PASSWORD ggs
RMTHOST sdtarget
RMTTRAIL /d1/oracle/ggs/dirdat/rt
TABLE scott.emp;
```

For Windows servers that have multiple Oracle database instances, you can set the environment variable for ORACLE_HOME and ORACLE_SID by adding these settings to the registry for Windows. This can be performed by opening My Computer ➤ Settings ➤ Properties ➤ Advanced tab then Environment Variables and System Variables.

GoldenGate and Oracle RAC Considerations

Oracle RAC is certified by Oracle to support Goldengate software. However, you will need to keep the following things in mind when performing installation for Oracle Goldengate with RAC environments:

- All GoldenGate software binary and executable files, trail files, and log files should be on shared storage accessible by all cluster nodes.

- System clocks must be synchronized for all RAC nodes using the Goldengate software. You can set up the network time protocol (NTP) to ensure that cluster nodes are kept in sync. In addition you can use the Goldengate IOLATENCY option with the THREADOPTIONS parameter for Extract and Replicat parameter files.

Installing Goldengate for Microsoft SQL Server on Windows

The Oracle GoldenGate installation process for Microsoft SQL Server requires additional configuration setups to ensure that it functions successfully. The following versions of Microsoft SQL Server are supported with Oracle GoldenGate:

- SQL Server 2000

- SQL Server 2005

- SQL Server 2008

To verify that your specific Windows platform and MS SQL Server version is supported, you can check the certification matrix online at My Oracle Support (http://support.oracle.com).

Software for non-Oracle platforms can be obtained online from the E-Delivery site at http://edelivery.oracle.com.

Now that we have discussed the installation process for Oracle RDBMS with GoldenGate, we will discuss how to prepare other database platforms with Oracle GoldenGate. One thing to keep in mind is that the installation steps for the Oracle GoldenGate software are the same for other RDBMS platforms such as Teradata and Sybase. However, the subtle nuances lie in the preparation for these environments with Oracle GoldenGate.

Installing Goldengate for Teradata on Windows and UNIX

Alas, by default, there is no built-in replication facility within the Teradata RDBMS platform. As such, Teradata requires Goldengate to perform replication activities. Teradata communicates with Oracle

Goldengate via the Teradata Access Module (TAM) and through the Teradata Change Data Capture (CDC) on the source Teradata server. Oracle Goldengate functions as the replication server and receives the transactions from the Teradata CDC source server.

Oracle Teradata has a number of requirements that must be performed prior to installing Oracle Goldengate. Before Oracle Goldengate can be installed for Teradata, the following items must be configured and available:

- Change Data Capture (CDC)

- Replication Groups

- Teradata Access Module (TAM)

- Relay Services Gateway (RSG)

The setup and configuration of these tasks for Teradata is beyond the scope of this chapter. For details on how to configure these features with Teradata, please consult the Teradata documentation available online at `www.info.teradata.com/`.

System Requirements for Teradata with Oracle GoldenGate

Oracle GoldenGate has unique requirements for setup with Teradata. The Oracle GoldenGate replication server must be configured along with setups for the source and target Teradata systems (if used).

Oracle GoldenGate Replication Server

It is important to keep the following points in mind when deploying Oracle GoldenGate for Teradata:

- Install Oracle 11g GoldenGate on a separate physical server. Do not install on any of the Teradata Servers.

- The Teradata Access Module (TAM) must be installed on the Oracle GoldenGate replication server under the root directory for the Oracle GoldenGate installation directory. TAM communicates with an Oracle GoldenGate API called the Vendor Access Module (VAM). Details for TAM configuration are provided in the Teradata Replication Services documentation available online at `www.info.teradata.com/`.

Disk Requirements

Teradata for Oracle GoldenGate has the following disk space requirements:

- 50–150MB of space plus 40 MB of additional disk space for the Oracle GoldenGate binaries and directory structures for the Oracle GoldenGate software.

Additional guidelines for Teradata and Oracle GoldenGate can be found in the Oracle® GoldenGate Teradata Installation and Setup Guide 11g Release 1 (11.1.1) available online at `http://download.oracle.com/docs/cd/E18101_01/index.htm`.

Installing Goldengate for Sybase on Windows and UNIX

Like all database platforms, Sybase presents unique requirements for installation of the Oracle GoldenGate software. Disk space requirements for Sybase with Oracle GoldenGate are the same as those for Oracle with GoldenGate. In addition to the disk space storage requirements, you will need to grant operating system–level privileges based on UNIX or Windows permissions so that the Sybase schema accounts and Oracle GoldenGate operating system–level accounts can read and write at the database and operating system level between source and target systems involved with the Sybase and Oracle GoldenGate installation. Otherwise, errors will occur when the replication processes attempt to perform their functions. The following database requirements must be completed as part of the Sybase and Oracle GoldenGate installation process:

- Configure DSQUERY variable in Sybase source database.

- Quiesce the Sybase RepServer before starting GoldenGate Extract process. You need to do so because Oracle GoldenGate Extract process uses Sybase LTM to read from the Sybase transaction log.

- Grant permission to Oracle GoldenGate Extract process to allow the ability to manage secondary log truncation point.

- The Sybase source database must be an active server. It cannot be in warm standby mode.

Further details with respect to the Sybase and GoldenGate installation procedures are available in the Oracle® GoldenGate Sybase Installation and Setup Guide 11g Release 1 (11.1.1) available online at http://download.oracle.com/docs/cd/E18101_01/index.htm.

Installing GoldenGate for IBM DB2 UDB on Windows and UNIX

We will focus on the database requirements for the Oracle 11g GoldenGate installation with IBM DB2 UDB database with Windows and UNIX platforms. Disk space storage requirements are the same as for general Oracle GoldenGate installation, as already discussed. In addition, you will need to grant read and write permissions at both the database and operating system–level for the Oracle GoldenGate user accounts on source and target DB2 systems with GoldenGate. The following items must be configured as part of the DB2 and GoldenGate installation:

- Read and write permissions at database and operating system–level to access the DB2READLOG functions so that the Oracle GoldenGate Extract process can read the DB2 UDB transaction logs.

- IBM DB2 UDB command-line interface (CLI) must be available on the target database environment because the Oracle GoldenGate Replicat process uses this CLI to apply data to the target system.

- Both IBM DB2 UDB Control Center graphical user interface (GUI) and command-line interface (CLI) are highly recommended to be installed and available on source and target DB2 systems.

After you have verified that the minimum disk space is available and that you have installed the required IBM DB2 UDB system tools, you need to grant privileges to the Oracle GoldenGate user. You will need to grant the SYSADM privilege or the DBADM database-level access to the Oracle GoldenGate database schema account and operating system–level account.

■ **Note** For IBM DB2 UDB you can grant permissions by executing the command GRANT DBADM ON DATABASE TO USER <ggs_user> or by using the IBM DB2 UDB Control Center utility.

Grant the following privileges to the Oracle GoldenGate schema database user within IBM DB2 UDB:

- Local CONNECT to the target IBM DB2 UDB database environment
- SELECT on the IBM DB2 UDB system catalog views
- SELECT, INSERT, UPDATE, and DELETE on the target IBM DB2 UDB tables

Additional information regarding the IBM DB2 UDB installation with GoldenGate is available in the Oracle GoldenGate DB2 LUW Installation and Setup Guide 11g Release 1 (11.1.1) online at: http://download.oracle.com/docs/cd/E18101_01/index.htm. You can also find the installation guides for other DB2 platforms such as IBM DB2 z/OS.

Installing Oracle GoldenGate Director 11g

Oracle GoldenGate Director is an optional software module that provides an end-to-end management and administration console for Oracle GoldenGate environments. Director uses a rich graphical interface similar to that found in network monitoring tools such as Tivoli and HP OpenView as well as Oracle Enterprise Manager (OEM). Director allows you to start and stop GoldenGate processes and to execute custom scripts as well. The installation procedure is quite a bit different for this product in contrast to that used for the base Oracle GoldenGate transaction software. Previous releases of the Oracle GoldenGate Director software had a different architecture and software installation process. We will discuss only the current release of the Oracle GoldenGate Director software in this chapter.

Further details regarding how to configure Oracle GoldenGate Director will be discussed in upcoming chapters. In addition, we recommend that you consult the Oracle GoldenGate Director Administrator's Guide 11g Release 1 (11.1.1) available online at http://download.oracle.com/docs/cd/E18101_01/doc.1111/e18482.pdf.

The installation process for Oracle 11g GoldenGate Director includes the following components:

- Oracle 11g Director Server Application
- Monitor Agent
- Director Client
- Director Administrator Client
- Oracle GoldenGate instances that will be monitored

The first step prior to performing the actual installation is to review the system requirements for the Oracle 11g GoldenGate Director software. Let's take a look at the installation requirements for the Oracle GoldenGate Director Server.

System Requirements

The following system configurations are necessary for the Oracle 11g GoldenGate Director installation to be performed successfully:

- At least 1GB of RAM (more memory is always better).

- Minimum of 1–1.5 GB of disk space allocated for Director software.

- Dedicated port for Oracle GoldenGate Director Server. The default port used is 7001.

- At least 200 MB of disk space in the repository database for the Oracle GoldenGate Director Server to be used for schema objects.

Next, you need to ensure that the particular platform used with Director is a supported configuration. Following are the supported platforms.

Supported Platforms

Oracle GoldenGate Director is available and supported on the following platforms:

- UNIX: Solaris, IBM AIX, HP-UX

- Linux: RedHat x86/x64, Oracle Enterprise Linux (OEL)

- Windows x86/x64

For the Oracle GoldenGate Director Server, you will also need to verify the following software has been installed and available for the Oracle GoldenGate Director Server before you perform the installation.

Software Requirements

The following software must be installed prior to deploying Oracle GoldenGate Director:

- Java Runtime Environment (JRE) release 6 (1.6 or later) required on the system that will house Oracle GoldenGate Director Server

- Oracle Weblogic Server 11g (10.3.1/10.3.2/10.3.3) Standard Edition Server

---

▓ **Note** Oracle 11g Weblogic Server must be installed and configured prior to performing the Oracle 11g GoldenGate Director Server installation. Please consult the Oracle 11g Weblogic documentation for details on how to install Oracle 11g Weblogic.

In addition to the above software requirements, you will also need to install a new repository database for the Oracle 11g GoldenGate Director Server during the installation process. The following RDBMS database platforms are supported as the repository database for Oracle GoldenGate Director Server:

- Oracle 9i or later

- MS SQL Server 2000 or 2005

- MySQL 5.x Enterprise Edition

For UNIX and LINUX platforms, a graphical (GUI) windowing environment such as X-Windows must be installed and configured.

GoldenGate Director Client Installation Requirements

Before you install the client for Oracle GoldenGate Director, be advised that you will need to complete the following preparations:

- The monitor screen display resolution must be at a level of 1024 × 768 or higher on the client machine.

- JRE version 6 software for the Java Runtime Environment must be installed on the client machine.

- Client host must be on the same physical network as that for the Oracle GoldenGate Director Server.

GoldenGate Director Web Client Installation Guidelines

The Oracle GoldenGate Director web client machine must contain a valid and supported Internet web browser. The following browsers are supported:

- Mozilla Firefox 1.4 or later

- Microsoft Internet Explorer 5.0 or later

- Apple Safari 1.2 or later

Installing Oracle GoldenGate Director Server

Once you have satisfied all of the above prerequisites, the installation for the Oracle GoldenGate Director Server can be performed. First you will need to create a new database schema account in the repository database on the Oracle GoldenGate Director Server. Then you can perform the installation of the Oracle GoldenGate Director software.

Grant Database Privileges and Credentials to Oracle GoldenGate Director Server Schema

If you choose to use Oracle for the repository database, you will need to create a schema user account and grant the QUOTA UNLIMITED privilege to the user's default tablespace. For details on using other database platforms, such as MySQL and Microsoft SQL Server, as the Oracle GoldenGate Director repository database, please consult the Oracle GoldenGate Director Administrator's Guide 11g Release 1 (11.1.1) documentation available online at http://download.oracle.com/docs/cd/E18101_01/doc.1111/e18482.pdf.

To perform the Oracle GoldenGate Director Server software installation, execute the setup script called ggdirector-serverset_<version> and follow the screen prompts.

Install Oracle GoldenGate Director

Now it is time to install the Oracle GoldenGate Director software. The following steps must be performed to ensure a successful installation of the Oracle GoldenGate Director software:

1. Download the Oracle 11g GoldenGate Director software .

2. Download and install the Microsoft Visual C++ 2005 SP1 Redistributable Package from http://microsoft.com

3. Install and configure Oracle 11g Weblogic Standard Server on the Oracle GoldenGate Director Server.

4. Download Oracle 11g database software to the Oracle 11g GoldenGate Director Server. This will be used for the repository database with the Director Server.

Installing Oracle GoldenGate Veridata

Oracle GoldenGate Veridata performs data synchronization functionality that allows you to ensure that all of the source and target Goldengate environments are in sync in terms of data replicated between source and target. Veridata uses the concept of a compare pare set of algorithms to measure synchronization changes between source and target Goldengate environments. Veridata consists of one or more agents and the repository server that houses the metadata objects for Oracle GoldenGate Veridata operations. For a standard Oracle GoldenGate Veridata installation, you will need to install and configure the following systems:

- Oracle GoldenGate Veridata Web

- Oracle GoldenGate Veridata Server

- Oracle GoldenGate Veridata Agent

- Oracle GoldenGate Veridata CLI

- Source and Target databases to be compared

We will cover administration of these Oracle GoldenGate Veridata components in Chapter 9. For now, we will provide you with details on the installation process. First, we will discuss the requirements for the Oracle GoldenGate Veridata Agent.

GoldenGate Veridata Agent System Requirements

You will need to install an Oracle GoldenGate Veridata agent for each database instance to be compared in the comparison check. In addition, the following software is required for the Oracle GoldenGate Veridata Agent:

- Java is required for the agent to function. Install either the Java Runtime Environment

- (JRE) 1.5, Java 6, or the Java Software Developer Kit (JSDK) for UNIX and LINUX systems that will be used with the Veridata Agent.

■ **Note**   A TCP/IP network port must be available and configured for all database platforms that will interact with Veridata Agent and Server. For instance, with Oracle, you must have the Oracle listener configured and online.

GoldenGate Veridata Agent Disk Requirements

While there is no exact disk space requirement for the Oracle GoldenGate Veridata Agent, we recommend that at least 200MB of disk space be granted for the software installation.

GoldenGate Veridata Agent Memory Requirements

- 1GB or more of RAM memory is required for the Oracle GoldenGate Veridata Agent software.

GoldenGate Veridata Agent Database Privileges

Depending on the specific database platform chosen for the Veridata comparison, you will need to grant database-level privileges to the Oracle GoldenGate Veridata Agent. For example, Oracle requires the following database privileges:

- GRANT SELECT on tables that will be compared by Veridata

- GRANT CONNECT
- SELECT_CATALOG_ROLE

MS SQL Server requires the following database privileges for the Veridata Agent:

- VIEW DEFINITION for databases that are compared
- db_datareader on tables compared
- SQL Server authentication must be used

For IBM DB2 and Veridata agent, you need to configure the SELECT privileges for all tables used in the comparison. Teradata also requires SELECT privileges for tables used by Veridata as part of the comparison check.

GoldenGate Veridata Server System Requirements

Disk Requirements

Oracle GoldenGate Veridata has the following disk space requirements:

- 30MB of disk storage for basic setup

Memory Requirements

Oracle Veridata has the following memory requirements:

- 1GB or more of available system memory is required for the Oracle GoldenGate Veridata Server.

We recommend 64-bit OS for best performance with Oracle GoldenGate Veridata processing operations. By using a 64-bit operating system, you will be able to take advantage of additional memory for virtual memory requirements should you perform large sorting operations with Veridata.

GoldenGate Veridata Server Software Requirements

Repository database is installed on the Oracle GoldenGate Veridata Server host.
The following database platforms are supported for the Veridata Server repository:

- Oracle
- MySQL
- MS SQL Server

The Veridata installer will create the database for you during the installation process. However, you will need to have staged the database repository software prior to running the installer. For instance, if you choose to use Oracle as the repository for the Veridata server, you will need to make sure that the client and server software for Oracle is available and staged on the Veridata Server host before you begin the installation process. Furthermore, for Oracle, you will need to use either the TNSNAMES or EZCONNECT method for the database network services. All of the correct values MUST be provided for the Oracle network services such as the database instance name in the tnsnames.ora and listener.ora file if you choose to use the TNSNAMES with the Oracle repository database for Veridata.

Database Privileges for GoldenGate Veridata Server

As part of the pre-installation tasks for the Oracle GoldenGate Veridata Server, you must grant the appropriate database privileges to the Veridata schema account to be used in the installation of the Veridata Server. For instance, if you choose to use MySQL for the repository with Veridata Server, you will need to first create a user and database and then grant DDL and DML privileges to this account. With Oracle as the repository database for Veridata, you need to grant database privileges to the newly created Veridata repository schema account.

GRANT the following privileges to the VERIDATA_ROLE:

- CREATE TABLE
- CREATE VIEW
- CREATE SESSION
- CREATE PROCEDURE

In addition, you will need to grant the VERIDATA_ROLE to the user for Oracle as well as grant the QUOTA UNLIMITED privilege to the Veridata user as default tablespace.

If you should choose to use Microsoft SQL Server for the Veridata Server repository database platform, you will need to create a new database and login for the Veridata user. Furthermore, the following privileges will need to be granted:

- ALTER SCHEMA
- CREATE, DROP TABLE, ALTER
- CONNECT
- CREATE INDEX
- DROP INDEX
- INSERT, UPDATE, DELETE
- SELECT

GoldenGate Veridata Web Requirements for Installation

For the Oracle GoldenGate Veridata web requirements, you will need to ensure that one of the following Internet browsers is available on the client web host:

- Mozilla Firefox 1.0.4 or later version

- Microsoft Internet Explorer 6 or later version

Oracle GoldenGate Veridata makes usage of various default ports via TCP/IP networking. The following ports are used by default and should be made available:

- 4150: Server communication port

- 8820: shutdown port

- 8830: HTTP port

▓ **Note** These default ports for Oracle GoldenGate Veridata can be changed after the installation.

In chapter 9, we will perform an installation of the Oracle GoldenGate Veridata components. Additional information on how to install Oracle GoldenGate Veridata is also available from the Oracle GoldenGate Veridata Administrator's Guide available online at: `http://download.oracle.com/docs/cd/E15881_01/doc.104/gg_veridata_admin.pdf`.

Install Oracle Goldengate Veridata

The following steps are required to get started with the Oracle GoldenGate Veridata installation:

1. Download the Oracle 11g Goldengate Veridata software.

2. Unzip the Veridata software to a directory that you will use to stage the software.

Summary

In this chapter we provided you with a detailed roadmap to install the Oracle GoldenGate product family of data replication applications. Common installation issues such as infrastructure setup for network, operating systems, and storage were provided to help you understand common pitfalls frequently encountered in the deployment process for Oracle GoldenGate.

CHAPTER 3

Architecture

This chapter looks at the typical GoldenGate replication flow and examines each of the architectural components in detail. It also looks at some of the different replication topologies supported by GoldenGate. Finally, you take a quick glance at some of the GoldenGate tools and utilities.

You should keep some key GoldenGate architectural concepts in mind from the start: the GoldenGate architecture is non-invasive, modular, and flexible, and it can support many different replication scenarios and use cases. GoldenGate components can be rearranged and scaled up or down to meet specific replication scenario requirements. And GoldenGate can replicate high volumes of data in real time with low server and database impact and never miss or duplicate a transaction.

Typical GoldenGate Flow

Most replication scenarios involve, at a minimum, the components discussed in this chapter. Figure 3-1 shows how these components combine to form what this book refers to as the *typical GoldenGate flow*.

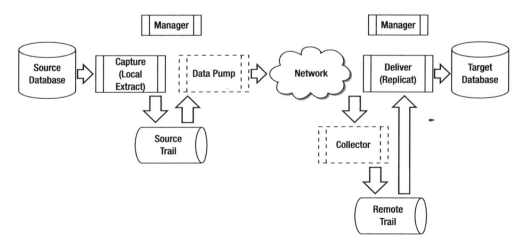

Figure 3-1. The typical GoldenGate flow

The typical GoldenGate flow shows new and changed database data being *captured* from the *source database*. The captured data is written to a file called the *source trail*. The trail is then read by a *data pump*, sent across the *network*, and written to a *remote trail* file by the *Collector* process. The *delivery* function reads the remote trail and updates the *target database*. Each of the components is managed by the *Manager* process.

You may notice that the data pump and the Collector process are formatted slightly differently than the others. The data pump is surrounded by dots to indicate that it's an optional process. The Collector is bordered with dashes to show that it's a dynamic process that starts automatically and runs in the background. I'll explain why and go into more detail about those and the other components in the next sections.

GoldenGate Components

Figure 3-1 illustrates the various components you're most likely to work with. Each of the components serves a different purpose in the overall GoldenGate configuration. In this section, you learn about the purpose of each component and how it fits into the overall replication flow. In later chapters, you learn how to set up and configure each of the components. Let's now look at the components in more detail.

Source Database

You may recognize that the source database isn't really a GoldenGate component but rather a vendor database that is part of your existing infrastructure. GoldenGate supports a wide variety of heterogeneous source databases and platforms. Table 3-1 shows the databases GoldenGate supports as source databases as of GoldenGate version 11g.

▓ **Note**   Be sure to check the GoldenGate product documentation for the most current list of supported databases.

Table 3-1. GoldenGate 11g Source Databases

Source Database
c-tree
DB2 for Linux, UNIX, Windows
DB2 for z/OS
MySQL
Oracle
SQL/MX
SQL Server
Sybase
Teradata

Capture (Local Extract) Process

Capture is the process of extracting data that is inserted into, updated on, or deleted from the source database. In GoldenGate, the capture process is called the *Extract*. In this case, the Extract is called a *Local Extract* (sometimes called the *Primary Extract*) because it captures data changes from the local source database. There are several types of extracts. Another type of Extract that's discussed later is the data-pump Extract, which passes the Local Extract changes to the target server. You can also have an initial-load Extract to capture database records to perform an initial load of the target database. You see an example of the initial-load Extract in Chapter 4, "Basic Replication."

Extract is an operating-system process that runs on the source server and captures changes from the database transaction logs. For example, in an Oracle database, Extract captures changes from the redo logs (and in some exceptional cases, the archived redo logs) and writes the data to a file called the *Trail File*. For Microsoft SQL Server, Extract captures changes from the transaction log. To reduce the amount of processing, Extract only captures committed changes and filters out other activity such as rolled-back changes. Extract can also be configured to write the Trail File directly to a remote target server, but this usually isn't the optimum configuration.

In addition to database data manipulation language (DML) data, you can also capture data definition language (DDL) changes and sequences using Extract if properly configured. You can use Extract to capture data to initially load the target tables, but this is typically done using DBMS utilities such as export/import or Data Pump for Oracle.

You can configure Extract as a single process or multiple parallel processes depending on your requirements. Each Extract process can act independently on different tables. For example, a single Extract can capture all the changes for of the tables in a schema, or you can create multiple Extracts and divide the tables among the Extracts. In some cases, you may need to create multiple parallel Extract processes to improve performance, although this usually isn't necessary. You can stop and start each Extract process independently.

You can set up Extract to capture an entire schema using wildcarding, a single table, or a subset of rows or columns for a table. In addition, you can transform and filter captured data using the Extract to only extract data meeting certain criteria. For example, you may want to filter a Customer table to only extract customer data if the customer's name is equal to "Jones".

You can instruct Extract to write any records that it's unable to process to a discard file for later problem resolution. And you can generate reports automatically to show the Extract configuration. You can set these up to be updated periodically at user-defined intervals with the latest Extract processing statistics.

Source Trail

The Extract process sequentially writes committed transactions as they occur to a staging file that GoldenGate calls a *source trail*. Data is written in large blocks for high performance. Data that is written to the trail is queued for distribution to the target server or another destination to be processed by another GoldenGate process, such as a data pump. Data in the trail files can also be encrypted by the Extract and then unencrypted by the data pump or delivery process.

You can size the trail files based on the expected data volume. When the specified size is reached, a new trail file is created. To free up disk space, you can configure GoldenGate to automatically purge trail files based on age or the total number of trail files.

By default, data in the trail files is stored in a platform-independent, GoldenGate proprietary format. In addition to the database data, each trail file contains a file header, and each record also contains its own header. Each of the GoldenGate processes keeps track of its position in the trail files using checkpoints, which are stored in separate files.

▓ **Note** GoldenGate uses a Commit Sequence Number (CSN) to identify and keep track of transactions processed by GoldenGate and to ensure data integrity. The CSN is a GoldenGate platform-independent representation of unique serial numbers that each DBMS uses to track the transactions it has processed. For example, in an Oracle database, GoldenGate uses the Oracle System Change Number (SCN) to represent the CSN. For a SQL Server database, GoldenGate uses a concatenation of the virtual log-file number, a segment number within the virtual log, and the entry number. Extract writes the CSNs to the checkpoint and trail files that you can view using the Logdump utility. You can use the CSN when starting the Replicat to begin processing at or after a specific CSN.

If needed, you can examine the trail files in detail using the GoldenGate Logdump utility. This is sometimes necessary for debugging purposes. You can also use Logdump to filter records and save a subset of your trail file for special processing. You learn more about the Logdump utility in Chapter 11, "Troubleshooting."

Data Pump

The data pump is another type of GoldenGate Extract process. The data pump reads the records in the source trail written by the Local Extract, *pumps* or passes them over the TCP/IP network to the target, and creates a target or remote trail. Although the data pump can be configured for data filtering and transformation (just like the Local Extract), in many cases the data pump reads the records in the source trail and simply passes all of them on as is. In GoldenGate terminology, this is called *passthru* mode. If data filtering or transformation is required, it's a good idea to do this with the data pump to reduce the amount of data sent across the network.

Although technically a data pump isn't necessary, you should usually configure a data pump anyway as good practice. As mentioned earlier, you could set up the Local Extract to send changes directly from the source server to the remote target without a data pump, as shown in Figure 3-2.

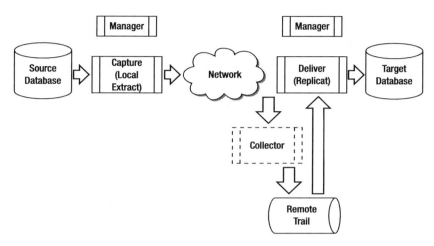

Figure 3-2. GoldenGate flow without a data pump

As you can see from Figure 3-2, in this configuration the Extract process can be directly affected by the network. Adding a data pump to the configuration, however, introduces a layer to insulate the Local Extract from any disruptions caused by the network connection to the target or a problem with the target itself.

For example, if there was a network issue between the source and the target, this could cause the Local Extract to fail. By having a data pump, the Local Extract can continue to extract changes, and *only the data pump is impacted*. This way, when the network issue is resolved, the data pump can be restarted and will quickly process the previously queued changes from the source trail that the Local Extract has already captured.

You can configure a single data pump or multiple data pumps, depending on the requirements. For example, a data pump on the source system can pump data to an intermediate or middle-tier system. The data on the middle tier can be further filtered by multiple pumps running in parallel and passed on to multiple heterogeneous targets. In this case, no database is required on the middle tier, only the data pumps. Figure 3-3 demonstrates multiple data pumps running in parallel. Data Pump #1 and Data Pump #2 can pump data on to another pump or to one or more Replicats.

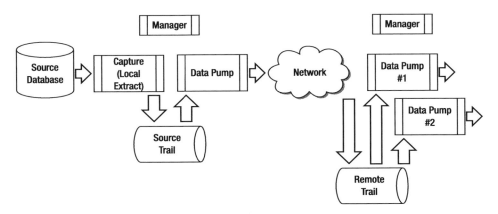

Figure 3-3. GoldenGate flow with multiple data pumps

Just as with the Local Extract, you can write any records the data pump is unable to process to a discard file for problem resolution. Reports can be automatically generated to show the data-pump configuration and updated periodically at user-defined intervals with the latest processing statistics.

Network

GoldenGate sends data from the source trail using the Local or data pump Extract over a TCP/IP network to a remote host and writes it to the remote trail file. The Local or data pump Extract communicates with another operating-system background Extract process called the *Collector* on the target. The Collector is started dynamically for each Extract process on the source that requires a network connection to the target. The Collector listens for connections on a port configured for GoldenGate. Although it can be configured, often the Collector process is ignored because it's started dynamically and does its job without requiring changes or intervention on the target.

During transmission from the source to the target, you can compress the data to reduce bandwidth. In addition, you can tune the TCP/IP socket buffer sizes and connection timeout parameters for the best performance across the network. If needed, you can also encrypt the GoldenGate data sent across the network from the source and automatically decrypt it on the target.

Collector

The Collector process is started automatically by the Manager as needed by the Extract. The Collector process runs in the background on the target system and writes records to the remote trail. The records are sent across the TCP/IP network connection from the Extract process on the source system (either by a data pump or a Local Extract process).

Remote Trail

The *remote trail* is similar to the *source trail*, except it is created on the remote server, which could be the target database server or some other middle tier server. The source trails and the remote trails are stored in a filesystem directory named dirdat by default. They are named with a two-character prefix followed by a six-digit sequence number. The same approach for sizing for the source trail applies to the remote trail. You should size the trail files based on the expected data volume. When the specified size is reached, a new trail file will be created. You can also configure GoldenGate to automatically purge the remote trail files based on age or the total number of trail files to free up disk space.

Just like the source trail, data in the remote trail files is stored in platform-independent, GoldenGate-proprietary format. Each remote trail file contains a file header, and each record also contains its own header. The GoldenGate processes keep track of its position in the remote trail files using *checkpoints*, which are stored in separate GoldenGate files or optionally in a database table.

You can also examine the remote trail files in detail, just like the source trails, by using the GoldenGate *Logdump* utility. You learn more about the *Logdump* utility in Chapter 11. One thing to keep in mind is you should never manually edit and change the trail files using a text editor.

Delivery (Replicat)

Delivery is the process of applying data changes to the target database. In GoldenGate, delivery is done by a process called the Replicat using the native database SQL. The Replicat applies data changes written to the trail file by the Extract process in the same order in which they were committed on the source database. This is done to maintain data integrity.

In addition to replicating database DML data, you can also replicate DDL changes and sequences using the Replicat, if it's properly configured. You can configure a special Replicat to apply data to initially load the target tables, but this is typically done using DBMS utilities such as Data Pump for Oracle.

Just like the Extract, you can configure Replicat as a single process or multiple parallel processes depending on the requirements. Each Replicat process can act independently on different tables. For example, a single Replicat can apply all the changes for all the tables in a schema, or you can create multiple Replicats and the divide the tables among them. In some cases, you may need to create multiple Replicat processes to improve performance. You can stop and start each Replicat process independently.

Replicat can replicate data for an entire schema using wildcarding, a single table, or a subset of rows or columns for a table. You can configure the Replicat to map the data from the source to the target database, transform it, and filter it to only replicate data meeting certain criteria. For example, Replicat can filter the Customer table to only replicate customer data where the name is equal to "Jones". Typically, filtering is done by the Extract process and not the Replicat, for performance reasons.

You can write any records that Replicat is unable to process to a discard file for problem resolution. Reports can be automatically generated to show the Replicat configuration; these reports can be updated periodically at user-defined intervals with the latest processing statistics.

Target Database

Like the source database, the target database isn't really a GoldenGate component but rather a vendor database that is part of your infrastructure. GoldenGate supports a variety of target databases. Table 3-2 shows the databases GoldenGate supports as target databases as of version 11g.

■ **Note** Be sure to check the GoldenGate product documentation for the most current list of supported targets.

Table 3-2. GoldenGate 11g Supported Target Databases

Target Database
c-tree
DB2 for iSeries
DB2 for Linux, UNIX, Windows
DB2 for z/OS
Generic ODBC
MySQL
Oracle
SQL/MX
SQL Server
Sybase
TimesTen

Manager

The GoldenGate Manager process is used to manage all of the GoldenGate processes and resources. A single Manager process runs on each server where GoldenGate is executing and processes commands from the GoldenGate Software Command Interface (GGSCI). The Manager process is the first GoldenGate process started. The Manager then starts and stops each of the other GoldenGate processes, manages the trail files, and produces log files and reports.

Topologies and Use Cases

Now that you're familiar with the GoldenGate architecture components, let's discuss the various GoldenGate topologies and use cases. GoldenGate supports a wide variety of replication topologies such as one-way replication, bidirectional replication, peer-to-peer replication, broadcast replication, and integration replication. Each of these topologies can be utilized to support many use cases. The topologies and examples of some use cases are discussed in the following sections.

One-Way Replication

One-way replication, as shown in Figure 3-4, is the simplest topology and is often used for reporting or query-offloading purposes. Data is replicated from a single source to a single target in only one direction. Changes to database data are only made at the source database. The target database is read-only.

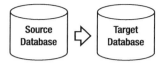

Figure 3-4. One-way replication

A one-way configuration is useful for offloading intensive queries and reports from the source database. It can also be used for maintaining a hot-standby database for failover purposes.

Another concept you should keep in mind is that the source and target databases can be different database technologies. For example, the source database can be Oracle for OLTP processing, and the target database can contain a filtered subset of tables from the source database using the SQL Server database for reporting and analysis purposes. A typical GoldenGate configuration to implement one-way replication is shown in Figure 3-5.

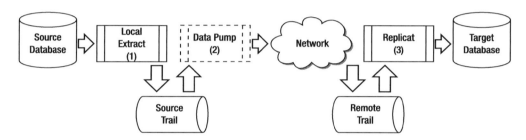

Figure 3-5. One-way replication GoldenGate configuration

Following is a description of the process as implemented in the figure:

1. A Local Extract running on the source server extracts data and writes to the source trail.

2. A data pump is running on the source server. This is optional but recommended. The data pump reads data from the source trail and transmits it over the network to the remote trail.

3. A Replicat running on the target updates the target database. Multiple parallel Replicats can be configured if needed to improve performance.

A special case of one-way replication is one-way-at-a-time replication, as illustrated in Figure 3-6. In this scenario, replication goes one way from the source to the target database and then is reversed from the target to the source. The replication doesn't occur simultaneously like bidirectional replication, which is discussed next. One-way-at-a-time replication can be used for *zero-downtime database upgrades or migrations.* Zero-downtime upgrades and migrations are covered in more detail in Chapter 13, "Zero Downtime Migrations and Upgrades."

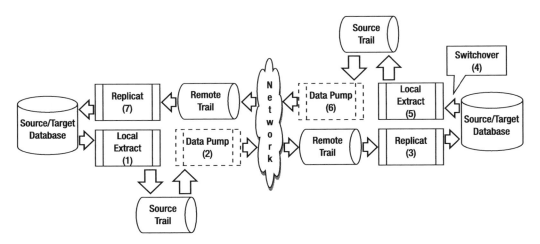

Figure 3-6. One-way-at-a-time replication GoldenGate configuration

Use the following process to implement one-way-at-a-time replication as shown in the figure:

1. Start one-way replication from the source database to the target database, as shown in the bottom half of Figure 3-6. A Local Extract running on the source server extracts data and writes to the source trail.

2. A data pump is running on the source server. This is optional but recommended. The data pump reads data from the source trail and transmits it over the network to the remote trail.

3. A Replicat running on the target updates the target database. Multiple parallel Replicats can be configured if needed to improve performance.

4. The replication from the source to the target may continue for as long as needed. For example, with zero-downtime database upgrades, you continue replicating from the source to the target until you're ready to switchover to the newly upgraded database. At this point, the replication is reversed, and the target database becomes the new source database, as shown at the top of Figure 3-6.

5. A Local Extract running on the source server extracts data and writes to the source trail.

6. A data pump is running on the source server. This is optional but recommended. The data pump reads data from the source trail and transmits it over the network to the remote trail.

7. A Replicat running on the target server updates the target database. Multiple parallel Replicats can be configured if needed to improve performance.

Bidirectional Replication

In bidirectional replication, as shown in Figure 3-7, changes to data can occur on either database at the same time and are replicated to the other database. Each database contains an identical set of data. Bidirectional replication is sometimes called *active-active replication* because each side of the replication is *actively* processing data changes.

Figure 3-7. Bidirectional replication

Figure 3-8 illustrates a typical bidirectional configuration. Such a configuration is often used in environments where there are high-volume and high-performance requirements. By allowing both sides of the replication to be active, the database and hardware can be fully utilized.

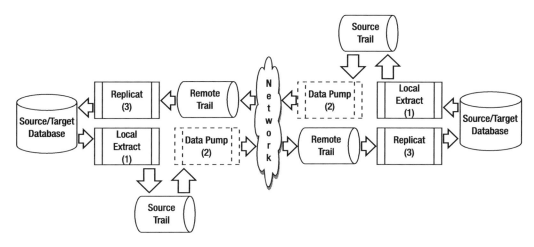

Figure 3-8. Bidirectional replication GoldenGate configuration

Following are some of the key components illustrated in Figure 3-8:

1. A Local Extract is running on *each* of the source servers.

2. A data pump is running on *each* of the source servers. This is optional but recommended. The data pumps can also be moved to a middle-tier server if needed to offload processing on the source server.

3. A Replicat is running on *each* target. Multiple parallel Replicats can be configured if needed to improve performance.

One drawback of bidirectional replication is that it can become complex. Strategies must be developed for handling collisions and avoiding key conflicts. For example, one strategy might be that each database can process only a certain range of key values to avoid conflicts.

Broadcast Replication

Broadcast replication, as shown in Figure 3-9, is used to replicate data from a single source to multiple targets. In this configuration, the target databases are read-only. Figure 3-10 shows a typical GoldenGate configuration.

Broadcast replication is often used in environments where a copy of the production data is needed in several different geographic locations. Distributing the data relieves the load on the primary database and gets the data closer to the end consumer of the data.

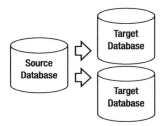

Figure 3-9. Broadcast replication

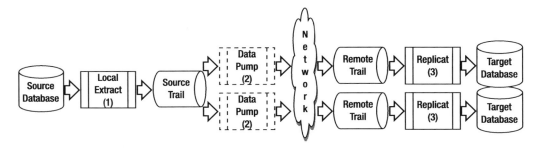

Figure 3-10. Broadcast replication GoldenGate configuration

Following are the key components from Figure 3-10 used to implement broadcast replication:

1. A Local Extract is running on the source servers.

2. Two data-pump Extracts are running on the source server, pumping data to each of the target databases in parallel. The data pumps can filter the data depending on the requirements of the target databases.

3. A Replicat is running on each target. Multiple Replicats can be configured if needed to improve performance.

Integration Replication

Integration replication, as shown in Figure 3-11, is used to consolidate and integrate data from multiple source databases into a single target. The target database is read-only.

Integration replication is often used in data-warehouse environments. Data is usually transformed and filtered, and only a subset of each of the source databases is needed for the data warehouse.

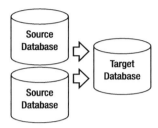

Figure 3-11. Integration replication

A typical GoldenGate configuration to implement integration replication involves the components shown in figure 3-12.

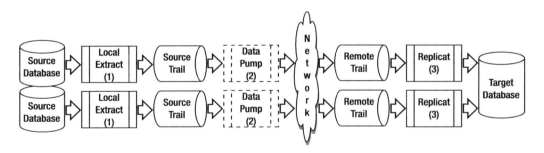

Figure 3-12. Integration replication GoldenGate configuration

Here is a more detailed description of each of the process components in the figure:

1. A Local Extract is running on *each* of the source servers.

2. A data pump is running on *each* source server, each pumping data to the target database. The data pumps can do transformation and filtering as needed.

3. Two Replicats are running in parallel on the target, one to process each trail file coming from the source.

Tools and Utilities

Now that you have an understanding of the GoldenGate flow and processes, let's take a quick look at some of the GoldenGate tools and utilities. The next sections provide a brief overview of the tools and utilities. You learn more about these in later chapters.

GGSCI

GGSCI is the GoldenGate Software Command Interface. GGSCI is delivered as part of the GoldenGate software and can be started from the software installation directory using the `ggsci` command. From the GGSCI command prompt, you can enter commands to manage all parts of the GoldenGate environment including Extracts, Replicats, trails, the Manager, and so on. The `Help` command is built into GGSCI to give information about each command and its syntax.

DEFGEN

You can use the GoldenGate DEFGEN utility to generate GoldenGate table-definition files when your source and target tables are different (if the source and target tables are identical, it isn't necessary to run DEFGEN). You can also use DEFGEN to generate a data-definitions file for a data-pump Extract that is doing data transformations on a middle-tier server. DEFGEN is included as part of the regular GoldenGate installation and is available in the GoldenGate software-installation directory.

Logdump

You can use the GoldenGate Logdump utility to view records in the GoldenGate trail files. The Logdump utility is part of the regular GoldenGate software installation. Logdump lets you view the unstructured trail data in hex and ASCII format and count the number of records in the trail for debugging purposes. You can also filter the trail for desired records and save them to a new trail for reprocessing if needed.

Reverse

If you ever need to undo database changes, you can use the GoldenGate Reverse utility. Reverse uses a special Extract to capture the before images of changes and then reverses the order of the transactions and writes a new trail file for doing the reversal. A Replicat then processes the special reversed trail to undo database changes. Reverse can be useful for backing out unwanted changes to the database or quickly restoring a test database back to its original state. Reverse is another utility that is included with the GoldenGate software installation.

Veridata

Veridata is an additional product from GoldenGate that you can use to verify that your source and target databases match. For critical business applications, you should always verify that your source and target databases match when doing replication. If the databases being replicated are used for failover, this is especially important. Data verification is usually time consuming and difficult to accomplish for large amounts of data. Veridata reduces the amount of time verification takes and does high-speed data verification while the databases are online. Results are presented on a web interface. Veridata is covered in detail in Chapter 9, "Veridata."

Director

Another add-on product available from GoldenGate is Director. Director is a graphical tool that you can use to centrally design, configure, manage, and monitor your entire GoldenGate environment. Director is made up of several components, including a centralized server and database repository, a client application, and a web browser interface. Director can also be integrated with third-party monitoring solutions. Director can manage all the databases and platforms that GoldenGate replication supports. It's covered in Chapter 10, "Director."

Summary

In this chapter, you learned about the GoldenGate replication flow and each of the components in detail. It's important to understand the components because almost all GoldenGate scenarios use these same components.

You also saw some typical replication topologies and how they can be implemented using GoldenGate. Specifically, you learned about the topologies listed in Table 3-3. As you move into the next chapters, you learn how to apply the GoldenGate architecture principles to implement GoldenGate replication.

Table 3-3. GoldenGate Topologies and Use Cases

Topology	Cardinality	Data State	Data Changes	Use Cases
One-way	One-to-one	Active/Passive	Source only	Reporting, query offloading, hot standby
Bidirectional	One-to-one	Active/Active	Source and target	High volume, high performance
Broadcast	One-to-many	Active/Passive	Source only	Data distribution to multiple sites
Integration	Many-to-one	Active/Passive	Source only	Data warehousing

CHAPTER 4

Basic Replication

This chapter provides a good understanding of basic GoldenGate replication, including an example of replicating a sample human resources schema. You learn how to set up, start, and verify the basic replication configuration, including the initial data-load process. You see examples in both Oracle Database on Linux and Microsoft SQL Server 2008 on Windows, but keep in mind that most of the same GoldenGate commands and concepts apply to all of the supported platforms. The chapter points out where a specific command or task applies only to an Oracle database or only to a SQL Server database.

Overview

Now that you've learned how to install the GoldenGate software and how the architectural components fit together, you can begin setting up the replication. This chapter covers setting up and configuring basic one-way GoldenGate replication. It discusses adding the local Extract, data-pump Extract, and Replicat for ongoing change synchronization. You also review initial data-loading methods, including using GoldenGate and native DBMS utilities.

More advanced configurations are covered in later chapters, such as bidirectional replication in Chapter 5, heterogeneous replication in Chapter 6, and zero-downtime migrations in Chapter 13. Keep in mind that the same concepts covered in this chapter are a foundation to build on for those more advanced configurations. Chapter 5 also builds on this basic replication configuration and adds some advanced features that you can use to enhance the basic configuration.

Prerequisites for Setting Up Replication

You need to have the following prerequisites in place before you can start setting up replication:

- The GoldenGate software installed on the source and target servers, as described in Chapter 2

- The GoldenGate database user ID created on the source and target databases

- The server name or IP address of the target database server

- The GoldenGate Manager process up and running on the source and the target

- TCP/IP network connectivity open from the source server to the target server's GoldenGate manager port

- An understanding of the business and technical replication requirements

Let's dig a little deeper on the last item in the next section about requirements. Understanding the requirements is probably the single most important factor in the success of a replication project.

Requirements

You need a solid understanding of the specific requirements that drive the replication technical design. Here are some of the factors that impact the replication design:

Source and target configurations: Describe the existing or planned source and target databases. What are the software releases for the database and operating system? Are the servers stand-alone or clustered? How is the data storage configured? What are the character sets for the source and target databases?

Data currency: How quickly and how often does the data need to be updated? Can any lag in the data replication be tolerated? If no lag can be tolerated and there is a high volume of changes, you may need to devote more time in the project to designing and tuning the replication to avoid any lag. Keep in mind that often, reporting systems can tolerate lag, and the target data doesn't need to be completely up to date with the source.

Data volume: How much data needs to be replicated? How often is it updated? You may be able to examine the existing database-transaction log files to determine the amount of data change that is occurring in the source database. The data-change volume will impact the network bandwidth requirements between the source and target and the amount of disk space required for trail files.

Data requirements: You should understand any unique or special data requirements so they can be handled properly in GoldenGate. For example, if there are triggers, they may need to be disabled in the target database. Sequences need special parameters added if they need to be replicated. Certain data types may need special handling or may not be supported. For example, in GoldenGate 11, data types such as BFILE and ANYDATA aren't supported. Other data types may be supported but with certain limitations. *Be sure to check the GoldenGate product documentation for a list of data types supported.*

Security requirements: How much security is required for the replication? For example, is it necessary to encrypt the data that GoldenGate is replicating? GoldenGate can encrypt both the data stored in trail files as well as the data being sent from the source to the target. Also, is the data in the database encrypted? For example, Oracle can encrypt database data using a feature called Transparent Data Encryption (TDE). If the database is using TDE, GoldenGate needs special parameters defined to unencrypt the data for replication.

Network requirements: Describe the network between the source and the target? Are there any firewalls that need to be opened for the replication? What is the distance between the source and target? How much bandwidth is required to handle the data volume, and how much is available?

Table 4-1 describes the environment used for discussion purposes in this chapter. Noted in parentheses are some settings for Windows with a SQL Server database environment. Remember, though, the sources and targets can be any platform and database supported by GoldenGate, as reviewed in Chapter 3. You may want to set up a table like this for your replication projects.

Table 4-1. Sample GoldenGate Replication Environment

Configuration Item	Value
GoldenGate software location	/gger/ggs (or c:\gger\ggs)
GoldenGate OS user ID/password	gguser/userpw
GoldenGate database user ID/password	gger/userpw
Source server name	sourceserver
Source manager port	7840
Source server OS/release	Linux 5.3 or Windows
Source database name	SourceDB
Source database vendor/release	Oracle 11.1 (or SQL Server 2008)
Source schema	HR
Target server name	targetserver
Target manager port	7840
Target server OS/release	Linux 5.3 (or Windows)
Target database vendor/release	Oracle 11.1 (or SQL Server 2008)
Target database name	TargetDB
Target schema	HR
Local extract name	LHREMD1
Data pump name	PHREMD1
Replicat name	RHREMD1
Local trail file	l1
Remote trail file	l2

The source and target schema used in the examples is the Human Resources or HR schema from the Oracle Database Sample Schemas. Listed next is a description of the Employees table from the HR schema, which is used in the examples:

```
Table EMPLOYEES
 Name                                        Null?     Type
 ------------------------------------------- --------- ---------------------------
 EMPLOYEE_ID    (PK)                         NOT NULL  NUMBER(6)
 FIRST_NAME                                            VARCHAR2(20)
 LAST_NAME                                   NOT NULL  VARCHAR2(25)
 EMAIL                                       NOT NULL  VARCHAR2(25)
 PHONE_NUMBER                                          VARCHAR2(20)
 HIRE_DATE                                   NOT NULL  DATE
 JOB_ID                                      NOT NULL  VARCHAR2(10)
 SALARY                                                NUMBER(8,2)
 COMMISSION_PCT                                        NUMBER(2,2)
 MANAGER_ID                                            NUMBER(6)
 DEPARTMENT_ID                                         NUMBER(4)
```

One-Way Replication Topology

The topology covered in this chapter is one-way replication, as shown in Figure 4-1. You may remember from Chapter 3 that one-way replication is the simplest topology and is often used for reporting or query-offloading purposes. Data is replicated from a single source database to a single target database in only one direction. Changes to database data are only made at the source database and are then replicated to the target database.

Figure 4-1. One-way replication

Basic Replication Steps

When the prerequisites are complete, setting up basic one-way replication can be accomplished in four steps, as shown in Figure 4-2. These steps include initially loading the data and then keeping the data synchronized after the initial load. The next sections cover each of these steps in detail.

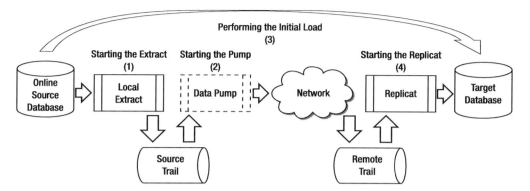

Figure 4-2. Basic replication steps

Following are descriptions of the steps in the figure:

1. Start the Extract. Configure and start the Extract to begin capturing database changes. You need to start the Extract *before* the initial load, so that any SQL data manipulation language (DML) changes made during the load process can be captured. The Extract captures the database changes from the source database-transaction log and writes them to the source trail file.

2. Start the data pump. Configure and start the data pump to send extracted changes captured by the local Extract into the source trail across the network to the target server. When on the target server, the changes are written to the remote trail file.

3. Perform the initial load. Load the data using either GoldenGate or vendor DBMS utilities. Doing so creates a synchronized copy of each database, except for changes that were captured during the load process by the Extract. These changes will be applied in the next step when the Replicat is started. You only need to run an initial data load the first time you setting up replication. After this, GoldenGate will keep the data synchronized on an ongoing basis using the Extract and Replicat processes.

4. Start the Replicat. Configure and start the Replicat to begin applying changes from the remote trail file. Changes that were captured while the initial-load process was executing have already been written to the remote trail file. It may take a Replicat some time to catch up with the changes, depending on the data volume and the length of time changes were captured during the load process. Also, some of these changes may cause data conflicts, because activity was occurring in the database at the same time the data load was running. Later, this chapter covers some GoldenGate parameters, such as HANDLECOLLISIONS, to automatically handle these data conflicts. When the Replicat has caught up and applied all the changes, the databases are synchronized.

> ■ **Note** These steps assume a zero-downtime replication configuration. Online DML changes will be occurring in the source database while the initial-load process is running. This is the most likely scenario in today's environments, where downtime usually needs to be avoided. If you can quiesce or stop DML activity against the source database *while* the initial load is occurring, it is *not* necessary to start the Extract *before* the initial load.

Let's look at each of the basic replication steps in detail, beginning with setting up and starting the Extract.

Starting the Extract

When you've verified that the prerequisites are complete, the first step you need to complete in setting up replication is to start the Extract. Remember that you should start the Extract first to begin capturing changes made while the initial data load is running. If you can afford to take an outage and stop all change activity on the source database while the initial load is running, then you can start the Extract after the initial load.

This section covers the various Extract configuration settings and options. After that, you see how to start the Extract and verify that it's properly capturing changes.

Verifying Database-Level Supplemental Logging

When replicating from Oracle databases, you need to enable database-level supplemental logging on the source database. Remember that if you're using bidirectional replication, you need to enable supplemental logging on both the source and the target databases. The supplemental logging is required to ensure that Oracle adds additional information to the redo logs that is required by GoldenGate.

First, you can verify whether Oracle database supplemental logging is already enabled by running the following SQLPLUS command:

```
SQL> SELECT SUPPLEMENTAL_LOG_DATA_MIN FROM V$DATABASE;

SUPPLEMENTAL_LOG_DATA_MIN
-------------------------
NO
```

For Oracle 9i, SUPPLEMENTAL_LOG_DATA_MIN must be YES. For Oracle 10g and later, SUPPLEMENTAL_LOG_DATA must be YES or IMPLICIT. Now that you've verified that database-level supplemental logging isn't currently enabled, you can enter the commands to make it enabled.

Enabling Database-Level Supplemental Logging

You can enable Oracle database-level supplemental logging by running the following SQLPLUS command as a user with the ALTER SYSTEM privilege:

```
SQL> ALTER DATABASE ADD SUPPLEMENTAL LOG DATA;

--Verify that it is enabled.

SQL> SELECT SUPPLEMENTAL_LOG_DATA_MIN FROM V$DATABASE;

SUPPLEMENTAL_LOG_DATA_MIN
-------------------------
YES
```

Remember, for Oracle 9i, SUPPLEMENTAL_LOG_DATA must be YES. For Oracle 10g and later, SUPPLEMENTAL_LOG_DATA must be YES or IMPLICIT.

Enabling Table-Level Supplemental Logging

Normally, databases such as Oracle, DB2, and SQL Server don't log enough data in the transaction logs for GoldenGate to be able to successfully replicate the change to the target database. GoldenGate requires the key values in addition to the changed data in order for the GoldenGate Replicat to apply the changed data to the target database. Adding supplemental logging to the source database tables ensures that the database logs the key values that GoldenGate needs in order to properly apply the updates on the target database.

You can use the GoldenGate ADD TRANDATA command to force the database to log primary-key columns for all updates on your source database. You don't need to enable supplemental logging on the target database for one-way replication. To add supplemental log data for key columns, issue the following commands from the GoldenGate Command Interface (GGSCI).

```
GGSCI (sourceserver) 1> dblogin userid gger password userpw
Successfully logged into database.
```

If you're logging in to SQL Server, the DBLOGIN command is slightly different, as shown in the following example:

```
GGSCI (sourceserver) 24> dblogin sourcedb sqlserver, userid sa, password userpw
Successfully logged into database.
```

SOURCEDB specifies the SQL Server ODBC data source, and USERID specifies the database user ID. If you're using Windows authentication, you can leave off the USERID and PASSWORD options.

Next you can use the ADD TRANDATA command to enable the supplemental logging required by GoldenGate:

```
GGSCI (sourceserver) 2> add trandata hr.employees

Logging of supplemental redo data enabled for table HR.EMPLOYEES.
```

The DBLOGIN command establishes a database connection for the gger database user. The ADD TRANDATA command causes the database to log primary-key columns for all update operations on the HR.EMPLOYEES table.

ADD TRANDATA performs different database commands in the background depending on the database. Behind the scenes, the ADD TRANDATA command is equivalent to the following command in an Oracle database:

```
ALTER TABLE HR.EMPLOYEES
ADD SUPPLEMENTAL LOG GROUP GGS_EMPLOYEES_19387 (EMPLOYEE_ID) ALWAYS;
```

For SQL Server 2008, you notice that ADD TRANDATA enables Change Data Capture (CDC) and sets up two new jobs to allow the GoldenGate Extract to use CDC. GoldenGate will minimize the amount of CDC data by using primary key or the smallest columns available.

You should verify the supplemental logging was successfully enabled with an Oracle query such as the following:

```
SQL> select owner, log_group_name, table_name
     from dba_log_groups where owner = 'HR';

OWNER  LOG_GROUP_NAME       TABLE_NAME
-----  -------------------  ----------
HR     GGS_EMPLOYEES_19387  EMPLOYEES
```

If you have a large number of tables, it may be time consuming to enter all the ADD TRANDATA commands individually. As an alternative, you can use a script, such as the following Oracle SQLPLUS script, to automatically generate the ADD TRANDATA commands for a large number of tables:

```
set echo off
set verify off
set pagesize 2000
set linesize 250
set trim on
set heading off
set feedback off

spool &&SCHEMA..add_trandata.obey

select 'add trandata &SCHEMA..'||table_name
  from dba_tables where owner = '&SCHEMA' ;

spool off
```

The preceding script generates an Oracle spool file, which you can then process in GGSCI using an OBEY command as follows:

```
GGSCI (sourceserver) 1> dblogin userid gger password userpw
Successfully logged into database.

GGSCI (sourceserver) 2> obey diroby/HR.add_trandata.obey
```

Once again, it's good practice that when the ADD TRANDATA commands complete, you should verify in SQLPLUS that the supplemental logging has been successfully enabled. You can do this with a query like the following:

```
SQL> select owner, log_group_name, table_name
     from dba_log_groups where owner = 'HR';

OWNER  LOG_GROUP_NAME        TABLE_NAME
-----  --------------------  ----------
HR     GGS_REGIONS_19375     REGIONS
HR     GGS_COUNTRIES_19377   COUNTRIES
```

```
HR      GGS_LOCATIONS_19379      LOCATIONS
HR      GGS_DEPARTMENTS_19382    DEPARTMENTS
HR      GGS_JOBS_19385           JOBS
HR      GGS_EMPLOYEES_19387      EMPLOYEES
HR      GGS_JOB_HISTORY_19391    JOB_HISTORY
```

For SQL Server 2008, you can query the Change Data Capture tables to determine if changed data capture has been enabled, as follows:

```
select * from cdc.change_tables
```

The next step is to disable any triggers or cascade-delete constraints, as discussed in the next section.

Disabling Triggers and Cascade-Delete Constraints

You need to disable any database triggers or cascade-delete referential integrity constraints on your *target* tables. The reason is to prevent duplicate changes, because GoldenGate is already replicating the *results* of the trigger and cascade-delete operations from the source database. If you didn't disable the constraints and triggers, GoldenGate would replicate those changes; then the triggers and cascade-delete constraints would also fire, causing duplicate changes on the target database.

Several methods are available for disabling the triggers and cascade-delete constraints. The first method is only available for newer Oracle versions and involves adding parameters to the Replicat. The second method is simply to alter the tables to disable the triggers and constraints and then enable them when replication is turned off.

Starting with GoldenGate version 11, a new SUPPRESSTRIGGERS option is available as part of the Replicat DBOPTIONS parameter, to automatically suppress the triggers from firing on the target. You can use it to avoid having to manually disable the triggers. This option is available for Oracle 10.2.0.5 databases and later, and for Oracle 11.2.0.2 databases and later. To disable constraints, if you have Oracle 9.2.0.7 database and later, you can use the Replicat parameter DBOPTIONS with the DEFERREFCONST option to delay checking and enforcement of integrity constraints until the Replicat transaction commits.

You can also use a SQL script such as the following Oracle database example to automatically generate your ALTER TABLE enable and disable commands for the cascade-delete constraints and triggers. Using a script to dynamically generate the commands from the database saves time and ensures more accuracy. In this example, the script prompts for the schema owner name:

```
set echo off
set verify off
set pagesize 2000
set linesize 250
set trim on
set heading off
set feedback off

spool &&SCHEMA..disable_cascade_delete_constraints.sql

select 'alter table '||owner||'.'||table_name||
' disable constraint '||constraint_name||';'
from all_constraints
where delete_rule = 'CASCADE'
and owner = '&SCHEMA';
```

```
spool off

spool &SCHEMA..disable_triggers.sql

select 'alter trigger '||owner||'.'||trigger_name||
' disable ;'
from all_triggers
where owner = '&SCHEMA';

spool off

spool &SCHEMA..enable_cascade_delete_constraints.sql

select 'alter table '||owner||'.'||table_name||
' enable constraint '||constraint_name||';'
from all_constraints
where delete_rule = 'CASCADE'
and owner = '&SCHEMA';

spool off

spool &SCHEMA..enable_triggers.sql

select 'alter trigger '||owner||'.'||trigger_name||
' enable;'
from all_triggers
where owner = '&SCHEMA';

spool off
```

The script generates four spool files, which you can then execute in SQLPLUS to disable and enable the triggers and cascade-delete constraints.

Verifying the Manager Status

You may remember from Chapter 2 and Chapter 3 the discussion of the GoldenGate Manager process, which manages all of the GoldenGate processes and resources. Before you can start the Extract and Replicat processes, you need to verify that the GoldenGate Manager process is running on the source and target servers. You can't start replication if the Manager isn't running. For the basic replication configuration, the Manager parameter file on the source and target servers needs to contain the port number, as shown in the following example:

```
GGSCI (server) 1> edit params MGR
------------------------------------------------------------------
-- GoldenGate Manager
------------------------------------------------------------------
port 7840
```

Chapter 5 significantly expands on the use of Manager parameters, but this is fine for now. You can use the INFO MGR command to verify that the Manager is running:

```
GGSCI (sourceserver) 1> info manager

Manager is running (IP port sourceserver.7840).
```

If the GoldenGate Manager isn't running, you can start it using the following command:

```
GGSCI (sourceserver) 1> start manager
```

■ **Tip** Many of the GoldenGate commands have abbreviations to save time and keystrokes. For example, instead of the command INFO MANAGER, you can abbreviate it as INFO MGR. The REPLICAT keyword can be abbreviated as REP and EXTRACT can be abbreviated as EXT.

Next, let's move on to configuring the GoldenGate Local Extract.

Configuring the Local Extract

Now that you've made sure the Manager is running, let's configure the Local Extract. In order to do this, you first need to create a parameter file for the Extract. Remember, for now, as the example, you're configuring the local Extract to capture all the SQL DML changes from the sample HR schema.

■ **Tip** You can edit the GoldenGate parameters directly from the GGSCI or using the native OS text editor outside of GGSCI, whichever is most convenient. To edit in GGSCI, you enter EDIT PARAMS *paramterfilename*. GGSCI brings up the parameter file in the default text editor, which is Notepad for Windows and vi for UNIX and Linux. You can change the default editor using the SET EDITOR command in GGSCI. If you're editing directly from the OS, save the parameter file in the /dirprm subdirectory under the GoldenGate software installation directory. In the example, the parameter file directory is /gger/ggs/dirprm.

Let's start by looking at the parameters for the Local Extract, as shown in the following example:

```
GGSCI (sourceserver) 1> edit params LHREMD1

Extract LHREMD1

-------------------------------------------------------------------
-- Local extract for HR schema
-------------------------------------------------------------------
```

```
SETENV (NLS_LANG = AMERICAN_AMERICA.AL32UTF8)

USERID GGER@SourceDB, PASSWORD userpw

ExtTrail dirdat/l1

Table HR.*;
```

The parameters and terminology may seem a little strange to you at first, but over time you get used to the format and usage. The next sections look at each of the parameters in more detail.

■ **Tip**   You can use two dashes (--) at the beginning of a line in the parameter file for comments.

Keep in mind that GoldenGate has many more configuration parameters than are used in these examples. You can refer to the *GoldenGate Reference Guide* for a detailed description of all the parameters. I usually refer to the "Alphabetical Reference" section in the *GoldenGate Reference Guide* to quickly find a parameter, its meaning, and its various options. The following sections also point out any applicable parameter differences for SQL Server.

EXTRACT

You can use the Extract parameter to define the GoldenGate Extract group. You should develop naming standards for your Extract group names. Having good naming standards will help you identify, at a glance, what the Extract is used for and where it's running. This is especially important in problem-solving situations where you need to get downed replication up and running again quickly. The current limit for Extract group names is eight characters. Here are some items you should include in your naming standard:

- The type of process, such as Extract, Data Pump, or Replicat
- The application that is using the process, such as human resources, payroll, sales, or billing
- The environment where the process is running, such as development or production
- A numeric indicator to show if there are multiple Extracts or Replicats

In the example, the Extract group is named LHREMD1. Let's review how you arrive at that Extract name. The *L* specifies it's the Local Extract. *HREM* specifies that you're using this Extract group for the human resources employee application in the HR schema. The *D* signifies that you're running in the development environment. And finally, the *1* indicates this is the first Extract group for this schema and application. You can add additional parallel Extract groups to improve performance, as discussed further in Chapter 7.

SETENV

You can use the SETENV parameter to override your default environment variable settings. In the example, you explicitly set NLS_LANG to AMERICAN_AMERICA.AL32UTF8. It's a good idea to set NLS_LANG and not let it unknowingly default to your environment setting. If NLS_LANG is incorrect, it could cause your replication to fail or replicate invalid data. For the Local Extract, NLS_LANG needs to match the source database character set. You can run a SQL query such as the following for Oracle to determine your NLS character set:

```
SQL> select * from v$nls_parameters where parameter like '%NLS_CHARACTERSET%';

PARAMETER          VALUE
-----------------  ----------
NLS_CHARACTERSET   US7ASCII
```

You can set other environment variables in addition to NLS_LANG using the SETENV parameter. For example, with an Oracle database, you can set ORACLE_HOME and ORACLE_SID as shown next. In the example, I chose instead to set the Oracle environment using the Oracle network TNS alias SourceDB instead of using SETENV. You can also set ORACLE_HOME and ORACLE_SID prior to entering GGSCI and not use a TNS alias or SETENV. Any of these methods will work, as long as the variable values are valid:

```
SETENV (ORACLE_HOME = "/u01/app/oracle/product/11.1.0")
SETENV (ORACLE_SID = "SourceDB")
```

For SQL Server, you can use SETENV to specify the number of times GoldenGate will try to read the transaction log before abending the time to delay between retries:

```
SETENV (GGS_CacheRetryCount = 25)
SETENV (GGS_CacheRetryDelay = 2000)
```

The preceding example tells GoldenGate to try reading the SQL Server transaction log 25 times (default is 10) and to wait 2000 milliseconds (default is 1000) between each try before abending.

USERID

In Chapter 2, you created the GoldenGate database user ID with appropriate security privileges. Using the USERID parameter, you can specify the GoldenGate database user ID and password to connect to the source database. The GoldenGate password can also be encrypted, as covered in Chapter 5.

To connect to SQL Server, you can use the SOURCEDB parameter with the USERID option, as shown in the following example:

```
SOURCEDB sqlserver, userid sa, PASSWORD userpw
```

SOURCEDB specifies the SQL Server ODBC data source, and USERID specifies the database user ID. If you're using Windows authentication, you can leave off the USERID and PASSWORD options.

▓ **Tip**   The order of the Extract parameters listed is important. For example, the EXTRACT parameter must be the first entry in the parameter file, and the EXTTRAIL parameter must precede any associated TABLE statements.

Next, let's look at the `EXTTRAIL` parameter.

EXTTRAIL

You can use the `EXTTRAIL` parameter to specify the two-character local Extract trail-file name. As discussed in Chapter 3, trail files are staging files used to store the committed transactions. In the example, the trail file holds the HR transactions extracted from the transaction log by the Local Extract. Next, the trail is processed by the data pump and sent across the network to the target server.

Trail files are usually written to the `dirdat` directory underneath the GoldenGate software installation directory. In this case, you're using a trail file named `l1`. GoldenGate automatically appends six characters to the trail-file name for aging purposes. For example, the first trail file is named `l1000000` in the `dirdat` directory. As this trail file fills up, GoldenGate will create the next new trail file, named `l1000001`, then `l1000002`, and so on.

You can specify a `FORMAT RELEASE` option with the `EXTTRAIL` parameter to instruct GoldenGate to write the trail file in an older release format for backward compatibility. This may be useful, for example, if you have an older version of GoldenGate on another system that you need to process trail files using a more recent version of GoldenGate.

For SQL Server, you should specify an additional parameter, as shown in the following example, to tell GoldenGate how to manage the secondary truncation points:

```
TRANLOGOPTIONS MANAGESECONDARYTRUNCATIONPOINT
```

You can specify `MANAGESECONDARYTRUNCATIONPOINT` If you want GoldenGate to maintain a secondary truncation point. You would specify this parameter if SQL Server replication wasn't running. If SQL Server replication was running concurrently with GoldenGate, then you would specify `NOMANAGESECONDARYTRUNCATIONPOINT` to allow SQL Server to manage the secondary truncation point.

TABLE

Use the `TABLE` parameter to specify from which source database tables you wish GoldenGate to extract changes. The `TABLE` parameter is a complex parameter; it has many options that allow you to filter rows, map columns, transform data, and so on. Chapter 5 covers some of these advanced options. For now, let's keep it simple and just instruct GoldenGate to extract all of the table data changes for the HR schema. You can do this easily by using a wildcard character, the asterisk (*), after the schema name. In the example, `HR.*`, tells GoldenGate to extract *all* the tables in the HR schema. You could also list each of the tables individually, but using the wildcard is much quicker and easier. The example also assumes that the source and target schemas match. If they didn't, you could use `TABLE` parameter options such as `COLMAP` to map the different source and target columns.

▓ **Tip**   Notice that the `TABLE` parameter must end in a semicolon.

Next, let's look at adding the Extract to the GoldenGate configuration.

Adding the Extract

Now that you've set up your Extract configuration parameters, the next step is to add the Extract group. You can do that using the following commands from GGSCI:

```
GGSCI (sourceserver) > ADD EXTRACT LHREMD1, TRANLOG, BEGIN NOW
GGSCI (sourceserver) > ADD EXTTRAIL dirdat/l1, EXTRACT LHREMD1, MEGABYTES 100
```

The first command, ADD EXTRACT, adds the Extract using the configuration parameters defined in the last section. After the Extract is added, it establishes checkpoints in the source trail file and on the database transaction log to keep track of processing. The TRANLOG parameter of the ADD EXTRACT command tells GoldenGate to use the database transaction log as its source. In the Oracle example, the redo logs are the source. BEGIN NOW tells Extract to begin processing changes from the source database as soon as the Extract is started. Optionally, you can also instruct Extract to begin capturing changes at a specific timestamp or using a specific trail-file number.

The ADD EXTTRAIL command adds the local Extract trail file, assigns it to Extract LHREMD1, and gives it a size of 100MB. The default size of trail files is 10MB. You should size the trail files sufficiently large enough based on the transaction volume so that GoldenGate isn't creating new trail files too often and slowing performance.

■ **Tip**   You should store your commands such as ADD EXTRACT in an obey file in the diroby directory. You can execute these from the GGSCI command prompt using the obey *filename* command. This is good practice because the commands are readily available as a future reference or if you need to re-execute the commands at some point. Chapter 14 covers more about obey files.

Now, let's look at how to start and stop the Extract.

Starting and Stopping the Extract

After adding the Extract, you need to start it to begin capturing changes, as shown in the following example:

```
GGSCI (sourceserver) > START EXTRACT LHREMD1
```

If needed, you can stop the Extract using a similar method. For example, you may need to make a change to the GoldenGate parameters. In this case, you would stop the Extract, make your changes to the parameters, and then start the Extract for the new changes to take effect. Here is an example of how to stop the LHREMD1 Extract:

```
GGSCI (sourceserver) > STOP EXTRACT LHREMD1
```

Verifying the Extract

When the Extract has started, you can verify that it's running using the INFO EXTRACT command. You should see a status of RUNNING. If you see a status of STOPPED or ABENDED, there may be a problem. In the following example, you're checking the status of the LHREMD1 Extract:

```
GGSCI (sourceserver) 2> info extract LHREMD1

EXTRACT     LHREMD1    Last Started 2011-01-15 13:53   Status RUNNING
Checkpoint Lag         00:00:00 (updated 00:00:08 ago)
Log Read Checkpoint    Oracle Redo Logs
                       2011-01-17 22:55:08  Seqno 3261, RBA 7135232
```

If the Extract isn't running, you can review the GoldenGate error log file and try to resolve the problem. Often, the error is something simple like incorrect spelling. The error file is named ggserr.log and is located in the GoldenGate software installation directory location. In the example on Linux, the error log is located in /gger/ggs/ggserr.log. On Windows, the GoldenGate error log based on the example is located in c:\gger\ggs\ggserr.log.

If your Extract won't start, first check for obvious problems such as the wrong GoldenGate database user ID, a bad password, or typographical errors in your parameter file. You should also verify that the source database is online and that you can access it using the GoldenGate database user and password. Chapter 11 goes into more detail on troubleshooting.

You can see from the INFO command that the local Extract is RUNNING. *Checkpoint lag* is the time delay between the last checkpoint written to the trail and the time when the record was processed by GoldenGate. You currently don't have any checkpoint lag. If you had a high checkpoint lag, it could indicate a performance problem or perhaps the local Extract just catching up on a large volume of changes. You can also see that Oracle redo logs are the source for the Extract, the last read checkpoint time, the transaction log sequence number, and the relative byte address (RBA) of the record in the transaction log.

You can add the DETAIL option to the INFO command to see even more information about the Extract. You may find the detail display helpful to see where the important files for the Extract are located, such as the parameter and report files. The following example uses the INFO command to display details about the LHREMD1 Local Extract"

```
GGSCI (sourceserver) 3> info ext LHREMD1, detail

EXTRACT     LHREMD1    Last Started 2011-01-15 13:53   Status RUNNING
Checkpoint Lag         00:00:00 (updated 00:00:01 ago)
Log Read Checkpoint    Oracle Redo Logs
                       2011-01-17 22:57:50  Seqno 3262, RBA 138240

  Target Extract Trails:

  Remote Trail Name                        Seqno       RBA     Max MB

  dirdat/l1                                    3      1489        100

  Extract Source                         Begin              End

  /data/SourceDB/database/redo01_01.rdo  2011-01-15 13:53   2011-01-17 22:57
  /data/SourceDB/database/redo01_01.rdo  2011-01-13 22:29   2011-01-15 13:53
  /data/SourceDB/database/redo01_01.rdo  2011-01-05 02:13   2011-01-13 22:29
  /data/SourceDB/database/redo02_01.rdo  2010-12-16 15:28   2011-01-05 02:13
  Not Available                          * Initialized *    2010-12-16 15:28
```

```
Current directory        /gger/ggs

Report file              /gger/ggs/dirrpt/LHREMD1.rpt
Parameter file           /gger/ggs/dirprm/LHREMD1.prm
Checkpoint file          /gger/ggs/dirchk/LHREMD1.cpe
Process file             /gger/ggs/dirpcs/LHREMD1.pce
Stdout file              /gger/ggs/dirout/LHREMD1.out
Error log                /gger/ggs/ggserr.log
```

Finally, you can run the `stats` command on your Extract. This shows whether the Extract has actually processed any DML changes. In the example, the Extract has processed four inserts and two deletes since it was started, as shown here:

```
GGSCI (sourceserver) 2> stats ext LHREMD1

Sending STATS request to EXTRACT LHREMD1 ...

Start of Statistics at 2011-01-18 18:50:38.

Output to /gger/ggs/dirdat/l1:

Extracting from HR.EMPLOYEES to HR.EMPLOYEES:

*** Total statistics since 2011-01-15 13:54:52 ***
        Total inserts                     4.00
        Total updates                     0.00
        Total deletes                     2.00
        Total discards                    0.00
        Total operations                  6.00
```

You're now finished starting the Local Extract, so let's move on to the next step: starting the data-pump Extract.

Starting the Data Pump

Now that the Local Extract is started, you can proceed with configuring, adding, and starting the data pump. First, let's refresh your memory a bit on the purpose of the data pump, from Chapter 3. The data pump is another type of GoldenGate Extract process. It reads the records in the source trail written by the Local Extract, pumps or passes them over the network to the target, and creates a target or remote trail.

In the example, you configure the data pump to read the l1 trail file written out by the Local Extract named LHREMD1 and pump it over the TCP/IP network to the target server to be processed by the Replicat.

Configuring the Data Pump

From GGSCI, let's edit the parameters for the data pump as shown in this example:

```
GGSCI (sourceserver) 1> edit params PHREMD1

Extract PHREMD1

-------------------------------------------------------------------
-- Data Pump extract for HR schema
-------------------------------------------------------------------

PassThru

RmtHost targetserver, MgrPort 7840
RmtTrail dirdat/l2

Table HR.* ;
```

Now, let's look at each of the parameters in more detail. As mentioned with the Local Extract, GoldenGate has many more configuration parameters than are used in the basic example. You can refer to the *GoldenGate Reference Guide* for a detailed description of all the parameters. I usually refer to the "Alphabetical Reference" section in the *GoldenGate Reference Guide* to quickly find a parameter and its meaning and various options.

EXTRACT

You probably already noticed that the data pump is simply another type of GoldenGate Extract. Use the `Extract` parameter to define the GoldenGate data-pump Extract group name. Just as with the Local Extract, you're limited to eight characters for Extract group name. Follow the same naming standard covered in the previous "Extract" section.

The example named the data-pump Extract group PHREMD1. The *P* specifies that it's the data-pump Extract. The rest of the name is the same as the Local Extract, covered in the previous section. You can add additional parallel data-pump Extract groups to improve performance, as discussed more in Chapter 7.

■ **Tip**   You don't specify a `SETENV` in the data pump. `SETENV` for `NLS_LANG` isn't needed for the data-pump Extract because it has no effect. It should be specified in the Local Extract and Replicat parameters.

Next, let's discuss the `PASSTHRU` parameter.

PASSTHRU

You can specify the `PASSTHRU` parameter on the data pump if you aren't doing any filtering or column mapping and your source and target data structures are identical. For GoldenGate to consider the tables identical, they must have the same column names, data types, sizes, and semantics and appear in the same order. Using `PASSTHRU` improves performance by allowing GoldenGate to bypass looking up any table definitions from the database or the data-definitions file. You may also find this helpful if you need to put your data-pump Extract on an intermediate or middle-tier server that doesn't have a database running.

RMTHOST

Use RMTHOST and MGRPORT to tell the data-pump Extract the remote server name and the port on which the GoldenGate manager is running. This is the destination location where the data pump sends the local trail file over the TCP/IP network. You should verify that you have network connectivity between your source server and the MGRPORT on the RMTHOST. If needed, you can specify multiple remote hosts in the same parameter file to send trails to different servers.

RMTTRAIL

You can use RMTTRAIL to specify the two-character remote trail name for your data pump. In this case, you use l2 as the remote trail name. Remember that l1 is the local trail. The data pump reads the local l1 trail file and pumps it to the remote or target server as l2. Also notice that GoldenGate adds the same six-character sequence number onto the trail-file name, starting with l2000000, then l2000001, then l2000002, and so on.

TABLE

The TABLE parameter may look familiar by now. This is the same TABLE parameter described for the Local Extract. In the example, you use wildcarding to pump all the tables in the HR schema (HR.*) to the target server. If needed, you coulf filter or transform data at this point using the data pump. Instead, you just pass on all the data that the Local Extract has captured.

Adding the Data Pump

Now that you've set up the data-pump Extract configuration parameters, the next step is to add the data-pump Extract group. You can do that using the commands shown in the following example:

```
GGSCI (sourceserver) > ADD EXTRACT PHREMD1, EXTTRAILSOURCE dirdat/l1
GGSCI (sourceserver) > ADD RMTTRAIL dirdat/l2, EXTRACT PHREMD1, MEGABYTES 100
```

Let's look at each of the commands in more detail.

The first command, ADD EXTRACT, adds the data-pump Extract using the configuration parameters defined in the last section. The EXTTRAILSOURCE parameter of the ADD EXTRACT command tells GoldenGate to use the trail file created by the Local Extract as the source for the data-pump Extract. In the Oracle example, the l1 trail file is the source. BEGIN NOW tells Extract to begin processing changes from the source trail as soon as the data-pump Extract is started. You can also tell the data-pump Extract to begin capturing changes at a specific timestamp or using a specific trail-file number.

The ADD RMTTRAIL command adds the data-pump Extract remote trail file, assigns it to Extract PHREMD1, and gives it a size of 100MB. The default size of trail files is 10MB. As with the Local Extract, you should size the trail files sufficiently large enough based on the transaction volume so that GoldenGate isn't creating new trail files too often and slowing performance.

▨ **Tip**   You can get help in GGSCI on any of the commands by entering the HELP command. More detailed help is available on specific commands, such as HELP ADD EXTRACT.

Starting and Stopping the Data Pump

After adding the data-pump Extract, you need to start it to begin processing records from the source trail file, as shown in this example:

```
GGSCI (sourceserver) > START EXTRACT PHREMD1
```

If needed, you can stop the data-pump Extract using the STOP EXTRACT command. For example, you may need to make a change to the data-pump Extract parameters. To do that, you stop the data-pump Extract, change the parameter file, and then start the data-pump Extract for the new changes to take effect. Here is an example of the STOP EXTRACT command:

```
GGSCI (sourceserver) > STOP EXTRACT PHREMD1
```

Let's look at a few commands to verify that the data-pump Extract is working.

Verifying the Data Pump

When the data-pump Extract has started, you can verify that it's running using the INFO EXTRACT command. This is similar to verifying the local Extract, as shown in the following example for the PHREMD1 data-pump Extract:

```
GGSCI (sourceserver) 2> info extract PHREMD1

EXTRACT      PHREMD1    Last Started 2011-01-14 10:25    Status RUNNING
Checkpoint Lag           00:00:00 (updated 00:00:01 ago)
Log Read Checkpoint     File dirdat/l1000001
                        2011-01-17 15:05:33.485076   RBA 977
```

You should see a status of RUNNING. If you see a status of STOPPED or ABENDED, there may be a problem. As with the Local Extract, you can review the GoldenGate error-log file and try to resolve the problem. Often, the error is something simple like incorrect spelling. The error file is named **ggserr.log** and is located in the GoldenGate software location.

If your data-pump Extract won't start, first check for obvious problems such as typographical errors in your parameter file, and verify that the source trail file exists in the dirdat directory and that you can access it using the GoldenGate OS user. Also make sure the target server is specified correctly in the parameters and verify that you have network connectivity from the source server to the GoldenGate manager port on the target server. Chapter 11 goes into more detail about troubleshooting.

You can see from the INFO command that the data pump status is RUNNING. As described earlier, checkpoint lag is the time delay between the last checkpoint written to the trail and the time when the record was processed by GoldenGate. You currently don't have any checkpoint lag. If you had high checkpoint lag, it could indicate a performance problem or the data-pump Extract catching up on a large volume of changes. Usually, the data-pump Extract in PASSTHRU mode doesn't experience lag because it's simply transferring data. You can also see the source of your data pump as the l1 trail created by the local extract, the time of the last read checkpoint, and the RBA of the record in the trail file.

You can add the DETAIL option to the INFO command to see even more information about the data-pump Extract. You may find the detail display helpful to see where the important files for the extract are located, such as the parameter and report files. This example shows the detail for the PHREMD1 data-pump Extract:

```
GGSCI (sourceserver) 3> info ext PHREMD1, detail

EXTRACT     PHREMD1    Last Started 2011-01-23 16:28    Status RUNNING
Checkpoint Lag         00:00:00 (updated 00:00:00 ago)
Log Read Checkpoint    File dirdat/l1000009
                       First Record   RBA 3431

  Target Extract Trails:

  Remote Trail Name                         Seqno        RBA     Max MB

  dirdat/l2                                     4       1151        100

  Extract Source                    Begin              End

  dirdat/l1000009                   2011-01-20 14:04   First Record
  dirdat/l1000009                   2011-01-14 10:22   2011-01-20 14:04
  dirdat/l1000007                   2011-01-12 10:59   2011-01-14 10:22
  dirdat/l1000005                   2011-01-07 08:38   2011-01-12 10:59
  dirdat/l1000004                   2011-01-07 08:38   2011-01-07 08:38
  dirdat/l1000004                   * Initialized *    2011-01-07 08:38
  dirdat/l1000000                   * Initialized *    First Record


Current directory      /gger/ggs/ora10

Report file            /gger/ggs/dirrpt/PHREMD1.rpt
Parameter file         /gger/ggs/dirprm/PHREMD1.prm
Checkpoint file        /gger/ggs/dirchk/PHREMD1.cpe
Process file           /gger/ggs/dirpcs/PHREMD1.pce
Stdout file            /gger/ggs/dirout/PHREMD1.out
Error log              /gger/ggs/ggserr.log
```

Finally, you can run the STATS command on your data-pump Extract. This shows whether the data-pump Extract has actually processed any DML activity. In the example, the data-pump Extract has processed four inserts and two deletes since it was started:

```
GGSCI (sourceserver) 2> stats ext PHREMD1

Sending STATS request to EXTRACT PHREMD1 ...

Start of Statistics at 2011-01-18 18:50:38.

Output to /gger/ggs/dirdat/l2:

Extracting from HR.EMPLOYEES to HR.EMPLOYEES:
```

```
*** Total statistics since 2011-01-15 13:54:52 ***
        Total inserts                      4.00
        Total updates                      0.00
        Total deletes                      2.00
        Total discards                     0.00
        Total operations                   6.00
```

After you've started the Local Extract and the data-pump Extract, you can run the initial data load from your source to the target databases. You can use either GoldenGate itself or the DBMS vendor load utilities to do the initial data load. The DBMS vendor load utilities are optimized to load the vendor database, so you may find that they perform better than the GoldenGate load. On the other hand, if you need to do complex transformations or are doing heterogeneous replication, the GoldenGate initial load may work better. The following sections discuss each load method.

Loading with GoldenGate

You have several choices to make if you decide to perform the initial load with GoldenGate. You can choose to have the Extract write the initial load records to a file that is then processed by the Replicat. You can also have the Extract write out the initial load records in a format that can be processed by DBMS utilities like Oracle SQL*Loader and the SQL Server Bulk Copy Program (BCP). Another method, which is the one covered here, is the Oracle GoldenGate direct-load method. With the Oracle direct-load method, no trail files are written to disk. Instead, GoldenGate extracts the data from the source database and sends it directly to a Replicat task on the target server, which loads the data into the target database. If you need further information, you can find instructions for using the GoldenGate initial-load methods in the *Oracle GoldenGate Windows and UNIX Administrator's Guide*.

In order to load the database using Oracle GoldenGate direct-load, you need to set up an initial-load Extract and an initial-load Replicat. These are similar to the Extract and Replicat you already added for ongoing synchronization, but with a few new parameters to let GoldenGate know these are to be used specifically for the initial load.

■ **Tip** You can set up multiple Extracts and Replicats to handle different sets of tables and run them in parallel to speed up the GoldenGate initial load. This is covered in more detail in Chapter 7.

First, let's look at some of the prerequisites for using the GoldenGate initial load.

Prerequisites for the GoldenGate Initial Load

Before starting the GoldenGate initial load, make sure the following tasks have been completed:

- You must disable any foreign-key constraints on the target tables to prevent errors. You may also choose to disable check constraints to speed up performance.

- Disable any triggers on the target tables. Triggers firing while the data is being loaded can cause errors.

- You may want to drop indexes on your target tables to speed up performance. This is optional.

When you've made sure the prerequisites have been met, you can begin setting up the initial-load Extract.

Configuring the Initial-Load Extract

Let's review the Oracle direct-load Extract parameter file used for the example. Remember, you need to load all the records in the HR schema from the source database into the same schema on the target database. You name the new initial-load Extract starting with the letter *I* to indicate that it's being used for the initial load:

```
GGSCI (sourceserver) 1> edit params IHREMD1

Extract IHREMD1

--------------------------------------------------------------------
-- Initial Load extract for HR schema
--------------------------------------------------------------------

SETENV (NLS_LANG = AMERICAN_AMERICA.AL32UTF8)

USERID GGER@SourceDB, PASSWORD userpw

RmtHost targetserver, mgrport 7840
RmtTask Replicat, Group DHREMD1

Table HR.*;
```

One new parameter is required for the initial-load Extract. The RMTTASK parameter is used to have GoldenGate automatically start and stop a Replicat on the target server for the direct load. During the direct load, the Extract communicates directly with the initial-load Replicat over the network. Records are loaded by the Replicat directly into the target database as the Extract captures them from the source database. The Replicat keyword tells GoldenGate that the remote task is a GoldenGate Replicat. The Group parameter is used to specify the name of the Replicat on the target server, in this case Replicat DHREMD1.

Adding the Initial-Load Extract

Now that you've set up your initial-load Extract configuration parameters, the next step is to add the initial-load Extract group. You can do that using the following commands from GGSCI:

```
GGSCI (sourceserver) > ADD EXTRACT IHREMD1, SOURCEISTABLE
```

Notice that adding the initial-load Extract is similar to adding the Local and data-pump Extracts. One difference is that you need to specify the SOURCEISTABLE option. SOURCEISTABLE tells GoldenGate that this Extract is used only for initial loading and to capture *all* the records from the source database for loading into the target database. Another difference is that there is no need to specify any trail files for the Oracle direct-load Extract.

Before you start the initial-load Extract, you need to configure and add the initial-load Replicat.

Configuring the Initial-Load Replicat

Next, let's examine the Oracle direct-load Replicat parameter file used for the example. Once again, you're loading all the records in the HR schema from the source database into the same schema on the target database. The Replicat is started and stopped automatically by GoldenGate when you start the initial-load Extract:

```
GGSCI (targetserver) 1> edit params DHREMD1

Replicat DHREMD1

-------------------------------------------------------------------
-- Initial load replicat for HR schema
-------------------------------------------------------------------

SETENV (NLS_LANG = AMERICAN_AMERICA.AL32UTF8)

USERID GGER@TargetDB, PASSWORD userpw

AssumeTargetDefs

Map HR.*, Target HR.* ;
```

Let's look at each of the Replicat parameters in more detail.

REPLICAT

You can use the REPLICAT parameter to define the GoldenGate initial-load Replicat group. You should develop naming standards for your Replicat groups. This will help you quickly identify what the Replicat is used for and where it's running. This is especially important in problem-solving situations where you need to quickly get the replication up and running again if it's down. The current limit for Replicat group names is eight characters. Here are some items you should include in your naming standard:

- The type of process: in this case, a Replicat. As shown in the example, you should also name initial-load Extracts and Replicats differently if you use GoldenGate for the initial load.

- The application that is using the process, such as human resources, payroll, sales, or billing.

- The environment where the process is running, such as development or production.

- An indicator to show if there are multiple Replicats.

In the example, the Replicat group is named DHREMD1. The first character, *D*, specifies that it's the direct-load Replicat. *HREM* specifies that you're using this Replicat group for the human resources employee application and the HR schema. The second *D* signifies that you're running in the development environment. Any finally, the *1* indicates that this is the first Replicat group for this schema and application. You can add additional Replicat groups to improve performance, as discussed further in Chapter 7.

SETENV

You can use the SETENV parameter to override default environment variable settings. The example explicitly sets NLS_LANG to AMERICAN_AMERICA.AL32UTF8. It's a good idea to set NLS_LANG and not let it default to the environment setting. If NLS_LANG is incorrect, it can cause your replication to fail or replicate incorrect data. For the Replicat, NLS_LANG needs to match the NLS character set of the data in the trail file it's reading, which was created from the source database.

You can set other environment variables in addition to NLS_LANG using the SETENV parameter. For example, you can set ORACLE_HOME and ORACLE_SID as shown next. In the example, I chose instead to set the Oracle environment using the TNS alias of TargetDB instead of using SETENV. You could also set ORACLE_HOME and ORACLE_SID prior to entering GGSCI and not use a TNS alias or SETENV. Any of these methods will work, as long as the variable values are valid:

```
SETENV (ORACLE_HOME = "/u01/app/oracle/product/11.1.0")
SETENV (ORACLE_SID = "TargetDB")
```

Next, let's review the USERID parameter.

USERID

In Chapter 2, you created the GoldenGate database user ID with appropriate security privileges. Using the USERID parameter, you can specify the GoldenGate database user ID and password to connect to the target database. The GoldenGate password can also be encrypted, as covered in Chapter 5.

As mentioned earlier on the Extract, for SQL Server, you can use the SOURCEDB parameter with the USERID option:

```
SOURCEDB sqlserver, userid sa, PASSWORD userpw
```

SOURCEDB specifies the SQL Server ODBC data source, and USERID specifies the database User ID. If you're using Windows authentication, you can leave off the USERID and PASSWORD options.

ASSUMETARGETDEFS

You can use the ASSUMETARGETDEFS parameter when the source and target tables are identical. In the example, the HR schema on the source and target is identical. If the database tables being used on the source and target are different, you need to generate a data-definitions file instead. Chapter 5 covers using a data-definitions file.

MAP

You use the MAP parameter to specify the mapping from your source tables to the target tables. The source tables were specified previously in the Extract with the TABLE parameter. In the example, you're using wildcarding to map all the tables in the HR schema on the source database to the same tables in the HR schema on the target database.

Similar to the TABLE parameter, the MAP parameter is a complex parameter with many options that allow you to filter rows, map columns, transform data, and so on. Some of these options are covered in Chapter 5. For now, let's keep it simple and just instruct GoldenGate to replicate all the changes for the HR schema. You can do this easily by using the wildcard character, an asterisk, as in HR.*. The wildcard tells GoldenGate to replicate *all* of the tables in the HR schema. You could also list each of the tables individually, but using the wildcard is much easier. You also assume that the source and target schemas match. If they didn't, you could use MAP parameter options such as COLMAP to map the different source and target columns.

Adding the Initial-Load Replicat

Before you can use the initial-load Replicat, you need to add the Replicat group. You can do that using the ADD REPLICAT command, as shown in the following example:

```
GGSCI (targetserver) > ADD REPLICAT DHREMD1, SPECIALRUN
```

The ADD REPLICAT command tells GoldenGate to add the Replicat group. You can use the SPECIALRUN parameter to let GoldenGate know that this is a special Replicat to be used only for the initial load. Later, this chapter covers setting up another Replicat for ongoing synchronization.

Now that you have the initial-load Extract and Replicat configured and added to GoldenGate, you can start the load process.

Starting the GoldenGate Initial Load

You start the GoldenGate initial-load process by starting the Extract. Remember, it isn't necessary to start the Replicat, because GoldenGate does this automatically for the initial load when the initial-load Extract is started. GoldenGate only automatically starts the Replicat for an initial-load Replicat, not for the ongoing-change Replicat. When the load is complete, GoldenGate automatically stops the initial-load Extract and Replicat. Let's start the IHREMD1 Extract, as shown in the following example:

```
GGSCI (sourceserver) > START EXTRACT IHREMD1
```

If needed for some reason, you can stop the initial-load Extract using a similar method. For example, you may need to make a change to the GoldenGate parameters on the initial-load Extract. You stop and then start the initial-load Extract for the new changes to take effect. You must remember to check whether any rows have already been loaded to the target table. If so, you need to delete those rows on the target before restarting the extract. Following is an example of stopping the IHREMD1 Extract:

```
GGSCI (sourceserver) > STOP EXTRACT IHREMD1
```

Verifying the Initial Load

You can verify the initial load by viewing the GoldenGate report file on the target server. Following is an excerpt from the report file that shows the number of rows that have been loaded:

```
GGSCI (targetserver) > VIEW REPORT DHREMD1


...
...
...

**********************************************************************
*                    ** Run Time Statistics **                      *
**********************************************************************
```

```
Report at 2011-01-21 23:31:42 (activity since 2011-01-21 23:31:36)

From Table HR.COUNTRIES to HR.COUNTRIES:
       #                    inserts:        25
       #                    updates:         0
       #                    deletes:         0
       #                    discards:        0
From Table HR.DEPARTMENTS to HR.DEPARTMENTS:
       #                    inserts:        27
       #                    updates:         0
       #                    deletes:         0
       #                    discards:        0
From Table HR.EMPLOYEES to HR.EMPLOYEES:
       #                    inserts:       117
       #                    updates:         0
       #                    deletes:         0
       #                    discards:        0
From Table HR.JOBS to HR.JOBS:
       #                    inserts:        19
       #                    updates:         0
       #                    deletes:         0
       #                    discards:        0
From Table HR.JOB_HISTORY to HR.JOB_HISTORY:
       #                    inserts:        10
       #                    updates:         0
       #                    deletes:         0
       #                    discards:        0
From Table HR.LOCATIONS to HR.LOCATIONS:
       #                    inserts:        23
       #                    updates:         0
       #                    deletes:         0
       #                    discards:        0
From Table HR.REGIONS to HR.REGIONS:
       #                    inserts:         4
       #                    updates:         0
       #                    deletes:         0
       #                    discards:        0

...
...
...
```

You need to wait until the initial load is completely finished before starting the Replicat for ongoing change synchronization. Later, this chapter reviews starting the ongoing synchronization Replicat. First, let's review the steps for loading with DBMS vendor utilities.

Loading with DBMS Utilities

The DBMS vendor load utilities are optimized to load the particular vendor database, so you may find that they perform better than the GoldenGate load. For example, for an Oracle database, you can choose from the original export/import, the Data Pump export/import, RMAN copy, transportable tablespaces, and so on. You should choose the load utility that works best for your particular needs. For example, if you're using GoldenGate to replicate from Oracle 9i to Oracle 11g, the original export/import may be your best option for the initial load. If you're replicating from Oracle 10g to Oracle 11g, then you may decide to use Oracle Data Pump export/import. You can refer to the specific DBMS manuals for requirements and instructions on running the load utilities.

Prerequisites for Loading with DBMS Utilities

Before starting the initial load using DBMS utilities, make sure the following tasks have been completed:

- You should disable any foreign-key constraints and triggers on the target tables to prevent data errors. Check constraints can be disabled during the load to speed up performance. Remember, if you're going to use GoldenGate to keep the data synchronized ongoing after the load, delete-cascade constraints and triggers will need to remain disabled.

- You may want to drop indexes on your target tables during the load to speed up performance. You can add these back when the load is complete. This is optional.

Steps for Loading with DBMS Utilities

You can use the following steps to load your target database using DBMS utilities in preparation for GoldenGate replication:

1. Make sure you've met the prerequisites described in the previous sections for starting replication and loading with the DBMS utilities.

2. Start the ongoing synchronization Local and data-pump Extracts to capture changes while the load is running. See the previous sections on starting the local and data-pump Extracts for details.

3. Execute the initial load using the DBMS utility you have chosen. After the load is completely finished, proceed with the next step.

4. Start the ongoing synchronization Replicat to apply changes made while the initial data-load DBMS utility was running. This also begins to apply new changes to keep the tables synchronized on an ongoing basis. The next section goes over this.

Starting the Replicat

After you've loaded your data, you can start the Replicat to apply the changes that were captured by the Extract while the load was running. These changes were queued up in the trail files while the load was running and are waiting to be applied by the Replicat. After you've configured, added, and successfully started the Replicat, the changes from the trail are applied to the target tables.

In some cases, you may run into errors with duplicate or missing data caused by the ongoing changes made during the initial-load process. For example, if a row was updated and then deleted during the initial load, GoldenGate may try to apply the update to the missing row that was never loaded. You can make GoldenGate try to resolve these errors automatically by adding the HANDLECOLLISIONS parameter to the Replicat. You may also notice that it takes some time for the Replicat to catch up with applying all the changes made during the load, particularly for a large database with heavy change volume and a long load time.

When the initial changes have been applied and there is no GoldenGate lag left, the databases are fully synchronized. At this point, the Local and data-pump Extracts and Replicat can continue to run and keep the databases synchronized in real time with the ongoing changes.

This section covers the various ongoing change Replicat configuration settings and options. After that, you see how to start the Replicat and verify that it's properly applying changes to the target. Let's begin with configuring the Replicat.

Configuring the Replicat

Before starting to configure the Replicat, you should go back and double-check the prerequisites on the target server, as covered in the section, "Prerequisites for Setting Up Replication." When you've confirmed that the prerequisites are met, you can begin configuring the Replicat. In order to do this, you first need to create a parameter file for the Replicat. Remember, you're configuring the Replicat to apply all the DML changes from the HR schema.

■ **Note** You can edit the GoldenGate parameters directly from the GGSCI or using the native OS text editor outside of GGSCI, whichever is most convenient. To edit in GGSCI, you enter EDIT PARAMS *paramterfilename*. GGSCI brings up the parameter file in the default text editor, which is Notepad for Windows and vi for UNIX and Linux. You can change the default editor using the SET EDITOR command in GGSCI. If you're editing directly from the OS, save the parameter file in the /dirprm subdirectory under the GoldenGate software installation directory. In the example, this is /gger/ggs/dirprm.

Let's begin by taking a look at the Replicat parameters for RHREMD1 as shown in the following example:

```
GGSCI (targetserver) 1> edit params RHREMD1

Replicat RHREMD1

------------------------------------------------------------------
-- Replicat for HR Schema
------------------------------------------------------------------

SETENV (NLS_LANG = AMERICAN_AMERICA.AL32UTF8)
```

```
USERID GGER@TargetDB, PASSWORD userpw

HandleCollisions

AssumeTargetDefs

Map HR.*, Target HR.* ;
```

Let's examine the parameters in more detail. Keep in mind that GoldenGate has many more configuration parameters than are used in the example. You can refer to the *Oracle GoldenGate Reference Guide* for a detailed description of all the parameters. I usually refer to the "Alphabetical Reference" section in the *Oracle GoldenGate Reference Guide* to quickly find a parameter and its meaning and various options.

■ **Tip**   You can use two dashes (--) at the beginning of a line in the parameter file for comments.

Let's start by reviewing the `Replicat` parameter in the next section.

Replicat

As with the initial-load Replicat, use the `Replicat` parameter to define the GoldenGate ongoing change Replicat group. You should follow naming standards, as covered earlier.

In the example, the Replicat group is named RHREMD1. The *R* specifies that it's the ongoing change Replicat. *HREM* specifies that you're using this Replicat group for the human resources employee application and the HR schema. The *D* signifies that you're running in the development environment. Any finally, the *1* indicates this is the first Replicat group for this schema and application. You can add additional parallel Replicat groups to improve performance, as covered in Chapter 7.

SETENV

As we showed in the initial-load Replicat, you can use the `SETENV` parameter to override default environment variable settings. In the example, you explicitly set `NLS_LANG` to `AMERICAN_AMERICA.AL32UTF8`. It's a good idea to set `NLS_LANG` and not let it default to the environment setting. It is possible we could have a different `NLS_LANG` for the Local Extract and the Replicat. If `NLS_LANG` is incorrect, it can cause the replication to fail or replicate incorrect data. For the Replicat, `NLS_LANG` needs to match the NLS character set of the data in the trail file it's reading, which was created from the source database.

You can set other environment variables in addition to `NLS_LANG` using the `SETENV` parameter. For example, you can set `ORACLE_HOME` and `ORACLE_SID` as shown next. In the example, I chose instead to set the Oracle environment using the Oracle network TNS alias of `TargetDB` instead of using `SETENV`. You can also set `ORACLE_HOME` and `ORACLE_SID` prior to entering GGSCI and not use a TNS alias or `SETENV`. Any of these methods will work as long as the variable values are valid:

```
SETENV (ORACLE_HOME = "/u01/app/oracle/product/11.1.0")
SETENV (ORACLE_SID = "TargetDB")
```

Next, let's review the `USERID` parameter.

USERID

Using the USERID parameter, you can specify the GoldenGate database user ID and password to connect to the target database. The GoldenGate password can be encrypted. Chapter 5 discusses encryption.

For SQL Server, you can use the SOURCEDB parameter with the USERID option, as shown here:

```
SOURCEDB sqlserver, userid sa, PASSWORD userpw
```

SOURCEDB specifies the SQL Server ODBC data source, and USERID specifies the database user ID. If you're using Windows authentication, you can leave off the USERID and PASSWORD options.

▓ **Note** The order of the parameters listed is important. For example, the REPLICAT parameter must be the first entry in the parameter file.

Next, let's review the HANDLECOLLISIONS parameter.

HANDLECOLLISIONS

You can use the HANDLECOLLISIONS parameter to have the Replicat attempt to resolve data errors or collisions when applying changes on the target. A collision can happen when the target row is either missing or a duplicate. The default processing for GoldenGate is not to automatically handle collisions, which can be set using the NOHANDLECOLLISIONS parameter.

HANDLECOLLISIONS is used mostly during initial loads, but it can also be used with care at other times for error resolution. During the initial load, you may run into errors with duplicate or missing data caused by the ongoing changes during the load. For example, if a row was updated and then deleted during the initial load, GoldenGate may try to apply the update to the deleted row that was never loaded. Another example is in problem situations where you need to have the Replicat reprocess transactions by repositioning it backward in the trail file. If you add the HANDLECOLLISIONS parameter, GoldenGate tries to resolve these errors automatically.

HANDLECOLLISIONS does the following when processing changes:

- Updates to rows that are missing are ignored.

- Deletes to rows that are missing are ignored.

- Inserts that are duplicated are changed to updates.

You should turn off HANDLECOLLISIONS as soon as possible after GoldenGate has completed processing past the point of the initial data load or past the problem situation. You can do this by removing the HANDLECOLLISIONS parameter in the Replicat parameter file (or adding the NOHANDLECOLLISIONS parameter) and restarting the Replicat. Another way to turn off HANDLECOLLISIONS is to use the SEND command, as shown next, to communicate directly with the running Replicat. If you choose this method, don't forget to also go back and remove the HANDLECOLLISIONS parameter from your Replicat parameter file so you don't inadvertently turn it on again the next time the Replicat is restarted. The following example sets the RHREMD1 Replicat to use NOHANDLECOLLISIONS:

```
GGSCI (targetserver)> send replicat RHREMD1 NOHANDLECOLLISIONS HR.*
Sending NOHANDLECOLLISIONS request to REPLICAT RHREMD1 ...
RHREMD1 NOHANDLECOLLISIONS set for 1 tables and 1 wildcard entries
```

The reason for turning off HANDLECOLLISIONS is that under normal processing conditions, you want GoldenGate to create an error condition if a collision occurs and to stop processing. There may be a serious problem that needs to be investigated. In those cases, you need to research the root cause of the problem rather than have HANDLECOLLISIONS mask the problem and GoldenGate continue processing.

You can see if the Replicat encountered any collisions by using the STATS REPLICAT command. It shows you if there were any collisions and how many for each type of DML statement. See the section "Verifying the Replicat" for an example of the output.

■ **Tip**   Techniques are available with specific load utilities that allow you to avoid using the HANDLECOLLISIONS parameter. For example, you can use the Oracle RMAN clone process for the initial load and start the GoldenGate Replicat to position after a specific Commit Sequence Number (CSN) in the trail corresponding to the Oracle System Change Number (SCN) from RMAN. For more details, download the white paper *Oracle GoldenGate Best Practices: Instantiation from an Oracle Source*. You can find the white paper at support.oracle.com, Article ID 1276058.1.

Next, let's review at the ASSUMETARGETDEFS parameter.

ASSUMETARGETDEFS

You can use the ASSUMETARGETDEFS parameter when your source and target tables are identical. In the example, the HR schema on the source and target is identical. For GoldenGate to consider the tables identical, they must have the same column names, data types, sizes, and semantics, and appear in the same order. If the database tables being used on the source and target are different, you need to generate a data-definitions file instead. Chapter 5 covers using a data-definitions file.

MAP

You use the MAP parameter to specify the mapping from your source tables to the target tables. The source tables you specified previously in the Extract with the TABLE parameter. In the example, you use wildcarding to map all the tables in the HR schema on the source database to the HR schema on the target database.

Similar to the TABLE parameter, the MAP parameter is a complex parameter that has many options that allow you to filter rows, map columns, transform data, and so on. Chapter 5 covers some of these options. For now, let's keep it simple and just instruct GoldenGate to replicate all the changes for the HR schema. You can do this easily by using wildcarding with HR.*, which tells GoldenGate to replicate *all* of the tables in the HR schema. You could also list each of the tables individually, but using the wildcard is much easier. You also assume that your source and target schemas match. If they didn't, you could use MAP parameter options such as COLMAP to map the different source and target columns.

■ **Note** Notice that the MAP parameter must end in a semicolon.

Next, let's look at adding the Replicat group.

Adding the Replicat

Now that you've set up the Replicat configuration parameters, the next step is to add the Replicat group. The following example adds the RHREMD1 Replicat to the GoldenGate configuration:

```
GGSCI (targetserver) > ADD REPLICAT RHREMD1, EXTTRAIL dirdat/l2
```

Let's look at each of the commands in more detail.

The first command, ADD REPLICAT, adds the Replicat using the configuration parameters defined in the last section. After the Replicat is added, it establishes checkpoints in the trail file to keep track of processing. The EXTTRAIL parameter of the ADD REPLICAT command tells GoldenGate to use a specific trail file for the Replicat to process. The example uses trail file l2 as the source for the Replicat. This is the trail file that was written by your data-pump Extract. In the example, you take the defaults and start processing at the beginning of the first trail file. You can also tell Replicat to begin applying changes at a specific timestamp or using a specific trail-file number.

■ **Tip** You should store commands such as ADD REPLICAT in an obey file in the diroby directory. You can execute these from the GGSCI command prompt using the obey *filename* command. This is good practice because the commands are readily available as a future reference or if you need to repeat the commands at some point. Chapter 14 covers obey files in more detail.

Now you can proceed with starting the Replicat.

Starting and Stopping the Replicat

After adding the Extract, you need to start it to actually begin applying changes to the target database. The following example starts the Replicat RHREMD1:

```
GGSCI (targetserver) > START REPLICAT RHREMD1
```

If needed, you can stop the Replicat using a similar method. For example, you may need to make a change to the GoldenGate Replicat parameters. To do that, you stop the Replicat, make the changes to the parameter file, and then start the Replicat for the new changes to take effect. The following example shows how to stop the Replicat RHREMD1:

```
GGSCI (targetserver) > STOP REPLICAT RHREMD1
```

The next section looks at verifying the Replicat.

Verifying the Replicat

When the Replicat has started, you can verify that it's running using the INFO REPLICAT command. You should see a status of RUNNING. If you see a status of STOPPED or ABENDED, there may be a problem. You can review the GoldenGate error log file and try to resolve the problem. Often, the error is something simple like incorrect spelling. The error file is named ggserr.log and is located in the GoldenGate software installation location. In the example, the error log on Linux is /gger/ggs/ggserr.log. On Windows, the GoldenGate error log based on the example is located in c:\gger\ggs\ggserr.log.

If your Replicat won't start, first check for obvious problems such as the wrong GoldenGate database user ID and password or typographical errors in your parameter file. You should also verify that the target database is online and that you can connect to it using the GoldenGate database user. Chapter 11 goes more into more detail on troubleshooting.

Let's do an INFO command on the Replicat RHREMD1 to check the status:

```
GGSCI (targetserver) 2> info replicat RHREMD1

REPLICAT    RHREMD1    Last Started 2011-01-22 22:40    Status RUNNING
Checkpoint Lag         00:00:00 (updated 00:00:09 ago)
Log Read Checkpoint    File dirdat/l2000003
                       2011-01-20 14:04:28.998416   RBA 3695
```

You can see from the INFO command that the Replicat RHREMD1 is RUNNING. Checkpoint lag is the time delay between the last checkpoint written to the trail and the time when the record was processed by GoldenGate. You currently don't have any checkpoint lag. If you had a high checkpoint lag it could indicate a performance problem or the Replicat catching up on a large volume of changes. You can also see that trail file l2000003 is the source for your Replicat, the last log-read checkpoint time, and the RBA of the record in the trail file. GoldenGate also refers to the trail-file number as the external sequence number (EXTSEQNO). In this case, EXTSEQNO is 3. You can start the GoldenGate Replicat processing at a specific EXTSEQNO if needed.

You can add the DETAIL option to the INFO command to see even more information about the Replicat. You may find the detail display helpful to see where the important files for the Replicat are located, such as the parameter and report files. The following example performs an INFO command on the Replicat RHREMD1 with the detail option:

```
GGSCI (targetserver) 3> info replicat RHREMD1, detail

REPLICAT    RHREMD1    Last Started 2011-01-22 22:40    Status RUNNING
Checkpoint Lag         00:00:00 (updated 00:00:07 ago)
Log Read Checkpoint    File dirdat/l2000003
                       2011-01-20 14:04:28.998416   RBA 3695

  Extract Source                         Begin              End

  dirdat/l2000003                        2011-01-20 13:57   2011-01-20 14:04
  dirdat/l2000003                        2011-01-20 13:57   2011-01-20 13:57
  dirdat/l2000003                        2011-01-20 13:57   2011-01-20 13:57
  dirdat/l2000003                        2011-01-12 10:59   2011-01-20 13:57
  dirdat/l2000001                        2011-01-07 08:38   2011-01-12 10:59
```

```
   dirdat/l2000000                    * Initialized *   2011-01-07 08:38
   dirdat/l2000000                    * Initialized *   First Record
   dirdat/l2000000                    * Initialized *   First Record


   Current directory       /gger/ggs

   Report file             /gger/ggs/dirrpt/RHREMD1.rpt
   Parameter file          /gger/ggs/dirprm/RHREMD1.prm
   Checkpoint file         /gger/ggs/dirchk/RHREMD1.cpr
   Process file            /gger/ggs/dirpcs/RHREMD1.pcr
   Stdout file             /gger/ggs/dirout/RHREMD1.out
   Error log               /gger/ggs/ggserr.log
```

Finally, you can run the STATS command on your Replicat. This shows if the Replicat has actually processed any DML activity. In the example, the Replicat has processed four inserts and two deletes since it was started. You may also notice the Replicat has handled two insert collisions, because you had to turn on the HANDLECOLLISIONS parameter to resolve errors.

Let's do a STATS command in the following example on the Replicat RHREMD1 to see if any data has been processed:

```
GGSCI (targetserver) 2> stats rep RHREMD1

Sending STATS request to REPLICAT RHREMD1 ...

Start of Statistics at 2011-01-18 18:50:38.

Replicating from HR.EMPLOYEES to HR.EMPLOYEES:

*** Total statistics since 2011-01-15 13:54:52 ***
        Total inserts                       4.00
        Total updates                       0.00
        Total deletes                       2.00
        Total discards                      0.00
        Total operations                    6.00
        Total insert collisions             2.00
```

You're now finished with setting up the basic replication. Let's summarize what you've learned.

Summary

This chapter covered how to set up, configure, and verify basic GoldenGate replication. You saw how to configure, add, and start a local Extract, a data-pump Extract, and a Replicat. You also examined the process for doing an initial data load using the Oracle GoldenGate direct-load method and using the vendor DBMS load utilities. The next chapter expands on these basic concepts and covers some advanced techniques to make your replication environment more secure and easier to manage and monitor.

CHAPTER 5

Advanced Features

This chapter gives you an in-depth understanding of some advanced features of GoldenGate replication. These features are often necessary to make your replication ready to handle a real-world production environment. In addition, you learn how to configure GoldenGate bidirectional replication to fully utilize both of your database servers in an active-active replication configuration.

In Chapter 4, you learned how to set up and configure basic GoldenGate replication. In this chapter, you build on the basic replication and add features to make the replication more robust and easier to manage and monitor. You also learn about some specific changes needed to make your replication work in specialized environments like Oracle Real Application Clusters (RAC). Later in the chapter, you expand the basic one-way replication into a bidirectional replication topology.

Enhancing the Replication Configuration

This section covers some recommended enhancements to your replication configuration. It begins with enhancements to the basic reporting configuration. Next, it covers the purging of old trail files and adding restartability to your Extracts and Replicats. Finally, you see how to add a checkpoint table in your database to make the replication more robust.

Before you get started, let's review the basic replication configuration parameters from Chapter 4. First, here's the basic Extract parameter file:

```
GGSCI (sourceserver) 1> edit params LHREMD1
Extract LHREMD1
-----------------------------------------------------------------
-- Local extract for HR schema
-----------------------------------------------------------------
SETENV (NLS_LANG = AMERICAN_AMERICA.AL32UTF8)
USERID GGER@SourceDB, PASSWORD userpw
ExtTrail /gger/ggs/dirdat/l1
Table HR.*;
```

Next is the basic Replicat parameter file:

```
GGSCI (targetserver) 1> edit params RHREMD1
Replicat RHREMD1
-----------------------------------------------------------------
-- Replicat for HR Schema
-----------------------------------------------------------------
```

```
SETENV (NLS_LANG = AMERICAN_AMERICA.AL32UTF8)
USERID GGER@TargetDB, PASSWORD userpw
HandleCollisions
AssumeTargetDefs
Map HR.*, Target HR.* ;
```

Finally, the Manager parameter file is as follows.

```
GGSCI (sourceserver) 1> edit params MGR
------------------------------------------------------------------
-- GoldenGate Manager
------------------------------------------------------------------
port 7840
```

You expand on these basic parameters throughout this chapter and see where to make changes and additions as you go along. Now, let's move on to enhancing your reporting configuration.

Enhancing Extract and Replicat Reporting

By default, the Extracts and Replicats generate a standard startup report every time they're started. The startup report contains a lot of useful information about the Extract or Replicat, such as the operating system, database version, character sets, and parameters used. For an example, let's look at the report for the human resources or HR schema Replicat you set up in Chapter 4, named RHREMD1:

```
**********************************************************************
                Oracle GoldenGate Delivery for Oracle
                    Version 11.1.1.0.0 Build 078
    Linux, x64, 64bit (optimized), Oracle 10 on Jul 28 2010 15:58:11

Copyright (C) 1995, 2010, Oracle and/or its affiliates. All rights reserved.



                    Starting at 2011-01-28 23:19:11
**********************************************************************


Operating System Version:
Linux
Version #1 SMP Tue Jan 23 12:49:51 EST 2007, Release 2.6.9-42.0.8.ELsmp
Node: targetserver
Machine: x86_64
                          soft limit    hard limit
Address Space Size    :    unlimited     unlimited
Heap Size             :    unlimited     unlimited
File Size             :    unlimited     unlimited
CPU Time              :    unlimited     unlimited

Process id: 15874
```

```
Description:

************************************************************************
**              Running with the following parameters              **
************************************************************************
Replicat RHREMD1


---------------------------------------------------------------------
-- Replicat for HR Schema
---------------------------------------------------------------------


SETENV (NLS_LANG = AMERICAN_AMERICA.AL32UTF8)

USERID GGER@TargetDB, PASSWORD userpw

HandleCollisions

AssumeTargetDefs

Map HR.*, Target HR.* ;


CACHEMGR virtual memory values (may have been adjusted)
CACHEBUFFERSIZE:                        64K
CACHESIZE:                              512M
CACHEBUFFERSIZE (soft max):             4M
CACHEPAGEOUTSIZE (normal):              4M
PROCESS VM AVAIL FROM OS (min):         1G
CACHESIZEMAX (strict force to disk):    881M

Database Version:
Oracle Database 10g Enterprise Edition Release 10.2.0.4.0 - 64bi
PL/SQL Release 10.2.0.4.0 - Production
CORE    10.2.0.4.0      Production
TNS for Linux: Version 10.2.0.4.0 - Production
NLSRTL Version 10.2.0.4.0 - Production

Database Language and Character Set:
NLS_LANG = "AMERICAN_AMERICA.AL32UTF8"
NLS_LANGUAGE     = "AMERICAN"
NLS_TERRITORY    = "AMERICA"
NLS_CHARACTERSET = "AL32UTF8"

For further information on character set settings, please refer to user manual.

************************************************************************
**                      Run Time Messages                          **
************************************************************************

Opened trail file dirdat/l2000006 at 2011-01-28 23:19:11
```

```
Switching to next trail file dirdat/l2000007 at 2011-01-28 23:20:02 due
to EOF, with current RBA 1281
Opened trail file dirdat/l2000007 at 2011-01-28 23:20:02

Processed extract process graceful restart record at seq 7, rba 1191.
Processed extract process graceful restart record at seq 7, rba 1253.
```

In addition to the standard reports, you can add parameters to instruct the Extract or Replicat to periodically add more information to the reports. As shown in the example, add the following parameters to your Extracts and Replicats to enhance the default reporting:

```
ReportCount Every 30 Minutes, Rate
Report at 01:00
ReportRollover at 01:15
```

The following sections look at each of these parameters in more detail.

REPORTCOUNT

You can use the REPORTCOUNT parameter to have the Extract or Replicat automatically add a count of the records GoldenGate has processed since startup. In the example, you request a record count every 30 minutes. Here is an example of what the reporting output looks like:

```
1000 records processed as of 2010-01-28 11:30:40 (rate 154,delta 215)
```

Since the Extract process started, it has processed 1,000 records as of the time displayed (11:30:40). You also asked for RATE information to be printed in the report. The rate calculations are as follows:

Rate = # of records processed since startup / total time since startup

Delta = # of records since last report / time since last report

In the example, the processing rate is 154 and the delta is 215. The delta is higher, which indicates that you're processing more records in the latest reporting period. You can compare the rate over time to see if it changes. Changes in rate could be due to more or less processing volume or perhaps performance issues with your Extract or Replicat or even the database itself.

REPORT

You can use the REPORT parameter to have the Extract or Replicat insert runtime statistics into your report, such as the following:

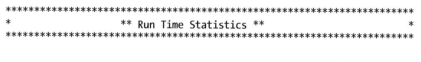

```
********************************************************************
*                    ** Run Time Statistics **                   *
********************************************************************


Report at 2011-01-15 13:53:30 (activity since 2011-01-13 23:23:10)

Output to /gger/ggs/dirdat/l2:
```

```
From Table HR.EMPLOYEES:
    #                    inserts:        6
    #                    updates:        2
    #                    deletes:        1
    #                    discards:       0
```

The example told the Extract or Replicat to generate statistics every day at 1 a.m. You can also pick a specific day of the week and generate statistics only once a week.

■ **Tip**   You can also manually add runtime statistics to your report using the SEND EXTRACT xxx REPORT or SEND REPLICAT xxx REPORT, where xxx is your Extract or Replicat name. Remember to update your parameter file if you want to see the statistics reported permanently.

REPORTROLLOVER

If an Extract or Replicat runs continuously for a long period, you may notice that the report file becomes rather large. To control the size of the report file, you can have GoldenGate automatically roll over the reports on a daily or weekly basis. The example rolls over the report file once a day at 1:15 a.m. Note that the report statistics continue to accumulate even after the reports are rolled over unless you specifically tell GoldenGate to reset them using the STATOPTIONS parameter with the RESETREPORTSTATS option.

Reporting Discarded Records

In some cases, you may notice that GoldenGate is unable to process particular records for one reason or another. These records are called *discards* by GoldenGate. For example, you may have changed a table layout and forgotten to update your GoldenGate configuration. In that case, GoldenGate may discard the records for that table because it doesn't know about the new table layout.

By default, GoldenGate won't produce a discard file to show you which records have been discarded. If you want to see the discards, you can instruct GoldenGate to write them out to a file using the DISCARDFILE parameter. The following example tells GoldenGate to generate a discard file for the human resources schema Extract named LHREMD1. You also have any new records appended to the discard file with the APPEND parameter. To keep the discard file from getting too large, you roll it over every Sunday at 2 a.m. with the DISCARDROLLOVER parameter:

```
DiscardFile dirrpt/LHREMD1.dsc, Append
DiscardRollover at 02:00 ON SUNDAY
```

You can choose to have GoldenGate report on discards for your local Extract, data-pump Extract, and Replicat.

Purging Old Trail Files

You can instruct GoldenGate to automatically purge your old trail files after they have been processed using the PURGEOLDEXTRACTS parameter. Although you can add this parameter to individual Extracts and

Replicats, it's best to add it to your Manager parameter file so purging can be managed centrally for all Extracts and Replicats.

Here is an example of the parameter you can add to your Manager parameter file to purge old trail files:

```
PurgeOldExtracts dirdat/*, UseCheckpoints, MinKeepDays 2
```

Let's take a closer look at the parameter and the options. First you tell GoldenGate to purge the extracts in your `dirdat` directory where the trail files are stored. The USECHECKPOINTS option tells GoldenGate to only delete the trail files after they have been fully processed by the Extracts and Replicats according to the checkpoint file. You should almost always specify the USECHECKPOINTS option along with PURGEOLDEXTRACTS because otherwise your trail files may be deleted before they're processed. Finally, you keep the trail files for a minimum of two days after they have been processed per the MINKEEPDAYS option. The Manager process automatically deletes any trail files that have been fully processed that are older than two days.

Adding Automatic Process Startup and Restart

Now you can add a couple of parameters to the Manager parameter file to try to avoid downtime for the Extracts and Replicats. The AUTOSTART parameter, as shown in the following example, automatically starts all the Extracts and Replicats when the Manager starts. The example uses wildcarding to tell the Manager to restart all Extracts and Replicats. You can specify that you want to start only individual Extracts and Replicats if needed:

```
AutoStart ER *
```

In some cases, an Extract or Replicat fails due to a temporary or intermittent problem such as a brief network outage. The AUTORESTART parameter shown in the following example automatically tries to restart the Extracts and Replicats if they fail because of such a problem.

▓ **Note** Use the AUTORESTART parameter with caution. To be sure you aren't unknowingly overlooking any problems, you may prefer to have an Extract or Replicat process fail and then resolve the issue manually instead of using AUTORESTART. AUTORESTART is best used as an exception for automatically resolving a known issue.

By default with AUTORESTART, GoldenGate tries to restart the Extracts and Replicats two times after waiting two minutes between restarts. Every two hours, GoldenGate tries again. You can adjust these defaults if needed.

Next, let's add a checkpoint table to the database.

Adding a Checkpoint Table

By default, GoldenGate maintains a checkpoint file on disk to keep track of transaction processing. In addition, you can create a checkpoint table in your target database. Doing so lets the Replicat include the checkpoint itself as part of the transaction processing and allows for better recoverability in certain circumstances. Let's add a checkpoint table in the target database.

First you need to add an entry to your GLOBALS file to tell GoldenGate the checkpoint file name. By adding this entry to the GLOBALS file, you tell GoldenGate to use the same checkpoint table for all of your Replicats. You can also add a specific checkpoint table for an individual Replicat as part of the ADD REPLICAT command:

```
CheckPointTable gger.chkpt
```

■ **Tip**   The GLOBALS file is used to specify GoldenGate parameters that apply to the entire GoldenGate instance, such as CHECKPOINTTABLE. The GLOBALS file is located in the GoldenGate software installation directory (in the example, /gger/ggs). This is different from the Extract and Replicat parameter files, which are located in the dirprm subdirectory. If the GLOBALS file doesn't exist, you may need to create it the first time you use it.

Next you create the checkpoint table in the target database:

```
GGSCI (targetserver) 1> dblogin userid gger password userpw
Successfully logged into database.

GGSCI (targetserver) 2> add checkpointtable

No checkpoint table specified, using GLOBALS specification (gger.chkpt)...

Successfully created checkpoint table GGER.CHKPT.
```

Now run another checkpoint command to verify that the checkpoint table exists:

```
GGSCI (targetserver) 1> info checkpointtable gger.chkpt

Checkpoint table GGER.CHKPT created 2011-01-30 22:02:03.
```

Here are the basic Extract and Replicat parameter files along with the changes you've introduced in this section, shown in italics. First let's look at the enhanced Extract parameter file:

```
GGSCI (sourceserver) 1> edit params LHREMD1
Extract LHREMD1
------------------------------------------------------------------
-- Local extract for HR schema
------------------------------------------------------------------
SETENV (NLS_LANG = AMERICAN_AMERICA.AL32UTF8)
USERID GGER@SourceDB, PASSWORD userpw
ReportCount Every 30 Minutes, Rate
Report at 01:00
ReportRollover at 01:15
DiscardFile dirrpt/LHREMD1.dsc, Append
DiscardRollover at 02:00 ON SUNDAY
ExtTrail dirdat/l1
Table HR.*;
```

Next is the enhanced Replicat parameter file:

```
GGSCI (targetserver) 1> edit params RHREMD1
Replicat RHREMD1
----------------------------------------------------------------------
-- Replicat for HR Schema
----------------------------------------------------------------------
SETENV (NLS_LANG = AMERICAN_AMERICA.AL32UTF8)
USERID GGER@TargetDB, PASSWORD userpw
AssumeTargetDefs
ReportCount Every 30 Minutes, Rate
Report at 01:00
ReportRollover at 01:15
DiscardFile dirrpt/RHREMD1.dsc, Append
DiscardRollover at 02:00 ON SUNDAY
Map HR.*, Target HR.* ;
```

Finally, the enhanced Manager parameter file is shown here:

```
GGSCI (server) 1> edit params MGR
----------------------------------------------------------------------
-- GoldenGate Manager
----------------------------------------------------------------------
port 7840
AutoStart ER *
AutoRestart ER *
PurgeOldExtracts /gger/ggs/dirdat/*, UseCheckpoints, MinKeepDays 2
```

Making the Replication More Secure

This section discusses a couple of items to make your GoldenGate replication environment more secure. First you look at encrypting the GoldenGate passwords, and then you examine encrypting the GoldenGate trail files. Of course, turning on these features is optional and depends on your specific security requirements.

Encrypting Passwords

You should encrypt the GoldenGate database user passwords in your parameter file in any secured environment. The following example shows how to encrypt the password *abc* and specify it in the parameter file. The example uses a default encryption key, but you can use a specific key if needed:

```
GGSCI (sourceserver) 1> encrypt password abc
No key specified, using default key...

Encrypted password:  AACAAAAAAAAAAADAVHTDKHHCSCPIKAFB
```

When you have the value for the encrypted password, you can update your parameter file with the value:

```
USERID 'GGER', PASSWORD "AACAAAAAAAAAAADAVHTDKHHCSCPIKAFB", ENCRYPTKEY default
```

In addition to encrypting passwords, you can encrypt the trail files, as you see next.

Encrypting the Trail Files

In some cases, you may want to encrypt the data stored in the trail files. You can do this by adding the ENCRYPTTRAIL and DECRYPTTRAIL commands to your parameter files. Let's look at an example of how you can use encryption for the trail files.

You can encrypt the source trail file created by the local Extract as shown next. Note that the ENCRYPTTRAIL parameter must come *before* the trail file to be encrypted—in this case, the l1 trail:

```
ENCRYPTTRAIL
ExtTrail dirdat/l1
```

Now the l1 source trail file is encrypted. The next step is to add encryption parameters to the data-pump Extract. First you must decrypt the trail file so it can be processed by the data pump, and then you can re-encrypt it as the l2 remote trail file:

```
PassThru
DECRYPTTRAIL
ENCRYPTTRAIL
RmtHost targetserver, MgrPort 7809
RmtTrail dirdat/l2
```

Notice that you can still use passthru mode for the data pump even with encrypted trail files. The data-pump Extract passes the encrypted trail data over the network and writes the encrypted remote trail.

The last step is for the Replicat to decrypt the trail file so it can be processed, as shown in the following example:

```
DECRYPTTRAIL
Map HR.*, Target HR.* ;
```

Let's take another look at your Extract and Replicat parameter files along with the new enhanced security changes introduced in this section (shown in italics). First is the enhanced Extract parameter file:

```
GGSCI (sourceserver) 1> edit params LHREMD1
Extract LHREMD1
-------------------------------------------------------------------
-- Local extract for HR schema
-------------------------------------------------------------------
SETENV (NLS_LANG = AMERICAN_AMERICA.AL32UTF8)
USERID 'GGER', PASSWORD "AACAAAAAAAAAAADAVHTDKHHCSCPIKAFB", ENCRYPTKEY default
ReportCount Every 30 Minutes, Rate
Report at 01:00
ReportRollover at 01:15
DiscardFile dirrpt/LHREMD1.dsc, Append
DiscardRollover at 02:00 ON SUNDAY
ENCRYPTTRAIL
ExtTrail dirdat/l1
Table HR.*;
```

Next is the enhanced Replicat parameter file:

```
GGSCI (targetserver) 1> edit params RHREMD1
Replicat RHREMD1
--------------------------------------------------------------------
-- Replicat for HR Schema
--------------------------------------------------------------------
SETENV (NLS_LANG = AMERICAN_AMERICA.AL32UTF8)
USERID 'GGER', PASSWORD "AACAAAAAAAAAAADAVHTDKHHCSCPIKAFB", ENCRYPTKEY default
AssumeTargetDefs
ReportCount Every 30 Minutes, Rate
Report at 01:00
ReportRollover at 01:15
DiscardFile dirrpt/RHREMD1.dsc, Append
DiscardRollover at 02:00 ON SUNDAY
DECRYPTTRAIL
Map HR.*, Target HR.* ;
```

In the next section, you add specialized filtering and mapping to your replication environment.

Adding Data Filtering and Mapping

You can use GoldenGate to filter the tables, columns, and rows you're replicating. You can also perform complex mapping of tables and columns from your source to target databases. The following sections look at these topics and use the same sample HR table introduced in Chapter 4. Following is the layout of the table as a reminder:

```
Table EMPLOYEES
 Name                                     Null?    Type
 ---------------------------------------- -------- ----------------------------
 EMPLOYEE_ID   (PK)                       NOT NULL NUMBER(6)
 FIRST_NAME                                        VARCHAR2(20)
 LAST_NAME                                NOT NULL VARCHAR2(25)
 EMAIL                                    NOT NULL VARCHAR2(25)
 PHONE_NUMBER                                      VARCHAR2(20)
 HIRE_DATE                                         NOT NULL DATE
 JOB_ID                                            NOT NULL VARCHAR2(10)
 SALARY                                            NUMBER(8,2)
 COMMISSION_PCT                                    NUMBER(2,2)
 MANAGER_ID                                        NUMBER(6)
 DEPARTMENT_ID                                     NUMBER(4)
```

Filtering Tables

You may remember from Chapter 4 that you instructed GoldenGate to extract all the changes for all tables in the HR schema using the following Extract parameter:

```
Table HR.*;
```

You did this by using the wildcard character asterisk after the schema name, HR.*, which tells GoldenGate to extract *all* the tables in the HR schema.

Now suppose your business requirements have changed and you don't need to extract all the tables in the HR schema. You only need to extract the EMPLOYEES and JOBS tables. You can do this by changing the Extract parameters as shown in the following example:

```
Table HR.EMPLOYEES;
Table HR.JOBS;
```

You removed the wildcard and added only the two tables you want to replicate. You may already be wondering whether you can accomplish the same thing by filtering using the Replicat instead of the Extract. The answer is yes, although there may be advantages to filtering using either the Extract or the Replicat, or both; it depends on your requirements and specific needs. For example, you may have multiple Replicats as targets that require different sets of data from different tables. In that case, it may be better to extract the data for all the tables and use each Replicat to filter out only the data it needs. Another option is to configure a data-pump Extract to do the filtering and send each Replicat only the data it needs. On the other hand, if you only need the two tables, it's probably better to filter out the data for those at the Extract and send the Replicat only the data it needs. You can see that you have to make some important design decisions as you configure your replication environment.

As a reminder, let's review the basic Replicat `MAP` parameter from Chapter 4. In the following parameter example, you replicate all the tables from the HR schema using the wildcard character:

```
Map HR.*, Target HR.* ;
```

If you want to replicate specific tables, you can filter the tables using the Replicat much in the same way you filter them in the Extract. The following example filters the tables to replicate only the EMPLOYEES and JOBS tables:

```
Map HR.EMPLOYEES, Target HR.EMPLOYEES ;
Map HR.JOBS, Target HR.JOBS ;
```

In addition to filtering tables, you can also filter columns. Let's look at that next.

Filtering Columns

Suppose that instead of extracting all the columns in the EMPLOYEES table, you're only interested in the EMPLOYEE_ID, FIRST_NAME, and LAST_NAME columns. You can do this by adding the following to your Extract `TABLE` parameter:

```
Table HR.EMPLOYEES
COLS (employee_Id, first_name, last_name);
```

In the example, all columns are ignored except the three columns listed in the `COLS` parameter. Keep in mind that it's probably a good idea to include your key columns in the `COLS` list; otherwise GoldenGate may choose all the columns listed as the key, which may not be a good idea.

▓ **Note** Keep in mind that if you use column filtering in your data-pump Extract, you can no longer use passthru mode.

Another example of column filtering is when you want all the columns in a table to be extracted *except* for a few columns. Let's assume you want to extract the entire EMPLOYEES table except for the EMAIL column. You can do that in the Extract with the COLSEXCEPT parameter, as shown in the following example:

```
Table HR.EMPLOYEES
COLSEXCEPT (email);
```

You may find that COLSEXCEPT is more convenient and efficient than using COLS, especially if you only want to exclude a few columns from a large table. Keep in mind that you can't exclude key columns with COLSEXCEPT.

In addition to filtering columns, you can filter rows.

Filtering Rows

The simplest way to filter rows is to add a WHERE clause to your TABLE statement on the Extract or to your MAP statement on the Replicat. Let's look at an example of each. First you add filtering to the Extract to only extract employees whose EMPLOYEE_ID is less than 100, as shown in the following example:

```
Table HR.EMPLOYEES,
WHERE (EMPLOYEE_ID < 100);
```

Now let's add filtering to the Replicat. Suppose you decide that you only want to replicate rows for your IT programmers. You can add that filter to the Replicat as follows:

```
Map HR.EMPLOYEES, Target HR.EMPLOYEES,
WHERE (JOB_ID = "IT_PROG");
```

▓ **Tip**   Double quotes are required when filtering for data values.

Another way you can perform complex filtering for numeric values is to use the GoldenGate FILTER parameter on either the Extract or the Replicat. In addition, you can use FILTER to restrict filtering to specific data manipulation language (DML) statements. The following example filters only for employees whose monthly salary is greater than 1000:

```
Map HR.EMPLOYEES, Target HR.EMPLOYEES,
FILTER (SALARY / 12 > 1000);
```

Let's look at another example using filtering based on the DML operation, such as insert, update, or delete. Suppose you only want to replicate deletes if the employee's monthly salary is less than 1000. You can set up a filter as shown next that only executes the filter for delete statements. This example filters using the Extract TABLE parameter:

```
Table HR.EMPLOYEES,
FILTER (ON DELETE, SALARY / 12 < 1000);
```

You've seen a few examples of the extensive capabilities of GoldenGate to filter tables, rows, and columns. Now let's look at some advanced column mapping.

Mapping Columns

You may remember from Chapter 4 that the Replicat parameter file used the `ASSUMETARGETDEFS` parameter. You used this parameter to tell GoldenGate that your source and target tables were identical. But what if the source and target tables are different? GoldenGate can easily handle these differences and even transform the data if needed.

Following is an enhanced version of the EMPLOYEES table that you use as your target table. On the target database, the table is named STAFF. This section also discusses a few more differences:

```
Table STAFF
 Name                                       Null?      Type
 ---------------------------------------    --------   ---------------------------
 EMPLOYEE_ID   (PK)                         NOT NULL   NUMBER(6)
 FIRST_NAME                                            VARCHAR2(20)
 LAST_NAME                                  NOT NULL   VARCHAR2(25)
 FULL_NAME                                  NOT NULL   VARCHAR2(46)
 EMAIL                                      NOT NULL   VARCHAR2(25)
 PHONE_NUMBER                                          VARCHAR2(20)
 HIRE_DATE                                  NOT NULL   DATE
 JOB_ID                                     NOT NULL   VARCHAR2(10)
 WAGES                                                 NUMBER(8,2)
 COMMISSION_PCT                                        NUMBER(2,2)
 MANAGER_ID                                            NUMBER(6)
 DEPARTMENT_ID                                         NUMBER(4)
```

Instead of using the column name SALARY as in the source database table; the target database table has a column named WAGES. You code the `MAP` parameter as shown in the following example:

```
Map HR.EMPLOYEES, Target HR.STAFF,
COLMAP (USEDEFAULTS,
WAGES = SALARY);
```

Before you can start the replication, you need to generate a GoldenGate data definitions file. This is required because the source and target tables are now different.

Generating a Data Definitions File

You must use a GoldenGate data definitions file whenever your source and target tables aren't considered identical by GoldenGate. In the example, there is one column with a different name, so you must create a data definitions file. The GoldenGate Replicat uses the data definitions file to map the source and target tables. Because you're doing the mapping on the target server using the Replicat, you generate the data definitions file on the source server and transfer it to the target server. If you're doing mapping on the source using the Extract, you create a data definitions file on the target server and transfer it to the source server.

▓ **Tip**   GoldenGate doesn't consider tables identical if any of the columns don't match or are in a different order. The names, lengths, data types, semantics, and column order must match exactly for GoldenGate to consider the tables identical.

The first step in generating a data definitions file is to create a defgen parameter file to tell GoldenGate what needs to be included in the file. The following example creates a defgen parameter file for all the source tables in the HR schema. In this case the defgen file has the same name as the Replicat, but with a different file name extension, defs:

```
defsfile ./dirdef/RHREMD1.defs
USERID GGER@sourcedb, PASSWORD userpw
TABLE HR.*;
```

Next you can generate the data definitions file using the GoldenGate defgen command:

```
defgen paramfile dirprm/hrdefs.prm
```

This generates the data definitions file RHREMD1.defs as specified in the defgen parameter file. The next step is to transfer this file from the source server to the target server. You should put the defgen file in the dirdef directory.

The last step is to tell GoldenGate that you're using a defgen file and no longer using the ASSUMETARGETDEFS parameter because the source and target tables are different. In the following example the ASSUMETARGETDEFS parameter is commented out, and you include a new SOURCEDEFS parameter that points to the defgen file:

```
--AssumeTargetDefs
SourceDefs dirdef/RHREMD1.defs
```

Now that you've set up the column mapping and generated a data definitions file, you're almost ready to start the Replicat. The next section addresses one additional requirement.

Transforming Columns

You must do one more thing before you can start replicating the EMPLOYEES table to the Staff table. The WAGES column in the target Staff table needs to reflect the *annual* employee salary. The SALARY column in the source database EMPLOYEES table stores only the *monthly* salary. So during replication, you must transform the *monthly* salary amount into an *annual* salary amount. You can do that using the Replicat MAP and COLMAP parameters, as shown in the following example:

```
Map HR.EMPLOYEES, Target HR.STAFF,
COLMAP (USEDEFAULTS,
WAGES = @COMPUTE(SALARY * 12));
```

The example maps the monthly SALARY column multiplied by 12 months into the annual WAGES column during replication. You can use the built-in GoldenGate @COMPUTE function for the calculation.

Another difference between the source and target EMPLOYEES tables is that the target has an additional column for FULL_NAME. The full name is a concatenation of the LAST_NAME, a comma, and the FIRST_NAME. You can perform this transformation using the Replicat MAP parameter as shown here:

```
Map HR.EMPLOYEES, Target HR.STAFF,
COLMAP (USEDEFAULTS,
WAGES = @COMPUTE(SALARY * 12)
FULL_NAME = @STRCAT(LAST_NAME,",",FIRST_NAME));
```

Now let's look at the Extract and Replicat parameter files with the mapping and filtering changes shown in italics. Here's the enhanced Extract parameter file:

```
GGSCI (sourceserver) 1> edit params LHREMD1
Extract LHREMD1
---------------------------------------------------------------------
-- Local extract for HR schema
---------------------------------------------------------------------
SETENV (NLS_LANG = AMERICAN_AMERICA.AL32UTF8)
USERID 'GGER', PASSWORD "AACAAAAAAAAAAADAVHTDKHHCSCPIKAFB", ENCRYPTKEY default
ReportCount Every 30 Minutes, Rate
Report at 01:00
ReportRollover at 01:15
DiscardFile dirrpt/LHREMD1.dsc, Append
DiscardRollover at 02:00 ON SUNDAY
ENCRYPTTRAIL
ExtTrail dirdat/l1
Table HR.EMPLOYEES
FILTER (ON DELETE, SALARY / 12 < 1000)
WHERE (EMPLOYEE_ID < 100);
Table HR.JOBS;
```

Next is the enhanced Replicat parameter file:

```
GGSCI (targetserver) 1> edit params RHREMD1
Replicat RHREMD1
---------------------------------------------------------------------
-- Replicat for HR Schema
---------------------------------------------------------------------
SETENV (NLS_LANG = AMERICAN_AMERICA.AL32UTF8)
USERID 'GGER', PASSWORD "AACAAAAAAAAAAADAVHTDKHHCSCPIKAFB", ENCRYPTKEY default
--AssumeTargetDefs
SourceDefs dirdef/RHREMD1.defs
ReportCount Every 30 Minutes, Rate
Report at 01:00
ReportRollover at 01:15
DiscardFile dirrpt/RHREMD1.dsc, Append
DiscardRollover at 02:00 ON SUNDAY
DECRYPTTRAIL
Map HR.EMPLOYEES, Target HR.STAFF,
COLMAP (USEDEFAULTS,
WAGES = @COMPUTE(SALARY * 12)
FULL_NAME = @STRCAT(LAST_NAME,",",FIRST_NAME));
Map HR.JOBS, Target HR.JOBS ;
```

Oracle-Specific DBMS Configuration Options

Let's review a few DBMS configuration options that are specific to those of you using an Oracle database in your replication configuration. First you see how to configure GoldenGate in an Oracle Real Application Clusters (RAC) environment. Then you review some special configuration options for Oracle Automatic Storage Management (ASM). Finally, you see how to set up DDL replication between Oracle databases. If you aren't using Oracle databases, you can skip this section.

Configuring for Oracle RAC

GoldenGate has had support for Oracle RAC for many years. There are some special considerations you should be aware of if you're running GoldenGate in Oracle RAC. Consult the *Oracle GoldenGate Oracle Installation and Setup Guide* for specific platform requirements.

You can choose to install and run GoldenGate from any of the nodes in your RAC cluster. You may decide to run GoldenGate on one of the nodes that is planned to have less workload than another node. GoldenGate can be installed on shared storage that is available to all the nodes in the RAC cluster or on local storage. If you install GoldenGate on shared storage, you can start the GoldenGate Manager and other GoldenGate processes from any of the nodes. If the node on which you started GoldenGate crashes, you can restart it on another node.

You can also set up GoldenGate to run under Oracle Clusterware and automatically fail over to another node in the cluster. Starting with Oracle 11gR2, you can use an ASM Clustered File System (ACFS) for the GoldenGate software and files. For more information, refer to the white paper *Oracle GoldenGate High Availability Using Oracle Clusterware,* available on the Oracle Technology Network at www.oracle.com/technetwork/index.html.

Synchronizing the Nodes

As part of the Oracle RAC installation, you should make sure the date and time for each of the nodes in the cluster are synchronized. Date and time synchronization is typically done using Network Time Protocol (NTP). Although synchronizing the date and time across nodes is part of the Oracle cluster installation, it's especially important for replication because GoldenGate makes processing decisions based on the system date and time settings. If the times are different on each node, it can cause replication issues or abends.

You should also be aware of a few GoldenGate parameters that allow you to control the I/O latency between the nodes. You can use the THREADOPTIONS IOLATENCY to compensate for differences in I/O latency between the nodes. The default value is 1.5 seconds, but you can increase this to 3 minutes if needed for significant latency. Another option of the THREADOPTIONS parameter lets you adjust for delays caused by disk contention on the redo logs: you can adjust the THREADOPTIONS MAXCOMMITPROPAGATIONDELAY up to 90 seconds to compensate for these delays. The default is 3 seconds.

Connecting to the Database

For Oracle RAC, you should set up a database service specifically for the GoldenGate connection and define the connection information in your tnsnames.ora file. You can set up the service using the Oracle Database Configuration Assistant (DBCA) or with Oracle Enterprise Manager, as shown in Figure 5-1.

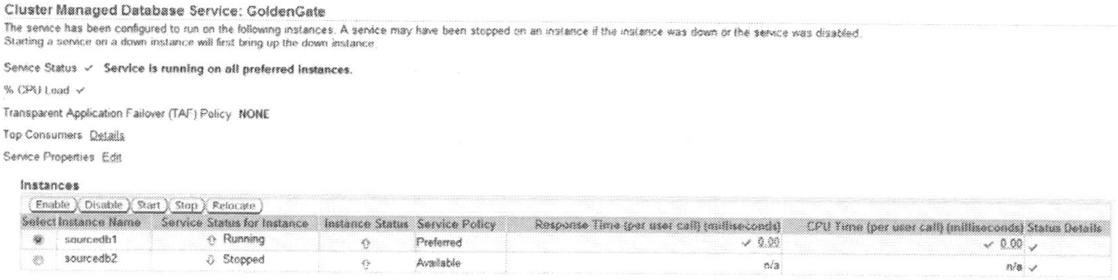

Cluster Managed Database Service: GoldenGate

The service has been configured to run on the following instances. A service may have been stopped on an instance if the instance was down or the service was disabled. Starting a service on a down instance will first bring up the down instance.

Service Status ✓ **Service is running on all preferred instances.**

% CPU Load ✓

Transparent Application Failover (TAF) Policy NONE

Top Consumers Details

Service Properties Edit

Instances

(Enable)(Disable)(Start)(Stop)(Relocate)

Select	Instance Name	Service Status for Instance	Instance Status	Service Policy	Response Time (per user call) (milliseconds)	CPU Time (per user call) (milliseconds)	Status Details
⦿	sourcedb1	⟳ Running	⇧	Preferred	✓ 0.00	✓ 0.00	✓
○	sourcedb2	⟳ Stopped	⇧	Available	n/a	n/a	✓

Figure 5-1. GoldenGate service defined in OEM

The example in Figure 5-1 defines the service on the preferred instance sourcedb1, and it's available on instance sourcedb2. After the service is defined, you can stop the Extract or Replicat and move the service from instance to instance as needed and then restart the Extract or Replicat. You can also display information about the service using the srvctl utility:

```
> srvctl config service -d sourcedb1 -s goldengate -a
goldengate PREF: sourcedb1 AVAIL: sourcedb2 TAF: NONE
```

When you've defined the service, you need to add the connection information to your tnsnames.ora file as shown here:

```
GoldenGate =
  (DESCRIPTION =
    (ADDRESS = (PROTOCOL = TCP)(HOST = sourceserver1-vip)(PORT = 1521))
    (ADDRESS = (PROTOCOL = TCP)(HOST = sourceserver2-vip)(PORT = 1521))
    (LOAD_BALANCE = NO)
    (CONNECT_DATA =
      (SERVER = DEDICATED)
      (SERVICE_NAME = GoldenGate)
    )
  )
```

Then, you can configure your Extract or Replicat to use the new service-based connection as follows:

```
USERID GGER@GoldenGate, PASSWORD userpw
```

This connection connects the Extract or Replicat to the 'GoldenGate' TNS alias you just added, which uses the service you defined in the database. Now let's look at another consideration you should be aware of when running GoldenGate on Oracle RAC.

Defining Threads

In an Oracle stand-alone database, there is typically only one redo thread. In Oracle RAC, there is typically one redo thread per instance. You need to tell the GoldenGate Extract process the number of redo threads defined in the Oracle RAC environment. The following example adds an Extract in an Oracle RAC environment with two instances and two threads:

```
GGSCI (sourceserver) > ADD EXTRACT LHREMD1, TRANLOG, THREADS 2, BEGIN NOW
```

■ **Tip**   If the number of threads ever changes (such as adding a new node and instance), you must remember to drop and re-add your Extracts with the correct number of threads.

Next, let's review how to configure GoldenGate for Oracle ASM.

Configuring for Oracle ASM

If you're using Oracle ASM, some special GoldenGate parameters are needed in order to allow the GoldenGate Extract to connect to ASM. In addition, you must configure the Oracle listener and `tnsnames.ora` to support the connection from GoldenGate. Let's look at the GoldenGate parameters first.

Specifying the ASM User

When using ASM, the GoldenGate local Extract must log in to the ASM instance in order to access the redo logs. You need to add an additional `TranLogOptions ASMUser` parameter in the local Extract parameter file to specify the ASM user ID and password, as shown in the following example:

```
TranLogOptions ASMUser "sys@asm", asmpassword "<encrypted password>",
ENCRYPTKEY default
```

The ASM user can be any user that has the SYSDBA privilege in the ASM instance (or the SYSASM privilege in 11g onwards. The example uses the sys user ID to connect to the ASM instance.

Updating the Listener

After updating your GoldenGate local Extract parameter file, you need to make sure your listener is listening for connections on the ASM instance. Add a clause as shown in the following Oracle 11g example to your `listener.ora` file:

```
(SID_DESC =
  (SID_NAME = +ASM1)
  (ORACLE_HOME = /u01/asm/oracle/product/11.1.0/asm_1)
```

This clause ensures that your listener is listening for connections on the ASM instance. Make sure to reload your listener for the changes to take effect.

Updating the TNSNAMES.ORA

Finally, you need an alias in your `tnsnames.ora` file for the ASM connection:

```
ASM =
  (DESCRIPTION =
    (ADDRESS = (PROTOCOL = TCP)(HOST = sourceserver1-vip)(PORT = 1521))
    (CONNECT_DATA =
      (SERVER = DEDICATED)
```

```
    (SERVICE_NAME = +ASM1)
    (INSTANCE_NAME = +ASM1)
  )
)
```

The entry should match the alias you specified earlier in your GoldenGate ASMUser parameter. The example uses an ASMUser of sys@asm to connect in the GoldenGate parameter file, which matches your TNS entry.

Adding Oracle DDL Replication

In addition to replicating DML statements, GoldenGate can replicate DDL statements for all Oracle database releases that support DML replication. You can configure GoldenGate to replicate only DDL, only DML, or both DDL and DML statements with the same Extract and Replicat parameter file. Before you jump into configuring the parameters for DDL replication, you should be aware of some of the major restrictions with GoldenGate DDL replication:

- You must turn off the Oracle recycle bin in Oracle 10g and later prior to Oracle 11gR1.

- GoldenGate can only automatically replicate DDL statements that are less than 2MB in length. Any DDL longer than that must be processed manually using a GoldenGate-provided script.

- DDL replication is supported for replication between *only* two systems. Bidirectional DDL replication is supported.

- The source and target schemas must be identical. This means you must be using the ASSUMETARGETDEFS parameter on your Replicat.

- You must use passthru mode on your data-pump Extracts for tables that require DDL replication.

- You should keep the DML and DDL replication for a single table and for related groups of tables together in the same Extract and Replicat groups.

Consult the Oracle *GoldenGate Windows and UNIX Administrator's Guide* for details on additional restrictions. Now, let's go though the steps to add Oracle DDL replication. This example uses the gger user schema to store the DDL tables, but you can choose another schema if needed:

1. Grant execute permission on UTL_FILE to the gger user:

   SQL> grant execute on utl_file to gger;

2. Add the following line to your GLOBALS file. Remember, this file is in your GoldenGate software installation directory. If it doesn't exist, you need to create it the first time:

   GGSCHEMA GGER

3. Run the marker_setup.sql script from the GoldenGate software installation directory, as shown next. This script is included as part of the GoldenGate software installation. It prompts for the schema name, which in this case is gger:

```
SQL> connect / as sysdba
Connected.
SQL> @marker_setup.sql

Marker setup script

You will be prompted for the name of a schema for the GoldenGate database objects.
NOTE: The schema must be created prior to running this script.
NOTE: Stop all DDL replication before starting this installation.


Enter GoldenGate schema name:gger


Marker setup table script complete, running verification script...
Please enter the name of a schema for the GoldenGate database objects:
Setting schema name to GGER

MARKER TABLE
------------------------------
OK

MARKER SEQUENCE
------------------------------
OK

Script complete.
```

4. Run the ddl_setup.sql from the GoldenGate software installation directory.
    This script is included as part of the GoldenGate software installation:

```
SQL> @ddl_setup.sql

GoldenGate DDL Replication setup script

Verifying that current user has privileges to install DDL Replication...
Checking user sessions...

Check complete.

You will be prompted for the name of a schema for the GoldenGate database objects.
NOTE: For an Oracle 10g source, the system recycle bin must be disabled.
For Oracle 11g and later, it can be enabled.
NOTE: The schema must be created prior to running this script.
NOTE: Stop all DDL replication before starting this installation.

Enter GoldenGate schema name:gger

You will be prompted for the mode of installation.
To install or reinstall DDL replication, enter INITIALSETUP
To upgrade DDL replication, enter NORMAL
Enter mode of installation:INITIALSETUP
```

```
Working, please wait ...
Spooling to file ddl_setup_spool.txt


Using GGER as a GoldenGate schema name, INITIALSETUP as a mode of installation.


Working, please wait ...

...

STATUS OF DDL REPLICATION
--------------------------------------------------------------------------------
SUCCESSFUL installation of DDL Replication software components

Script complete.
```

5. Run the role-setup script to set up the roles needed for DDL synchronization
    and grant the role to the gger database user:

```
SQL> @role_setup.sql

GGS Role setup script

This script will drop and recreate the role GGS_GGSUSER_ROLE
To use a different role name, quit this script and then edit the params.sql script
to change the gg_role parameter to the preferred name. (Do not run the script.)

You will be prompted for the name of a schema for the GoldenGate database objects.
NOTE: The schema must be created prior to running this script.
NOTE: Stop all DDL replication before starting this installation.

Enter GoldenGate schema name:gger
Wrote file role_setup_set.txt

PL/SQL procedure successfully completed.


Role setup script complete

Grant this role to each user assigned to the Extract, GGSCI, and Manager processes,
by using the following SQL command:

GRANT GGS_GGSUSER_ROLE TO <loggedUser>

where <loggedUser> is the user assigned to the GoldenGate processes.

SQL> GRANT GGS_GGSUSER_ROLE TO gger;

Grant succeeded.
```

6. Run the `ddl_enable.sql` script to enable the DDL trigger:

    ```
    SQL> @ddl_enable.sql
    Trigger altered.
    ```

7. Update the local Extract parameter file to include the DDL parameter, to tell GoldenGate you wish to replicate DDL. In this example you're only replicating DDL statements that are mapped in your replication scenario. You can choose to `INCLUDE` other tables or `EXCLUDE` them from DDL replication using different parameter options as well:

    ```
    DDL Include Mapped
    ```

At this point, you should be replicating DDL changes between your Oracle databases. Next you see how to set up bidirectional replication.

Adding Bidirectional Replication

In Chapter 4, you set up basic one-way replication. Let's expand that basic configuration now to support bidirectional replication. First, let's review from Chapter 3 the architecture for bidirectional replication.

In bidirectional replication, as shown in Figure 5-2, changes to data can occur on either database at the same time and are replicated to the other database. Each database contains an identical set of data. Bidirectional replication is sometimes called *active-active replication* because each side of the replication is *actively* processing data changes.

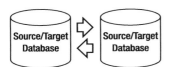

Figure 5-2. Bidirectional replication

Figure 5-3 illustrates a typical bidirectional GoldenGate configuration. Such a configuration is often used in environments where there are high-volume and high-performance requirements. By allowing both sides of the replication to be active, the database and hardware can be fully utilized.

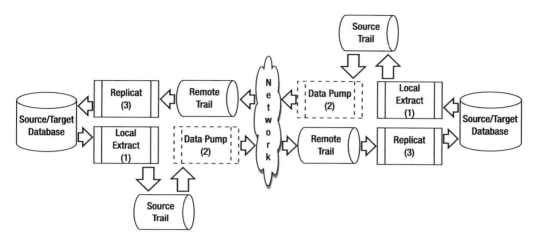

Figure 5-3. BiDirectional replication GoldenGate configuration

Following are some of the key components illustrated in Figure 5-3:

- A local Extract running on *each* of the the source servers.

- A data pump running on *each* of the source servers. This is optional but recommended. The data pumps can also be moved to a middle-tier server if needed to offload processing on the source server.

- A Replicat running on *each* target. Multiple parallel Replicats can be configured if needed to improve performance.

One drawback to bidirectional replication is that it can become extremely complex. You must develop strategies for handling data collisions and avoiding key conflicts. For example, one strategy might be that each database can only process a certain range of key values to avoid collisions.

The following sections look at these topics and use the same sample HR.EMPLOYEES table you've been using throughout the chapter. For bidirectional replication, the HR.EMPLOYEES table is *both* a source and a target on each database involved in the replication.

Before you start configuring the parameters for bidirectional replication, you should be aware of the following considerations:

- You can't replicate truncates in bidirectional replication. You can work around this restriction by configuring truncates for one-way replication as long as they always originate from the same server.

- From a practical standpoint, bidirectional replication is typically done with a maximum of two identical databases. Any more than that, and the configurations become extremely hard to manage.

- In an active-active configuration, it isn't possible to disable triggers, so you should add code to your triggers to ignore DML generated by the GoldenGate Replicat.

- If you're using cascade delete constraints, these need to be disabled and converted to triggers.

- You need to plan for database-generated sequential keys so there is no overlap across databases. For example, you can have one database generate odd key values and the other database generates even key values. Another option is to have one database use a specific range of keys and the other database use a different range of keys to avoid duplication.

- If you share the same key values across both databases, then you must develop some conflict-resolution routines. For example, if the same data on a row with the same key is being updated on both databases, which update should be applied? GoldenGate provides documentation examples for identifying and handling conflicts, but usually this depends on the application business rules.

Consult the Oracle *GoldenGate Windows and UNIX Administrator's Guide* for details on additional restrictions and considerations. Now, let's go though the steps for configuring bidirectional replication.

Excluding Transactions for Bidirectional Replication

In a bidirectional configuration, you have one or more Replicats running on each server applying SQL transactions. You can imagine that an endless looping scenario of SQL transactions could occur if each Replicat always applied SQL from the other Replicat back and forth. By default, GoldenGate doesn't replicate SQL transactions applied by the Replicats in order to prevent this endless looping. This is controlled by the GETREPLICATES or IGNOREREPLICATES parameter. For most databases, however, you still need to identify to GoldenGate which Replicat user transactions to exclude. You do so with different parameters depending on the DBMS, as shown in the following examples.

For DB2 z/OS and LUW, Ingres, and Sybase code, use the following local Extract parameter file to exclude the gger user:

```
TRANLOGOPTIONS EXCLUDEUSER gger
```

For Sybase, include the following in the local Extract parameter file to exclude the default transaction name of ggs_repl. For SQL Server, this parameter is required only if the Replicat transaction name is something other than the default ggs_repl:

```
TRANLOGOPTIONS EXCLUDETRANS ggs_repl
```

For Teradata, you don't need to identify the Replicat transaction; however, you must include the following SQLEXEC statements in the Replicat parameter file to execute a procedure that sets the Replicat session automatically at startup:

```
SQLEXEC "SET SESSION OVERRIDE REPLICATION ON;"
SQLEXEC "COMMIT;"
```

For SQL/MX, include the following in the local Extract parameter file to exclude the operations on the checkpoint table gger.ckpt:

```
TRANLOGOPTIONS FILTERTABLE gger.chkpt
```

For Oracle 10g and later, include the following local Extract parameter file to exclude the gger user:

```
TRANLOGOPTIONS EXCLUDEUSER gger
```

For Oracle 9i, include the following TRACETABLE parameter in both the Extract and Replicat parameter files before any TABLE or MAP statements. When an update occurs, the Replicat updates the trace table. This helps the Extract identify and exclude any GoldenGate transactions. You have to create the trace table first, using the ADD TRACETABLE command. This example uses the trace table ggs_trace:

```
TRACETABLE ggs_trace
```

Next, let's discuss how to handle conflict resolution for bidirectional replication.

Handling Conflict Resolution for Bidirectional Replication

In a bidirectional configuration, you must plan for, identify, and handle data conflicts. Conflicts can occur if data belonging to a record with the same key value is updated on both databases at the same time. Because GoldenGate is an asynchronous solution, it's possible for these conflicts to occur.

The following are a few techniques you can use to avoid conflicts and handle conflict resolution:

Low latency: You should make sure that the latency or lag between the two databases is minimized to prevent or at least minimize conflicts from occurring. For example, if a user on the first database updates Employee_ID 100's FIRST_NAME to Bill and a few minutes later a different user on the second database updates the same employee's FIRST_NAME to the correct name of William, you want to make sure the correct name is applied to both databases. If there is latency, Bill may be applied after William. If there is no latency the correct name of William will be applied in the proper order. If there is significant latency, then you may end up with more conflicts to resolve.

Key ranges: You can assign specific key ranges to applications and ensure that they only update that key range on a specific database. For example, to avoid conflicts in the EMPLOYEES table, you can assign EMPLOYEE_IDs 0–1000000 to the first database and EMPLOYEE_IDs 1000001–2000000 to the second database. The HR application will be aware of the key ranges and code their DML accordingly to point to the correct database based on the key value.

Key identifiers: Another technique is to add an additional key column to the existing key to identify the specific database where the record is owned or mastered. For example, database A can have an additional key column to indicate that the record belongs to database A. Database B can have a similar key added. You need to evaluate any disadvantages of having such a column in your database tables.

Automated key sequences: In some databases, you can use automatically generated sequence numbers for keys with different options. In the EMPLOYEES table, for example, you can generate even-numbered sequences for one database and odd-numbered sequence for the second database. Doing so ensures that there are no conflicts between the databases.

Conflict-resolution routines: If you can't avoid key conflicts, you need to identify that a conflict is about to occur and handle it appropriately based on business decisions and application logic. You can add filters to your MAP statements to determine that a conflict is about to occur and how to handle it. For example, you can add a filter to determine if a record comes in with the same key and an older timestamp column than an existing record. If so, you can discard the older record. For example, on the HR.EMPLOYEES table, you can add a timestamp column to help you determine which row to discard on a SQL update statement conflict. An example of the MAP statement to handle the conflict is as follows:

```
MAP HR.EMPLOYEES, TARGET HR.EMPLOYEES, &
REPERROR (90000, DISCARD), &
SQLEXEC (ID checkemployee, ON UPDATE, &
QUERY "select count(*) empduplicate from HR.EMPLOYEES where employee_id = ? and &
employee_timestamp > ?", &
PARAMS (p1 = employee_id, p2 = employee_timestamp), BEFOREFILTER, ERROR REPORT, &
TRACE ALL),&
FILTER (checkemployee.empduplicate = 0, ON UPDATE, RAISEERROR 90000);
```

This example executes a GoldenGate filter before replicating an update to the row. The filter determines whether there are any rows already in the database with the same key and a newer timestamp than the row you're replicating. If no rows that are duplicates with a newer timestamp are found (checkemployee.empduplicate = 0), then you replicate the row. If there are already rows with a newer timestamp (checkemployee.empduplicate > 0), then you raise an error, keep the existing row in the database, and discard the row being replicated.

Refer to the Oracle *GoldenGate Windows and UNIX Administrator's Guide* for additional examples of conflict-resolution routines.

Summary

This chapter covered how to add advanced features to your basic GoldenGate replication configuration. You saw how to enhance your basic reporting capabilities and make replication more secure using encryption. You added some automatic start parameters to the Manager so your replication stays up and running longer. You also reviewed how to include advanced table, row, and column mapping and data filtering in your replication configuration to meet your complex business requirements. Finally, the chapter covered the GoldenGate bidirectional replication topology setup. The next chapter expands even further on replication scenarios by configuring GoldenGate for heterogeneous replication.

CHAPTER 6

Heterogeneous Replication

In previous chapters we discussed how to install and configure basic replication for an Oracle 11g GoldenGate environment. Based on experiences in the field at customer sites, most implementations for Oracle 11g GoldenGate involve complex heterogeneous environments with multiple platforms and database vendors. For instance, while implementing a recent configuration for a large telecommunications customer, we had to install and configure Oracle GoldenGate to replicate data from a Microsoft SQL Server 2005 data warehouse running under Microsoft Windows 2003 Server to an Oracle 11g data warehouse system on Linux. Before Oracle GoldenGate existed, data replication between different platforms and RDBMS systems was problematic at best and nigh well impossible at worst. It involved hundreds of man hours to create custom scripts and development to take advantage of poorly documented system-level APIs, and even then it was a crapshoot. Well, fret no more! With Oracle GoldenGate, the challenge of replicating data in real time between different platforms and databases is a cake walk by comparison. It is more difficult than basic replication setups for Oracle GoldenGate that only require that the data be replicated between like platforms such as from Oracle 10g to Oracle 11g environments. However, we will show you how to set up heterogeneous environments in the easiest manner possible.You will learn how to prepare the environment from source to target database configurations as well as administration tasks involved with heterogeneous replication with Oracle GoldenGate environments.

Since heterogeneous replication can involve a large variety of third-party database platforms, the amount of time and space to address each configuration would fill a volume in and of itself. As such, we have chosen to present a case study example of common platforms that we have implemented for customers in the field. Our case study will provide information on how to configure and implement heterogeneous replication for Oracle to Microsoft SQL Server. The first task in setting up heterogeneous replication for Oracle GoldenGate involves consultation of the Oracle GoldenGate documentation with a focus on review of the Oracle GoldenGate release notes to find up-to-date changes in heterogeneous replication with Oracle GoldenGate.

Microsoft SQL Server to Oracle Replication

Microsoft SQL Server is one of the most popular and widely known RDBMS platforms for small to mid-size corporate database environments for back-office operations. However, it does not scale well based on our experiences for large enterprise data warehouse environments that migrate to massive terabyte and even petabyte environments. As such, companies today look to migrating off of their smaller Microsoft SQL Server environments to Oracle for the robust performance that Oracle can provide. You can verify the currently supported third-party database platforms that Oracle 11g GoldenGate supports by logging into the My Oracle Support (MOS) site online at `http://support.oracle.com` with a valid customer account (CSI) number and checking the certification matrix as shown in Figure 6-1.

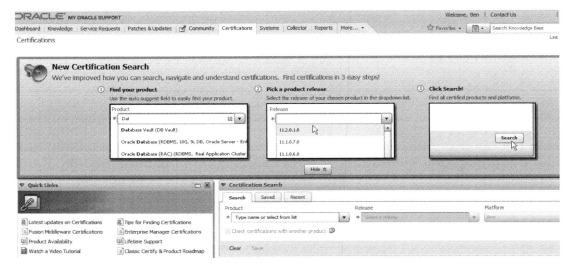

Figure 6-1. My Oracle Support certification matrix

Currently, Oracle GoldenGate replication from Microsoft SQL Server to Oracle is supported with the versions shown in Table 6-1.

Table 6-1. Supported Configurations for Oracle 11g GoldenGate with Microsoft SQL Server

Source	Source OS	Target	Target OS	GG Version
Microsoft SQL Server 2000	Microsoft Windows Server 2000, 2003, 2008	Oracle 9i, 10g, 11g	Windows, Linux, UNIX	Oracle 11g GoldenGate
Microft SQL Server 2005	Microsoft Windows Server 2000, 2003, 2008	Oracle 9i, 10g, 11g	Windows, Linux, UNIX	Oracle 11g GoldenGate
Microsoft SQL Server 2008	Microsoft Windows Server 2000, 2003, 2008	Oracle 9i, 10g, 11g	Windows, Linux, UNIX	Oracle 11g Goldengate

Preparing the Oracle GoldenGate Environments

You will first need to install the Oracle 11g GoldenGate software on the source Oracle and target Microsoft SQL Server environments. Be sure to install the sample database schemas and scripts included with GoldenGate and these database platforms.

Initial Data Load Completion for Oracle GoldenGate Environments

Before we can set up the Oracle GoldenGate process groups for Extract, data pump, and Replicat on the source and target environments, we need to load the sample data on both source and target systems. This is called the initial data load and, unfortunately, Oracle GoldenGate has no built-in procedure to automate this task. You can use a variety of vendor-supplied utilities for Oracle and Microsoft SQL Server. For Oracle, you can perform an export/import or data pump export and import. For Microsoft SQL Server, you can use the Microsoft native BCP and DTS bulk load utilities or perform a direct load with Replicat.

Source Oracle Database Configuration

Before you can replicate data to the target Micrososft SQL Server database environment, there are a number of preliminary setups that must be performed. Let's walk through each of these procedures.

Create the Manager parameter file on the source Oracle system and specify the port that it should use.

```
$ cd /ggs/source
$ ggsci
GGSCI> EDIT PARAMS MGR

--GoldenGate Manager parameter file
PORT 50001
```

Start the Manager process.

```
GGSCI> START MGR
```

Verify that the Manager process has started.

```
GGSCI> INFO MGR
Manager is running (IP port oracledba.50001).
```

Log in to the Oracle source database as the scott user. Create and populate the SCOTT.EMP and SCOTT.DEPT tables with sample data. Perform a CREATE TABLE AS SELECT to copy the table data to the GGS user schema. Next, by using GGSCI, you will need to log in to the source Oracle database and turn on supplemental logging for the EMP and DEPT tables for the SCOTT user schema. Supplemental logging must be enabled within the database environment so that changes made to data in the tables are captured during DML operations such as whenever Insert or Updates are performed against the tables for Oracle.

```
$ ggsci
GGSCI> DBLOGIN USERID GGS
GGSCI> ADD TRANDATA GGS.EMP
GGSCI> ADD TRANDATA GGS.DEPT
```

Next, you will need to verify that supplemental logging has been turned on for these tables.

```
GGSCI> INFO TRANDATA GGS.*
Logging of supplemental redo data enabled for table GGS.DEPT.

2011-04-03 22:31:21  WARNING OGG-00869  No unique key is defined for table EMP. All viable
columns will be used to represent the key, but may not guarantee uniqueness.  KEYCOLS may be
used to define the key.

Logging of supplemental redo data enabled for table GGS.EMP.
```
This warning is very important to keep in mind when you set up the GoldenGate environment since GoldenGate requires either a primary or unique key to be defined for tables in order to identify unique key columns as part of replication processing. Otherwise, all of the columns will be used thereby affecting performance adversely.

Configure Source Definition on Source Oracle Database System

The next step is to perform the source definition file creation mapping with the following commands on the source Oracle database system to create the DEFGEN parameter file and to add the additional parameters given below.

```
$ cd /ggs/$ ggsci
GGSCI> edit param defgen
DEFSFILE dirdef/source.def, PURGE
USERID GGS, PASSWORD xxxx
TABLE GGS.EMP;
TABLE GGS.DEPT;
GGSCI> exit
```

Execute the Source Definition Generator on the Oracle Source System

Execute the defgen commands on the source Oracle database system.

```
$ defgen paramfile dirprm/defgen.prm
```

Transfer the Source Definition File to the Target Microsoft SQL Server System

```
$ ftp mssql2k8
Password: xxxxx
ftp> ascii
ftp> cd ggs/dirdef
ftp> lcd ggs/dirdef
```

Now that we have configured the Oracle source database system for Oracle GoldenGate, we will discuss how to set up the target environment to replicate data from Oracle to Microsoft SQL Server.

Target Microsoft SQL Server Database Configuration

Before you can replicate data from the source Oracle database environment, there are a number of preliminary setups that must be performed. Let's walk through each of these procedures.

1. Configure ODBC source database connections.

2. Set up permissions and security in source database.

3. Create Extract and data-pump processes and parameter files.

4. Enable supplemental logging.

5. Add manager to Windows as a service (optional).

Install the Oracle 11g GoldenGate software for Microsoft SQL Server on the source Windows host.
For our case study, we will be using Microsoft SQL Server 2008 Express Edition with Windows XP 32-bit OS.

```
C:\ggs\mssqlserver>unzip V22241-01.zip
Archive:  V22241-01.zip
  inflating: mgr.exe
  inflating: ggsci.exe
  inflating: install.exe
  inflating: ggMessage.dat
  inflating: help.txt
  inflating: tcperrs
  inflating: bcrypt.txt
  inflating: libxml2.txt
```

Add the manager as a Windows service to simplify things and allow the manager process to run as a background Windows service. We recommend this for production environments so that this critical process always runs without stopping.

```
C:\ggs\mssqlserver> install addevents addservice
```

Check the Windows Event viewer to ensure that the Oracle GoldenGate Manager process has been added to Windows as a service, as shown in Figure 6-2.

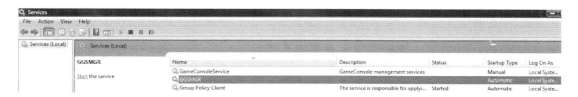

Figure 6-2. Adding the manager as a Windows Service

If the manager process has not been started, click the option to start it as shown in Figure 6-3.

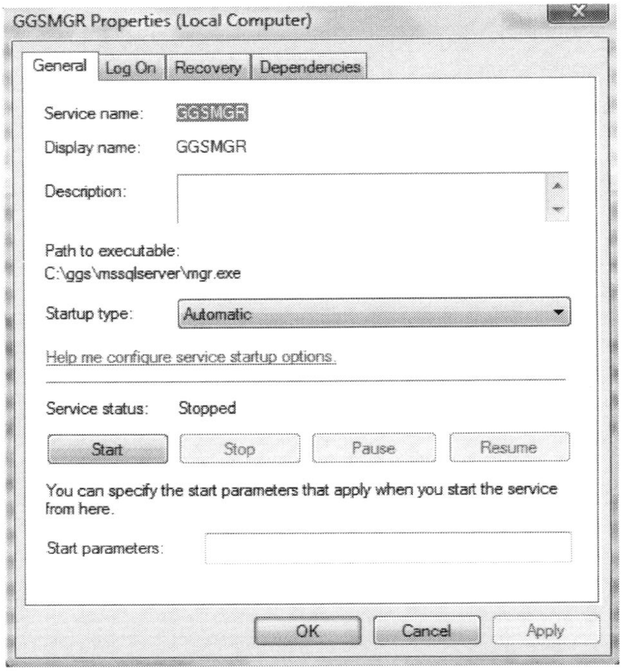

Figure 6-3. Checking status for manager process in Windows event viewer

Since the manager process on the source system for Microsoft SQL Server has not been started, we start the process. You can also configure the manager process to run as a Windows service so that it starts automatically upon server bootup or you can set it to require manual intervention to start the manager. Log in to the GGSCI interface and create the subdirectories for the Oracle GoldenGate software on the source system.

```
C:\ggs\mssqlserver>ggsci

Oracle GoldenGate Command Interpreter for ODBC
Version 11.1.1.0.0 Build 078
Windows (optimized), Microsoft SQL Server on Jul 28 2010 18:55:52

Copyright (C) 1995, 2010, Oracle and/or its affiliates. All rights reserve



GGSCI (oracledba) 1> create subdirs

Creating subdirectories under current directory C:\ggs\mssqlserver

Parameter files              C:\ggs\mssqlserver\dirprm: created
Report files                 C:\ggs\mssqlserver\dirrpt: created
```

```
Checkpoint files              C:\ggs\mssqlserver\dirchk: created
Process status files          C:\ggs\mssqlserver\dirpcs: created
SQL script files              C:\ggs\mssqlserver\dirsql: created
Database definitions files    C:\ggs\mssqlserver\dirdef: created
Extract data files            C:\ggs\mssqlserver\dirdat: created
Temporary files               C:\ggs\mssqlserver\dirtmp: created
Veridata files                C:\ggs\mssqlserver\dirver: created
Veridata Lock files           C:\ggs\mssqlserver\dirver\lock: created
Veridata Out-Of-Sync files    C:\ggs\mssqlserver\dirver\oos: created
Veridata Out-Of-Sync XML files C:\ggs\mssqlserver\dirver\oosxml: created
Veridata Parameter files      C:\ggs\mssqlserver\dirver\params: created
Veridata Report files         C:\ggs\mssqlserver\dirver\report: created
Veridata Status files         C:\ggs\mssqlserver\dirver\status: created
Veridata Trace files          C:\ggs\mssqlserver\dirver\trace: created
Stdout files                  C:\ggs\mssqlserver\dirout: created
```

```
GGSCI (oracledba) 2>
```

Windows Vista and Windows 2008 security options need to be configured to allow the manager and Extract processes to be started. Otherwise, you will receive the following error message when you try to start manager:

```
GGSCI (oracledba) 7> start mgr
```

```
Process creation error: WIN32 API CALL CreateProcess failed 740 (The requested operation
requires elevation.)
```

The solution is simple: run the command `msconfig` utility from a Windows shell prompt as shown in Figure 6-4.

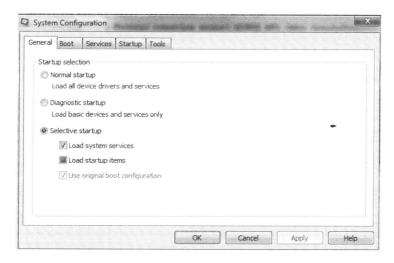

Figure 6-4. Security settings for manager on Windows and Microsoft SQL Server

Now you should be able to start the manager process on Windows for the source system from the services menu as the Administrator account.

```
C:\ggs\mssqlserver>ggsci
Oracle GoldenGate Command Interpreter for ODBC
Version 11.1.1.0.0 Build 078
Windows (optimized), Microsoft SQL Server on Jul 28 2010 18:55:52
Copyright (C) 1995, 2010, Oracle and/or its affiliates. All rights reserved.


GGSCI (oracledba) 1> info all
Program     Status       Group        Lag              Time Since Chkpt

MANAGER     RUNNING

GGSCI (oracledba) 2> status mgr
Manager is running (IP port oracledba.2000).

GGSCI (oracledba) 3> view params mgr
PORT 2000
```

Creating Sample Microsoft SQL Server Database

Now that we have the Oracle GoldenGate software installed on both source and target systems, we need to create and populate the target Microsoft SQL Server database. From Microsoft Windows, under the Start>Programs, run Microsoft SQL Server Enterprise Manager. You will then need to expand out the console navigation tree to the local SQL Server Instance. Right-click the Microsoft SQL Server database instance as shown in Figure 6-5 and select Properties.

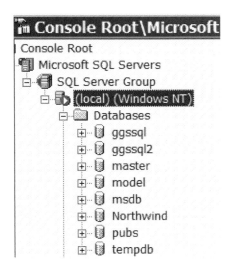

Figure 6-5. Creating the sample Microsoft SQL Server database

In the following Microsoft SQL Server Window, select the Security tab and then choose authentication for SQL Server and Windows as shown in Figure 6-6.

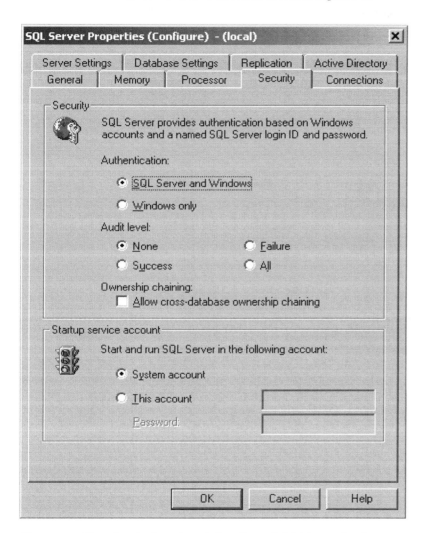

Figure 6-6. Choosing the Security tab for Microsoft SQL Server database

Create the sample database on the target Microsoft SQL Server environment as well as the GGS user security account. Make sure to assign the correct level of system and database privileges to the system and database account.

Since the Oracle GoldenGate Extract and Replicat process groups both connect to a Microsoft SQL Server database via an ODBC (Open Database Connectivity) connection, you will need to set up these Oracle GoldenGate components with a system data source name (DSN). To do so, perform the following tasks on the Microsoft SQL Server host:

1. Under Programs, select Start ➤ Settings ➤ Control Panel.

2. Choose ➤ Administrative Tools.

3. Open the ODBC Data Source Administrator dialog box by double-clicking the option for Data Sources (ODBC).

4. Next be sure to click the System DSN tab, and then hit the Add button. The Create New Data Source dialog box will then appear as shown in Figure 6-7.

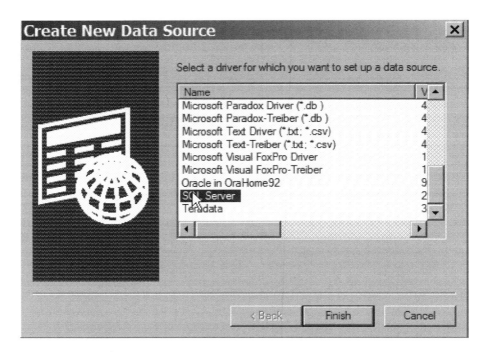

Figure 6-7.Create New Data Source for the Microsoft SQL Server database

5. Create the new data source on the target Microsoft SQL Server system as shown in Figure 6-8.

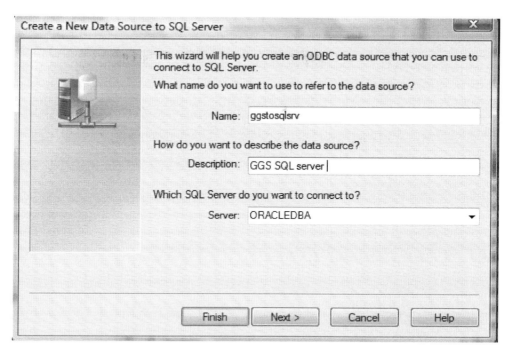

Figure 6-8. Add New Data Source for the Microsoft SQL Server database

Now that we have finished the initial setups on both source and target environments, we are ready to set up the parameter file configurations for Oracle and Microsoft SQL Server to use as part of data replication with Oracle GoldenGate.

Configure Change Data Capture on Source

Next you will need to configure the Change Capture Process on the Oracle Source database system.

```
GGSCI> ADD EXTRACT EXTORA, TRANLOG, BEGIN NOW
EXTRACT added.

GGSCI> INFO EXTRACT EXTORA
GGSCI (oracledba) 4> info extract extora

EXTRACT     EXTORA    Initialized   2011-04-03 23:15   Status STOPPED
Checkpoint Lag        00:00:00 (updated 00:00:31 ago)
VAM Read Checkpoint   2011-04-03 23:15:12.005000
```

The next step is to create and associate the trail files with our extract from the previous step. Using GGSCI and the ADD RMTTRAIL commands, add the trail file as shown below.

```
GGSCI (oracledba) 5> add rmttrail ./dirdat/lt,extract extora,megabytes 5
RMTTRAIL added.
GGSCI (oracledba) 6> info rmttrail *
        Extract Trail: ./dirdat/lt
              Extract: EXTORA
                Seqno: 0
                  RBA: 0
            File Size: 5M
```

Create the extract parameter as shown in the following sample parameter file.

```
--
-- Change Capture parameter file to capture
-- EMP and DEPT Changes
--
EXTRACT EXTORA
USERID GGS, PASSWORD "GGS"
RMTHOST localhost, MGRPORT 2000
RMTTRAIL ./dirdat/lt
TABLE GGS.EMP;
TABLE GGS.DEPT;
```

Start the capture process for Oracle on the source system by using the START command in GGSCI as shown. For the change capture delivery process, configure the Replicat parameter and add the trail files in the normal manner from previous chapter examples.

SQL Server to Oracle replication is performed in a similar manner to that shown earlier for replicating data from Oracle to SQL Server. The main difference is that you will create the Extract process groups on the source SQL Server system and the Replicat process groups on the Oracle target system.

MySQL to Oracle Replication

MySQL is a popular RDBMS platform widely implemented by Internet startup companies, media companies, and Internet Service Providers (ISPs) as part of the open standard Linux Apache MySQL PHP (LAMP) technology stack. Based on our experiences with Oracle GoldenGate customers, they have a need to replicate and migrate their MySQL data as they scale up to larger environments and move to Oracle environments, as shown in Table 6-2.

Table 6-2. Supported Configurations for Oracle 11g GoldenGate with MySQL

Source	Source OS	Target	Target OS	GG Version
MySQL 5.x	Microsoft Windows, Linux, UNIX	Oracle 9i, 10g, 11g	Windows, Linux, UNIX	Oracle 11g GoldenGate

Details on how to configure MySQL to Oracle replication can be found in the online Oracle GoldenGate documentation guides available at http://otn.oracle.com.

Teradata to Oracle Replication

Teradata is one of the key players in the enterprise data warehouse and business intelligence market. It scales well and has robust performance. However, lack of a built-in native replication feature has been the Achille's Heel of Teradata. As such, it requires Oracle GoldenGate software to perform database replication tasks. Many customers have a business need to replicate from Teradata to Oracle environments and GoldenGate fulfills this task perfectly.

Table 6-3 provides the currently supported configuration of Teradata with Oracle GoldenGate.

Table 6-3. Supported Configurations for Oracle 11g GoldenGate with Teradata

Source	Source OS	Target	Target OS	GG Version
Teradata 12.0	Microsoft Windows, Linux, UNIX	Oracle 9i, 10g, 11g	Windows, Linux, UNIX	Oracle 11g GoldenGate
Teradata 13.0				

Details on how to configure Teradata to Oracle replication can be found in the online Oracle GoldenGate documentation guides available at `http://otn.oracle.com`.

Sybase to Oracle Replication

Sybase was originally a joint venture between Microsoft and Sybase Corporation before SQL Server split off from Sybase and Microsoft to become two different database products. Sybase has two database products: Sybase IQ and Sybase SQL Server. Currently there is no support for Sybase IQ to replicate with Oracle GoldenGate. However, replication from Sybase SQL Server is supported with Oracle GoldenGate. Table 6-4 provides the currently supported versions of Sybase with Oracle GoldenGate.

Table 6-4. Supported Configurations for Oracle 11g GoldenGate with Sybase

Source	Source OS	Target	Target OS	GG Version
Sybase 12.x	Microsoft Windows, Linux, UNIX	Oracle 9i, 10g, 11g	Windows, Linux, UNIX	Oracle 11g GoldenGate
Sybase 15	Microsoft Windows, Linux, UNIX	Oracle 9i, 10g, 11g	Windows, Linux, UNIX	Oracle 11g GoldenGate

Details on how to configure Sybase to Oracle replication can be found in the online Oracle GoldenGate documentation guides available at `http://download.oracle.com/docs/cd/E18101_01/doc.1111/e17806.pdf`.

IBM DB2 UDB to Oracle Replication

IBM DB2 UDB provides an enterprise data warehouse and OLTP (Online Transaction Processing) database platform for Windows, UNIX, Linux, and mainframe platforms. With the advent of Oracle Fusion Middleware popularity and Oracle data warehouse capabilities, many IBM customers have a business need to maintain their current IBM DB2 database environments while maintaining their Oracle database environments. As a result, they have a need for a heterogeneous replication solution to keep all of their database environments in sync. Oracle GoldenGate fulfills this key requirement. Oracle 11g GoldenGate provides support for the following versions of IBM DB2 UDB with Oracle database environments, as shown in Table 6-5..

Table 6-5. Supported Configurations for Oracle 11g GoldenGate with IBM DB2 UDB

Source	Source OS	Target	Target OS	GG Version
IBM DB2 UDB 8.x	Microsoft Windows, Linux, UNIX	Oracle 9i, 10g, 11g	Windows, Linux, UNIX	Oracle 11g GoldenGate
IBM DB2 UDB 9.x	Microsoft Windows, Linux, UNIX	Oracle 9i, 10g, 11g	Windows, Linux, UNIX	Oracle 11g GoldenGate

Details on how to configure IBM DB2 UDB to Oracle replication can be found in the online Oracle GoldenGate documentation guides available at `http://download.oracle.com/docs/cd/E18101_01/doc.1111/e17795.pdf`.

Verifying Operational Readiness

Now that we have set up multiple replication environments with third-party databases to move data to Oracle, it's time to test and verify that the new Oracle GoldenGate environments function correctly. We also need to test and measure basic performance to ensure that sufficient resources are available to move data to Oracle from our different source systems. Operational readiness can be performed by using scripts to generate initial loads, perform DML and DDL transactions such as updates, deletes, and inserts, as well as using Oracle GoldenGate Veridata to check for data synchronization status between source and target heterogeneous environments with Oracle GoldenGate. Another way to measure operational readiness for your Oracle GoldenGate environments is to use the Oracle GoldenGate Director product to check on status for replication between source and target environments.

Summary

We provided a case study walkthrough on heterogeneous real-time data replication to Oracle from third-party database platforms with Oracle GoldenGate. We began with some basic installation guidelines and provided sample configuration steps along with the required commands to get up and running with minimal time and effort. In a large production environment with complex transformations, you would most likely need to build out these simple examples with more advanced features such as tokens and filters, along with macro libraries to enhance the business requirements of your replication environment.

CHAPTER 7

Tuning

GoldenGate is a proven high-performance product that replicates data for some of the busiest, high-volume applications in the world. To make GoldenGate perform efficiently in these types of environments, you need to have a solid understanding of how to tune GoldenGate. The process of tuning GoldenGate is similar to many software tuning exercises; however, the tuning tools and mechanisms are quite different. You should also keep in mind that although GoldenGate has its own tuning approaches, its performance depends on the performance of the underlying database, server, network, and storage. This chapter gives you an in-depth understanding of how to tune GoldenGate replication.

This chapter reviews a structured methodology for tuning GoldenGate replication and digs into each step of the methodology. You then focus on some specific tuning strategies and examples you can use to improve the performance of your GoldenGate replication environment.

Tuning Methodology

When tuning GoldenGate, it's important for you to follow a standard performance and tuning methodology. Otherwise, you may not know when there is a performance problem, or you may find yourself fixing the wrong problem. This chapter suggests a standard methodology, but it's not important that you follow it precisely. You can create your own methodology or adapt this methodology to work in your particular environment. The most important consideration is that you *do* follow a structured approach that has requirements defined up front and measurements and verification specified afterward. Using a structured approach helps ensure that you can respond properly to performance issues and meet the expectations of your users.

Here are the suggested steps in the GoldenGate performance and tuning methodology. Steps 1 and 2 should be completed early in the project:

1. Define the performance requirements.

2. Create a performance baseline.

Steps 3 through 6 should be done as tuning issues are identified:

3. Evaluate current performance.

4. Determine the problem.

5. Design and implement a solution.

6. Repeat steps 3 thru 5 as needed.

If you've ever performed database performance and tuning, these may look like familiar steps. But each step has specific considerations in a GoldenGate replication environment. This chapter explains and expands on the steps as you move along. Now, let's examine the first step in the methodology: defining the performance requirements.

Defining the Performance Requirements

The key to successfully meeting the performance expectations of your business users is to properly define the performance requirements. Without performance requirements, you never know if you've successfully met the users' expectations. When you have the requirements defined and agreed on, you can focus your tuning efforts on areas that don't conform to the requirements.

You should define the GoldenGate replication performance requirements early in the project, before GoldenGate is even installed and configured. You do this because these requirements can have a significant impact on how GoldenGate is set up and configured.

The most important performance requirement for replication is the amount of lag the application can tolerate. As you gather your replication requirements, you should think of lag in terms of the overall delay in replicating from the source to the target. Later, you'll break the lag down into specific Extract and Replicat lag for the GoldenGate environment.

In Chapter 4, you looked at some of the requirements that drive your replication technical design. The following two areas relate specifically to performance and tuning of replication:

> *Data currency*: How quickly and how often does the data need to be updated? Can any lag in the data replication be tolerated? If no lag can be tolerated and there is a high volume of changes, you may need to devote more time in the project to designing and tuning the replication to avoid any lag. Keep in mind that often, reporting systems can tolerate lag and the target data doesn't need to be completely up to date with the source.

> *Data volume*: How much data needs to be replicated? How often is it updated? You may be able to examine the existing database transaction log files to determine the amount of data change that is occurring in the source database. The data-change volume impacts the network bandwidth requirements between the source and target and the amount of disk space required for trail files.

After you've worked with your business users and stakeholders to answer these questions, you can begin to formulate your replication performance requirements. It's best to keep the requirements simple and easy to understand. Let's look at a few examples of performance requirements.

The first example is for an important high-volume Online Transaction Processing (OLTP) database involved in an active-active replication topology. It's critical to the business that the source and target databases be kept nearly synchronized all the time. After working with the business users, you've agreed on the following performance requirement:

The replication lag must be less than 1 minute at least 80 percent of the time. If the replication lag exceeds 1 minute, a warning should be issued and the replication should be closely monitored. If the replication lag exceeds 5 minutes, a critical alert should be issued and the problem needs to be addressed immediately.

Let's look at another example of replication that isn't as critical. In this example, you're running replication from an OLTP database to a reporting database. The reporting database is running on another highly utilized server with only limited server resources available to make the replication perform properly. The reporting is used for offline analytical purposes, and it isn't as critical to the business that the data is kept up to date. In this case, your performance requirement might look like this:

The replication lag from the OLTP database to the reporting database must be less than 1 hour at least 80 percent of the time. If the replication lag exceeds 8 hours, a warning should be issued. If the replication lag exceeds 24 hours, a critical alert should be issued and the problem needs to be addressed within the following day.

You can see that each of these replication scenarios has very different performance requirements. If you don't properly define the requirements up front, you may spend all your time tuning the reporting replication when the active-active replication is really the most critical. Next, let's look at creating a performance baseline.

Creating a Performance Baseline

You should capture a baseline of the performance of your replication environment as soon as possible after your environment goes live. A *baseline* is simply a set of performance metrics you can capture when your replication is running under normal conditions. Normal conditions mean you don't want to collect your baseline metrics while any special or unusual processing is running or if there are any existing performance problems. You don't want to capture the baseline when a performance spike is occurring.

After you've captured the baseline, you can use the baseline metrics for comparison purposes to identify possible performance problems. You should also capture new baselines periodically, particularly when there are major changes in your environment. For example, if a new server is added to your database cluster, you should capture new baseline metrics because the old metrics are no longer valid.

Let's look at a sample of the metrics you should collect for your performance baseline:

Server statistics: For the servers where you have replication running, you should collect CPU utilization, disk utilization, and memory usage. How you collect these statistics varies by platform. For example, on Linux you may use SAR or IOSTAT, and on Windows you can use perfmon. You may even have your own custom tools to collect these metrics.

Extract and Replicat statistics: For each Extract and Replicat, you should capture the following metrics:

- *Name and status of each processing group:* You can capture the output of the GoldenGate Software Command Interface (GGSCI) info * command.

- *Processing statistics:* You can use the stats command and get an aggregate processing rate for your Extracts and Replicats using a command such as STATS RHREMD1, TOTALSONLY *, REPORTRATE MIN. You can use this command, for example, to get the total operations per minute processed by the Replicat.

- *Processing rate:* Chapter 5 showed how to add reporting parameters to the Extract and Replicat to automatically report performance statistics. You can now view the report file for each Extract and Replicat and record the statistics. From the report file, you can record the number of records processed, the rate, and the delta.

- *Processing lag:* You can get the approximate lag from the info command and also the specific lag by running the lag command for each Extract and Replicat.

- *Server process statistics:* You can collect server statistics, such as memory and CPU usage, specifically for the Extract and Replicat processes. For example, on Linux, if you have the top command available, you can use a command like top -U gger to monitor just the GoldenGate gger operating system user processes.

Database performance statistics: As part of your baseline, you should include statistical reports on the source and target database usage, such as an Oracle AWR report or a SQL Server dashboard report. This gives you an indication of how much database activity is happening during your normal baseline.

Network performance statistics: You should capture some statistics to indicate the network throughput and utilization. You can use tools such as the Windows System Monitor or the netstat command on Linux to gather these statistics.

When you've collected a solid set of baseline statistics, you're well-armed to deal with any performance issue that may arise. Don't forget to update these baseline statistics periodically.

The next question you're probably asking is, what metrics should I collect, and for how long? This section offers guidelines for metrics you should collect in your performance baseline. Keep in mind that these are only suggestions, and you should collect any metrics that can have an influence on the performance of your particular replication environment. Collect the metrics for at least for one hour. You can collect them for a week or even a month if that makes sense for your particular environment. You can also capture metrics for special situations. For example, you may have some month-end processing that causes your replication volume to increase. You can capture a baseline for this activity when you consider it to be running normally and then use the baseline to compare to subsequent months.

Let's assume that you've done a good job of collecting your baseline statistics, and a few weeks later you get a report that the replication is running slowly. That triggers you to move to the next step in your process: evaluating the current performance.

Evaluating the Current Performance

When a potential GoldenGate replication performance problem has been reported, the next step in the process is to evaluate the current performance against the baseline that you recorded earlier. You should follow the exact same steps to collect the *current* statistics during the performance problem conditions as when you collected the *baseline* performance statistics under normal conditions.

Let's look at a sample of some baseline and current processing statistics collected for HR Extracts and Replicats as shown in Table 7-1.

Table 7-1. Extract and Replicat Performance Statistics

Statistics	Baseline	Current
Source CPU % Utilization	12	15
Target CPU % Utilization	17	73
Source Disk Reads/sec	2.1	2.9
Source Disk Writes/sec	10.1	10.6
Source Disk Service Time	3.4	3.2
Target Disk Reads/sec	2.1	2.8
Target Disk Writes/sec	10.1	10.9
Target Disk Service Time	3.4	3.2
Local Extract LHREMD1 Status	RUNNING	RUNNING
Data Pump PHREMD1 Status	RUNNING	RUNNING
Replicat RHREMD1 Status	RUNNING	RUNNING

Continued

Statistics	Baseline	Current
Local Extract LHREMD1 Rate/Delta	20/21	20/19
Data Pump PHREMD1 Rate/Delta	20/21	20/19
Replicat RHREMD1 Rate/Delta	15/16	9/6
Replicat RHREMD1 Operations/Min	1948	1232
Local Extract LHREMD1 Secs Lag	12	11
Data Pump PHREMD1 Sec Lag	8	9
Replicat RHREMD1 Secs Lag	15	127

You probably notice some major differences when comparing the baseline statistics to the current performance statistics. They may indicate a performance problem, but you should be careful not to jump to conclusions. Let's move on to the next step in the tuning process to determine the problem.

Determining the Problem

After you've collected the current performance statistics, you can move on to try to determine the actual performance problem. Even though you're now armed with plenty of statistics, there are still many unanswered questions. Let's look at some of the required tasks when going through your analysis to determine the problem:

1. Analyze the baseline statistics compared with the current statistics. Determine if there are significant differences. In the example, you can see that the CPU utilization on the target server is significantly higher. You can also see that the Replicat processing rate has dropped and the lag has increased significantly. This points you in the direction of a possible problem with the Replicat, but it could be something on the target database or the server or even something else.

2. Conduct a short meeting with the stakeholders to determine their perspective on what the current performance problems are and establish their expectations for tuning results. It's important to understand what they believe is their most significant problem. You can also share the initial findings from your comparison of baseline to current performance statistics. Here are some examples of questions you should ask during the meeting:

   - What are the most significant performance problems?

   - What business processes are being impacted?

   - What time of day does the performance problem occur, or is it constant?

- Does the performance problem affect only one user or all users?

- Is the performance problem related to any specific database table or all tables?

- Is the performance problem the result of increased workload or a system change?

- Can the problem be consistently reproduced in a testing environment?

You may be surprised at the answers to these questions. Perhaps the stakeholders consider the replication slowdown a low priority. Maybe they're only seeing a slowdown at certain times of the day. Or maybe the problem is the result of a system change or new business volume. In any case, it's important to get the stakeholders' perspective and expectations. You should document responses to the performance questions and obtain agreement from the stakeholders on the scope, impact, and expectations of the replication tuning effort.

3. Drill down on the GoldenGate processes that appear to be running slowly. View the GoldenGate reports in the `dirrpt` directory, and compare the processing rates to try to determine when the problem began. Look at the rate and delta values and see when they started to decrease, as shown in the following example from the Replicat report:

```
RHREMD1.rpt:    98650000 records processed as of 2011-03-09 19:27:48 (rate 4728,delta 3969)
RHREMD1.rpt:    98660000 records processed as of 2011-03-09 19:28:50 (rate 4728,delta 4439)
RHREMD1.rpt:    98670000 records processed as of 2011-03-09 19:29:53 (rate 3685,delta 4183)
RHREMD1.rpt:    98680000 records processed as of 2011-03-09 19:30:55 (rate 3247,delta 3366)
RHREMD1.rpt:    98690000 records processed as of 2011-03-09 19:31:57 (rate 2327,delta 2630)
RHREMD1.rpt:    98700000 records processed as of 2011-03-09 19:32:00 (rate 1727,delta 2257)
RHREMD1.rpt:    98710000 records processed as of 2011-03-09 19:33:02 (rate 1135,delta 1736)
RHREMD1.rpt:    98720000 records processed as of 2011-03-09 19:34:04 (rate 768,delta 1125)
RHREMD1.rpt:    98730000 records processed as of 2011-03-09 19:35:06 (rate 436,delta 923)
```

In the example, you're reporting on the Replicat processing rate every 10,000 records. You can see from the Replicat report listing that the processing rate began decreasing at 19:28 and continued to decrease.

4. Review the GoldenGate `ggserr.log` file, and look for any errors or warnings. Sometimes a warning message may be triggered that you may not be aware could be negatively impacting performance.

5. Review the server system logs for any error messages that could be contributing to the slow performance, such as a bad disk drive.

6. Review the built-in database performance reports (such as AWR for Oracle or the SQL Server dashboard), and compare them to the reports from the baseline period. See if there are any significant changes that could be causing poor performance.

When you've finished analyzing the statistics, stakeholder communication, and information about the performance problem, you should have a pretty good idea of what is causing the problem. You may not know the exact solution yet, but you should at least have some clear ideas to try to improve the performance. The next step is to design and implement a solution.

Designing and Implementing a Solution

Now you're at the point where you can move forward to design and implement a solution to tune the replication. At this point, you may have several possible solutions to the problem. You need to go through some analysis to determine which solution to implement first. One solution may be easier and have less impact to implement, so you may try it first to see if it works or rule it out. The important thing is to implement only one tuning change at a time and then measure the impact. That way, you have a better indication that your solution actually solved the problem and improved performance. If you implement multiple solutions at once, it may be difficult to determine which one fixed the problem (or made it worse).

The following sections go through some different tuning strategies for Extracts and Replicats. Of course, these aren't the only strategies, and you may discover your own based on your particular environment and experiences. Because the scope of this book is GoldenGate, it only covers tuning of components such as the database and servers as they relate to GoldenGate replication; but it's important to rule out general performance issues with these components before tuning GoldenGate.

Using Parallel Extracts and Replicats

Typically, most tuning is focused on the Replicats and not the Extracts. The reason is that the Extracts are usually reading from the database transaction log, whereas the Replicats are executing single-threaded SQL commands to change data in the database on the target. There may be situations, however, when an Extract needs some tuning. For example, in certain situations an Extract may need to fetch data from the database if there is a Large Object (LOB) column or if a column isn't in the transaction log. In those cases, you may want to isolate those tables into their own Extract group.

One common strategy for tuning GoldenGate is to create multiple parallel Extract or Replicat processing groups to balance the workload. GoldenGate supports up to 300 processing groups per GoldenGate Manager. As an example, let's split the data-pump Extract and Replicat for the HR schema. Before you get started, as a reminder, Figure 7-1 shows the basic replication configuration with no parallel groups.

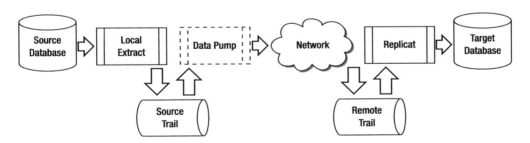

Figure 7-1. One-way replication without parallel Extract or Replicat groups

Now let's look at the same replication with two parallel data-pump Extract and Replicat groups, as shown in Figure 7-2.

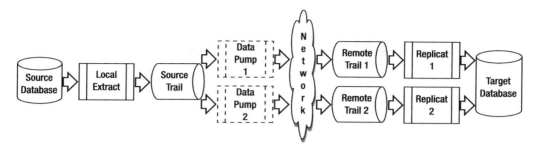

Figure 7-2. One-way replication with parallel data-pump Extract and Replicat groups

Let's look at a specific example of how to implement parallel Extracts and Replicats on the HR schema.

Implementing Parallel Extracts and Replicats with Table Filtering

In this example, all of your interviews, analysis, and problem solving point to a slowdown in the Replicat, so your first tuning change is to split the data-pump Extract and Replicat into two parallel processing groups. You do this to try to divide the replication workload, make the Replicat run faster, and reduce the Replicat lag. For now, in the example you split the GoldenGate process groups by filtering for specific SQL tables. Later, you see how to split the replication another way by using key ranges.

⬛ **Note**   When splitting GoldenGate processing groups, remember to keep tables related by SQL referential integrity constraints together in the same GoldenGate process groups.

Figure 7-3 shows more details on how you split the data-pump Extract and Replicat for the HR schema.

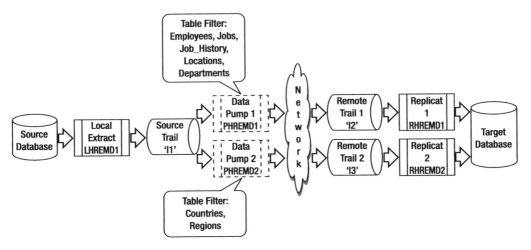

Figure 7-3. Parallel data-pump Extract and Replicat groups for the HR example

Local Extract LHREMD1 remains unchanged and still extracts all the tables for the HR schema. Using the Local Extract to extract *all* the data is a common approach. Typically, it's better to use the Local Extract to extract all o the data and then use the data-pump Extracts to do any filtering.

Data Pump PHREMD1 is changed from extracting all the tables in the HR schema to filtering only for HR tables EMPLOYEES, JOB_HISTORY, JOBS, and LOCATIONS. The other tables in the schema, COUNTRIES and REGIONS, are extracted by a new data-pump Extract, PHREMD2. Next, you use two Replicat groups to process the two remote trail files from the data pumps.

▓ **Tip**   To avoid contention, Oracle recommends that when reading trail files, you pair each Replicat with its own trail file. No more than three Replicats should be reading the same trail file.

Replicat RHREMD1 processes the data pumped from data pump PHREMD1 in the l2 trail file. The new Replicat, RHREMD1, processes the data pumped from data pump PHREMD2 in the new l3 trail file.

Next, let's go over the steps to implement your tuning changes. Because you already have replication running for the HR schema, you have to make the tuning changes to the existing running configuration as shown in Figure 7-1. Following are the steps to add the parallel data-pump Extract and Replicat to the existing replication configuration. As a reminder, although it isn't shown here (so you can see the command details), you should put the GoldenGate commands in these steps in an obey file, as covered in Chapter 4:

▓ **Tip**   Always make a backup of your GoldenGate parameter files before you make any changes.

---

1. Edit the existing data-pump Extract parameter file PHREMD1 to add the table filtering:

```
GGSCI (sourceserver) 1> edit params PHREMD1

Extract PHREMD1

--------------------------------------------------------------------
-- Data Pump extract for HR schema
--------------------------------------------------------------------

PassThru

RmtHost targetserver, MgrPort 7809
RmtTrail dirdat/l2

ReportCount Every 10000 Records, Rate
Report at 01:00
ReportRollover at 01:15

DiscardFile dirrpt/PHREMD1.dsc, Append
DiscardRollover at 01:00

Table HR.EMPLOYEES ;
Table HR.JOBS ;
Table HR.JOB_HISTORY ;
Table HR.LOCATIONS ;
Table HR.DEPARTMENTS ;
```

2. Add the parameter file for the new data-pump Extract, PHREMD2:

```
GGSCI (sourceserver) 1> edit params PHREMD2

Extract PHREMD2

--------------------------------------------------------------------
-- Data Pump extract for HR schema
--------------------------------------------------------------------

PassThru

RmtHost targetserver, MgrPort 7809
RmtTrail dirdat/l3

ReportCount Every 10000 Records, Rate
Report at 01:00
ReportRollover at 01:15

DiscardFile dirrpt/PHREMD2.dsc, Append
DiscardRollover at 01:00
```

```
Table HR.COUNTRIES;
Table HR.REGIONS;
```

3. Edit the existing Replicat parameter file RHREMD1 to add the table filtering:

```
GGSCI (targetserver) 1> edit params RHREMD1
Replicat RHREMD1
----------------------------------------------------------------------
-- Replicat for HR Schema
----------------------------------------------------------------------
USERID 'GGER', PASSWORD "AACAAAAAAAAAAADAVHTDKHHCSCPIKAFB", ENCRYPTKEY default
AssumeTargetDefs

ReportCount Every 30 Minutes, Rate
Report at 01:00
ReportRollover at 01:15

DiscardFile dirrpt/RHREMD1.dsc, Append
DiscardRollover at 02:00 ON SUNDAY

Map HR.EMPLOYEES, Target HR.EMPLOYEES;
Map HR.JOBS, Target HR.JOBS;
Map HR.JOB_HISTORY, Target HR.JOB_HISTORY;
Map HR.LOCATIONS, Target HR.LOCATIONS;
Map HR.DEPARTMENTS, Target HR.DEPARTMENTS;
```

4. Add the parameter file for the new Replicat, RHREMD2:

```
GGSCI (targetserver) 1> edit params RHREMD2
Replicat RHREMD2
----------------------------------------------------------------------
-- Replicat for HR Schema
----------------------------------------------------------------------
USERID 'GGER', PASSWORD "AACAAAAAAAAAAADAVHTDKHHCSCPIKAFB", ENCRYPTKEY default
AssumeTargetDefs

ReportCount Every 30 Minutes, Rate
Report at 01:00
ReportRollover at 01:15

DiscardFile dirrpt/RHREMD2.dsc, Append
DiscardRollover at 02:00 ON SUNDAY

Map HR.COUNTRIES, Target HR.COUNTRIES;
Map HR.REGIONS, Target HR.REGIONS;
```

5. Stop the existing data-pump Extract, PHREMD1, and record **EXTRBA** and **EXTSEQ** from the **info** command. You need those values when you add the new data-pump Extract so it begins processing at the correct location in the Local Extract trail file. From the **info** command shown in the following example, you can see that **EXTSEQ** is equal to the trail file number 18. **EXTRBA** is 8144:

```
GGSCI (sourceserver) 1> stop ext PHREMD1

Sending STOP request to EXTRACT PHREMD1 ...
Request processed.


GGSCI (sourceserver) 2> info ext PHREMD1

EXTRACT     PHREMD1   Last Started 2011-03-20 13:09    Status STOPPED
Checkpoint Lag        00:00:00 (updated 00:00:10 ago)
Log Read Checkpoint   File dirdat/l1000018
                      2011-03-20 13:19:23.000000  RBA 8144
```

6. When the Replicat RHREMD1 has processed all the remaining changes from
    the current data-pump Extract trail and has zero lag showing, stop it:

```
GGSCI (targetserver) 1> info rep RHREMD1

REPLICAT    RHREMD1   Last Started 2011-03-20 13:18    Status RUNNING
Checkpoint Lag        00:00:00 (updated 00:00:01 ago)
Log Read Checkpoint   File dirdat/l2000013
                      2011-03-20 13:19:23.000107  RBA 2351


GGSCI (targetserver) 2> stop rep RHREMD1

Sending STOP request to REPLICAT RHREMD1 ...
Request processed.
```

7. Add the new data-pump Extract, PHREMD2, and tell GoldenGate to start
    processing at the EXTRBA and EXTSEQ in the Local Extract trail l1 that you
    recorded in step 5. Be aware that if you don't tell GoldenGate to start at a
    specific location, you can end up re-extracting changes from the first trail and
    cause collisions downstream in the Replicat. Run the info command to verify
    that the Extracts were added properly:

```
GGSCI (sourceserver) > ADD EXTRACT PHREMD2, EXTTRAILSOURCE dirdat/l1,
EXTSEQNO 18, EXTRBA 8144

GGSCI (sourceserver) > ADD RMTTRAIL dirdat/l3, EXTRACT PHREMD2, MEGABYTES 100

GGSCI (sourceserver) > info ext PHREMD*

EXTRACT     PHREMD1   Last Started 2011-03-20 13:09    Status STOPPED
Checkpoint Lag        00:00:00 (updated 00:55:22 ago)
Log Read Checkpoint   File dirdat/l1000018
                      2011-03-20 13:19:23.000000  RBA 8144

EXTRACT     PHREMD2   Initialized   2011-03-20 22:12   Status STOPPED
Checkpoint Lag        00:00:00 (updated 00:00:24 ago)
Log Read Checkpoint   File dirdat/l1000018
                      First Record   RBA 8144
```

8. Add the new Replicat, RHREMD2, and tell GoldenGate to use the new l3 trail from data-pump Extract PHREMD2 for processing. Because l3 is a new trail, you can take the default to start processing from the beginning of the first l3 trail. Run an *info* command to verify the Replicat has been added properly:

```
GGSCI (targetserver) > ADD REPLICAT RHREMD2, EXTTRAIL dirdat/l3

GGSCI (targetserver) > info rep *

REPLICAT    RHREMD1   Last Started 2011-03-20 13:18    Status STOPPED
Checkpoint Lag        00:00:00 (updated 00:52:11 ago)
Log Read Checkpoint   File dirdat/l2000013
                      2011-03-20 13:19:23.000107   RBA 2351

REPLICAT    RHREMD2   Initialized   2011-03-20 22:41   Status STOPPED
Checkpoint Lag        00:00:00 (updated 00:00:03 ago)
Log Read Checkpoint   File /gger/ggs/dirdat/l3000000
                      First Record  RBA 0
```

9. Start the data-pump Extracts, and begin sending changes to the target server:

```
GGSCI (sourceserver) > start ext PHREMD*

Sending START request to MANAGER ...
EXTRACT PHREMD1 starting

Sending START request to MANAGER ...
EXTRACT PHREMD2 starting

GGSCI (sourceserver) > info ext PHREMD*

EXTRACT     PHREMD1   Last Started 2011-03-20 22:51    Status RUNNING
Checkpoint Lag        00:00:00 (updated 00:00:06 ago)
Log Read Checkpoint   File dirdat/l1000018
                      First Record  RBA 8144

EXTRACT     PHREMD2   Last Started 2011-03-20 22:51    Status RUNNING
Checkpoint Lag        00:00:00 (updated 00:00:06 ago)
Log Read Checkpoint   File dirdat/l1000018
                      First Record  RBA 8144
```

10. Start both Replicats to begin processing changes from the data pumps:

```
GGSCI (targetserver) > start rep RHREMD*

Sending START request to MANAGER ...
REPLICAT RHREMD1 starting

Sending START request to MANAGER ...
REPLICAT RHREMD2 starting

GGSCI (targetserver) > info rep RHREMD*
```

```
REPLICAT    RHREMD1    Last Started 2011-03-20 22:53    Status RUNNING
Checkpoint Lag         00:00:00 (updated 00:00:04 ago)
Log Read Checkpoint    File dirdat/l2000016
                       2011-03-20 22:51:22.493945    RBA 1559

REPLICAT    RHREMD2    Last Started 2011-03-20 22:53    Status RUNNING
Checkpoint Lag         00:00:00 (updated 00:00:04 ago)
Log Read Checkpoint    File dirdat/l3000000
                       First Record    RBA 0
```

11. After some changes are applied, you can again check the status of the Replicats to make sure they're processing properly. You can check the RBA and make sure it's increasing. You can also do a `stats replicat` *tablename* command and a `stats extract` *tablename* command to make sure the Extracts and Replicats are processing changes:

```
GGSCI (targetserver) > info rep *

REPLICAT    RHREMD1    Last Started 2011-03-20 22:53    Status RUNNING
Checkpoint Lag         00:00:00 (updated 00:00:00 ago)
Log Read Checkpoint    File dirdat/l2000016
                       2011-03-20 22:56:37.000067    RBA 1856

REPLICAT    RHREMD2    Last Started 2011-03-20 23:07    Status RUNNING
Checkpoint Lag         00:00:00 (updated 00:00:01 ago)
Log Read Checkpoint    File dirdat/l3000000
                       2011-03-20 23:00:05.000105    RBA 1086
```

Next let's look at another strategy for creating parallel Extracts and Replicats: using key ranges for your HR schema.

Implementing Parallel Extracts and Replicats Using Key Ranges

Another strategy for creating parallel Extracts and Replicats is to use the @RANGE function to split the incoming table rows into equal buckets using a GoldenGate hash algorithm on the key values. Using this technique, you can create even more parallel processes than you can just by splitting using table filtering. You do this to divide the replication workload into parallel processes by key ranges and make the replication process more data and reduce the Replicat lag.

Figure 7-4 shows more details about how you split the Replicat using key ranges for the HR schema.

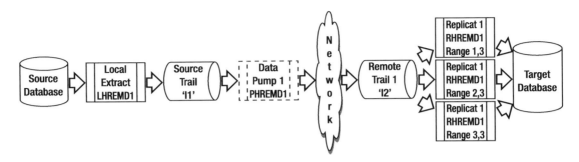

Figure 7-4. Parallel Replicat groups split by key range

Local Extract LHREMD1 remains unchanged and still extracts all the tables for the HR schema. Using the Local Extract to extract all the data is a common approach.

In this example you also leave the data pump unchanged to pass through the complete trail from the Local Extract. You could split the trails using the data pump, but this section shows another technique and splits processing using the Replicats.

Replicat RHREMD1 is split into three Replicats. The first Replicat, RHREMD1, processes the first range of keys. The second Replicat; RHREMD2, processes the second range of keys, and so on. You use the GoldenGate @RANGE function to split the keys into three buckets using a built-in hashing algorithm.

Now let's go over the steps to implement your tuning changes. Again, this example assumes you're implementing the tuning changes to the basic one-way replication topology shown in Figure 7-1.

Following are the steps to add the parallel data-pump Extract and Replicat to your replication configuration. As a reminder, this list doesn't show the commands in an obey file so you can see the command details, but you should put the GoldenGate commands in these steps in an obey file as covered in Chapter 4:

1. Edit the existing Replicat parameter file RHREMD1 to add the RANGE filtering:

```
GGSCI (targetserver) > edit params RHREMD1
Replicat RHREMD1
---------------------------------------------------------------------
-- Replicat for HR Schema
---------------------------------------------------------------------
USERID 'GGER', PASSWORD "AACAAAAAAAAAAADAVHTDKHHCSCPIKAFB", ENCRYPTKEY default
AssumeTargetDefs

ReportCount Every 30 Minutes, Rate
Report at 01:00
ReportRollover at 01:15

DiscardFile dirrpt/RHREMD1.dsc, Append
DiscardRollover at 02:00 ON SUNDAY

Map HR.EMPLOYEES, Target HR.EMPLOYEES,COLMAP (USEDEFAULTS), FILTER (@RANGE (1,3));
Map HR.JOBS, Target HR.JOBS,COLMAP (USEDEFAULTS), FILTER (@RANGE (1,3));
Map HR.JOB_HISTORY, Target HR.JOB_HISTORY,COLMAP (USEDEFAULTS),
FILTER (@RANGE (1,3));
Map HR.LOCATIONS, Target HR.LOCATIONS,COLMAP (USEDEFAULTS), FILTER (@RANGE (1,3));
```

```
Map HR.DEPARTMENTS, Target HR.DEPARTMENTS,COLMAP (USEDEFAULTS),
FILTER (@RANGE (1,3));
Map HR.COUNTRIES, Target HR.COUNTRIES,COLMAP (USEDEFAULTS), FILTER (@RANGE (1,3));
Map HR.REGIONS, Target HR.REGIONS,COLMAP (USEDEFAULTS), FILTER (@RANGE (1,3));
```

2. Add the parameter file for the new Replicat, RHREMD2:

```
GGSCI (targetserver) > edit params RHREMD2
Replicat RHREMD2
----------------------------------------------------------------------
-- Replicat for HR Schema
----------------------------------------------------------------------
USERID 'GGER', PASSWORD "AACAAAAAAAAAAADAVHTDKHHCSCPIKAFB", ENCRYPTKEY default
AssumeTargetDefs

ReportCount Every 30 Minutes, Rate
Report at 01:00
ReportRollover at 01:15

DiscardFile dirrpt/RHREMD2.dsc, Append
DiscardRollover at 02:00 ON SUNDAY

Map HR.EMPLOYEES, Target HR.EMPLOYEES,COLMAP (USEDEFAULTS), FILTER (@RANGE (2,3));
Map HR.JOBS, Target HR.JOBS,COLMAP (USEDEFAULTS), FILTER (@RANGE (2,3));
Map HR.JOB_HISTORY, Target HR.JOB_HISTORY,COLMAP (USEDEFAULTS),
FILTER (@RANGE (2,3));
Map HR.LOCATIONS, Target HR.LOCATIONS,COLMAP (USEDEFAULTS), FILTER (@RANGE (2,3));
Map HR.DEPARTMENTS, Target HR.DEPARTMENTS,COLMAP (USEDEFAULTS),
FILTER (@RANGE (2,3));
Map HR.COUNTRIES, Target HR.COUNTRIES,COLMAP (USEDEFAULTS), FILTER (@RANGE (2,3));
Map HR.REGIONS, Target HR.REGIONS,COLMAP (USEDEFAULTS), FILTER (@RANGE (2,3));
```

3. Add the parameter file for the new Replicat, RHREMD3:

```
GGSCI (targetserver) > edit params RHREMD3
Replicat RHREMD2
----------------------------------------------------------------------
-- Replicat for HR Schema
----------------------------------------------------------------------
USERID 'GGER', PASSWORD "AACAAAAAAAAAAADAVHTDKHHCSCPIKAFB", ENCRYPTKEY default
AssumeTargetDefs

ReportCount Every 30 Minutes, Rate
Report at 01:00
ReportRollover at 01:15

DiscardFile dirrpt/RHREMD3.dsc, Append
DiscardRollover at 02:00 ON SUNDAY

Map HR.EMPLOYEES, Target HR.EMPLOYEES,COLMAP (USEDEFAULTS), FILTER (@RANGE (3,3));
Map HR.JOBS, Target HR.JOBS,COLMAP (USEDEFAULTS), FILTER (@RANGE (3,3));
Map HR.JOB_HISTORY, Target HR.JOB_HISTORY,COLMAP (USEDEFAULTS),
FILTER (@RANGE (3,3));
```

```
Map HR.LOCATIONS, Target HR.LOCATIONS,COLMAP (USEDEFAULTS), FILTER (@RANGE (3,3));
Map HR.DEPARTMENTS, Target HR.DEPARTMENTS,COLMAP (USEDEFAULTS),
FILTER (@RANGE (3,3));
Map HR.COUNTRIES, Target HR.COUNTRIES,COLMAP (USEDEFAULTS), FILTER (@RANGE (3,3));
Map HR.REGIONS, Target HR.REGIONS,COLMAP (USEDEFAULTS), FILTER (@RANGE (3,3));
```

4. Stop the existing data-pump Extract, PHREMD1. You want it to stop extracting so you can make sure the lag on the Replicat goes down to zero and you can continue with the Replicat changes. The Local Extract can continue to run. Also run an **info** command to verify that it's stopped:

```
GGSCI (sourceserver) 1> stop ext PHREMD1

Sending STOP request to EXTRACT PHREMD1 ...
Request processed.


GGSCI (sourceserver) 2> info ext PHREMD1

EXTRACT      PHREMD1  Last Started 2011-03-20 13:09   Status STOPPED
Checkpoint Lag        00:00:00 (updated 00:00:10 ago)
Log Read Checkpoint   File dirdat/l1000018
                      2011-03-20 13:19:23.000000  RBA 8144
```

5. When the Replicat RHREMD1 has processed all the remaining changes from the current data-pump Extract trail and has zero lag showing, stop it and record the **EXTRBA** and **EXTSEQ** from the **info** command. You need those values when you add the new Replicats so they begin processing at the correct location in the data-pump Extract trail file l2. From the **info** command, you can see that EXTSEQ is equal to the trail file number of 13. **EXTRBA** is 2351:

```
GGSCI (targetserver) 1> info rep RHREMD1

REPLICAT     RHREMD1  Last Started 2011-03-20 13:18   Status RUNNING
Checkpoint Lag        00:00:00 (updated 00:00:01 ago)
Log Read Checkpoint   File dirdat/l2000013
                      2011-03-20 13:19:23.000107  RBA 2351


GGSCI (targetserver) 2> stop rep RHREMD1

Sending STOP request to REPLICAT RHREMD1 ...
Request processed.
```

6. Add the new Replicat, RHREMD2, and tell GoldenGate to begin processing at the **EXTRBA** and **EXTSEQ** in the Local Extract trail l2 that you recorded in step 5. Be aware that if you don't tell GoldenGate to start at a specific location, you can end up re-replicating changes from the first trail and cause collisions in the Replicat:

```
GGSCI (targetserver) > ADD REPLICAT RHREMD2, EXTTRAIL dirdat/l2,
EXTSEQNO 13, EXTRBA 2351

GGSCI (targetserver) > info rep RHREMD2

REPLICAT   RHREMD2   Initialized   2011-03-20 22:51   Status STOPPED
Checkpoint Lag        00:00:00 (updated 00:00:01 ago)
Log Read Checkpoint   File dirdat/l2000013
                      First Record  RBA 2351
```

7. Add the new Replicat, RHREMD3, and tell GoldenGate to begin processing at
    the EXTRBA and EXTSEQ in the Local Extract trail l2 that you recorded in step 5.
    Once again, if you don't tell GoldenGate to start at a specific location, you can
    end up re-replicating changes from the first trail and cause collisions in the
    Replicat:

```
GGSCI (targetserver) > ADD REPLICAT RHREMD3, EXTTRAIL dirdat/l2,
EXTSEQNO 13, EXTRBA 2351

GGSCI (targetserver) > info rep RHREMD3

REPLICAT   RHREMD3   Initialized   2011-03-20 22:51   Status STOPPED
Checkpoint Lag        00:00:00 (updated 00:00:01 ago)
Log Read Checkpoint   File dirdat/l2000013
                      First Record  RBA 2351
```

8. Start the data-pump Extract, and begin sending new changes to the target
    server:

```
GGSCI (sourceserver) > start ext PHREMD*

Sending START request to MANAGER ...
EXTRACT PHREMD1 starting

GGSCI (sourceserver) > info ext PHREMD*

EXTRACT    PHREMD1   Last Started 2011-03-20 22:51   Status RUNNING
Checkpoint Lag        00:00:00 (updated 00:00:06 ago)
Log Read Checkpoint   File dirdat/l1000018
                      First Record  RBA 8144
```

9. Start all three of your Replicats to begin processing changes. Run an info
    command to verify that they're running:

```
GGSCI (targetserver) > start rep RHREMD*

Sending START request to MANAGER ...
REPLICAT RHREMD1 starting

Sending START request to MANAGER ...
REPLICAT RHREMD2 starting
```

```
Sending START request to MANAGER ...
REPLICAT RHREMD3 starting

GGSCI (targetserver) > info rep RHREMD*

REPLICAT    RHREMD1    Last Started 2011-03-20 22:53    Status RUNNING
Checkpoint Lag         00:00:00 (updated 00:00:04 ago)
Log Read Checkpoint    File dirdat/l2000013
                       2011-03-20 22:51:22.493945  RBA 2351


REPLICAT    RHREMD2    Last Started 2011-03-20 22:53    Status RUNNING
Checkpoint Lag         00:00:00 (updated 00:00:04 ago)
Log Read Checkpoint    File dirdat/l2000013
                       First Record   RBA 2351


REPLICAT    RHREMD3    Last Started 2011-03-20 22:53    Status RUNNING
Checkpoint Lag         00:00:00 (updated 00:00:04 ago)
Log Read Checkpoint    File dirdat/l2000013
                       First Record   RBA 2351
```

10. After some changes are applied, you can check the status of the Replicats to
    make sure they're processing properly. You can check the RBA and make sure
    it's increasing. You could also do a `stats replicat` *tablename* command and a
    `stats extract` *tablename* command to make sure the Extracts and Replicats
    are processing changes:

```
GGSCI (targetserver) > info rep *

REPLICAT    RHREMD1    Last Started 2011-03-25 23:08    Status RUNNING
Checkpoint Lag         00:00:00 (updated 00:00:03 ago)
Log Read Checkpoint    File dirdat/l2000013
                       2011-03-25 23:21:48.001492  RBA 2852


REPLICAT    RHREMD2    Last Started 2011-03-25 23:11    Status RUNNING
Checkpoint Lag         00:00:00 (updated 00:00:03 ago)
Log Read Checkpoint    File dirdat/l2000013
                       2011-03-25 23:21:48.001492  RBA 2852


REPLICAT    RHREMD3    Last Started 2011-03-25 23:11    Status RUNNING
Checkpoint Lag         00:00:00 (updated 00:00:03 ago)
Log Read Checkpoint    File dirdat/l2000013
                       2011-03-25 23:21:48.001492  RBA 2852
```

Using BATCHSQL

BATCHSQL is another parameter you can add to your Replicats to improve performance. According to the
Oracle GoldenGate documentation, BATCHSQL can improve the performance of Replicats by as much as
300 percent. There are some usage restrictions for BATCHSQL, and it's only valid for Oracle, SQL Server,
DB2 LUW, DB2 on z/OS, and Teradata databases. You should check the *Oracle GoldenGate Windows and
UNIX Reference Guide* for the full list of restrictions.

In normal processing, GoldenGate groups transactions together but preserves transaction order from the source. With BATCHSQL, GoldenGate groups together similar transactions into a high-performance array and processes them at a much faster rate. To implement BATCHSQL using defaults, simply add the following parameter to your Replicat parameter file:

BATCHSQL

You can add several optional parameters to BATCHSQL if you need to tune the amount of memory BATCHSQL is consuming. You can refer to the GoldenGate Reference Guide for details on those parameters. Typically, you should start with the default value and then add the optional parameters if needed.

Let's look at a few examples to illustrate how BATCHSQL works. Figure 7-5 shows GoldenGate processing a remote trail normally. The remote trail has three transactions, each with an insert and a delete to the HR.EMPLOYEE table. The GoldenGate Replicat organizes those transactions into a larger Replicat transaction according to the minimum value of the GROUPTRANSOPS parameter setting. For this example, let's assume you're using the default GROUPTRANSOPS setting of a minimum of 1,000 SQL operations per Replicat transaction. Notice that GoldenGate normally preserves the order of SQL operations with inserts followed by deletes, just as in the remote trail.

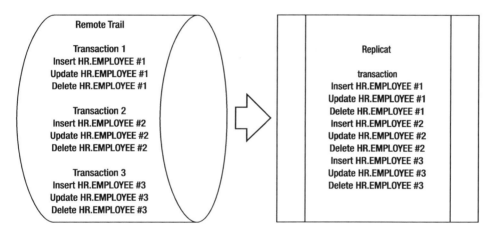

Figure 7-5. Normal GoldenGate transaction processing

Figure 7-6 shows GoldenGate processing a remote trail using BATCHSQL. The remote trail has three transactions, each with an insert and a delete to the HR.EMPLOYEE table. The GoldenGate replicat organizes those transactions into a larger Replicat transaction according to the GROUPTRANSOPS parameter setting. For this example, let's assume you're using the default GROUPTRANSOPS setting of 1,000 SQL operations per Replicat transaction. With BATCHSQL, notice that GoldenGate changes the order of SQL operations and groups together the inserts, updates, and the deletes for the same SQL table. BATCHSQL groups or batches together in a processing array the same SQL operations operating on the same table with the same columns.

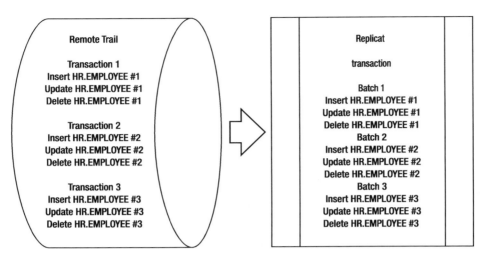

Figure 7-6. BATCHSQL GoldenGate transaction processing

You may be asking yourself if using BATCHSQL causes any issues with referential integrity. GoldenGate analyzes any foreign-key dependencies before applying the batch and makes adjustments. According to the GoldenGate documentation, in some cases, GoldenGate may need to apply more than one SQL statement per batch to maintain the referential integrity.

BATCHSQL also creates a new section in your report file. Here is an example of the new statistics you see in your report file when BATCHSQL is activated. Keep in mind that these tiny sample numbers are based on the simple example in Figure 7-6 for illustration purposes:

```
BATCHSQL statistics:

                Batch operations:       9
                        Batches:        3
                Batches executed:       2
                         Queues:        2
                Batches in error:       1
             Normal mode operations:    1
          Immediate flush operations:   0
                   PK collisions:       0
                   UK collisions:       0
                   FK collisions:       0
               Thread batch groups:     0
                         Commits:       2
                       Rollbacks:       1
               Queue flush calls:       2

                   Ops per batch:       3
           Ops per batch executed:     4.5
                   Ops per queue:      4.5
               Parallel batch rate:    N/A
```

Let's review a couple of the fields in the BATCHSQL report. Batch Operations are the total number of operations executed. Batches are the number of batches created. In this case you had three batches, which you can see by referring to Figure 7-6. Batches in Error was 1, which tells you that you had an error while BATCHSQL was processing. Because of the error, Normal Mode Operations equals 1 because BATCHSQL rolls back and reverts to normal transaction-processing mode operations when there is an error.

When BATCHSQL encounters processing errors, you see the following type of messages in your GoldenGate logs:

```
2011-03-22 17:12:14  WARNING OGG-00869  Aborting BATCHSQL transaction.
Database error 1 (ORA-00001: unique constraint (HR.PK_EMP_ID) violated).

2011-03-22 17:12:15  WARNING OGG-01137  BATCHSQL suspended, continuing in
normal mode.

2011-03-22 17:12:15  WARNING OGG-01003  Repositioning to rba 231493300 in seqno 49.
```

When these errors occur, GoldenGate automatically rolls back the BATCHSQL processing and attempts to process the transaction in normal mode. This slows down the BATCHSQL, so if you're seeing a lot of these errors you may find BATCHSQL won't improve your performance.

When you have BATCHSQL successfully enabled, you should review your Replicat report file and compare the processing rates to your baseline reports and determine if you're getting performance improvements.

Using GROUPTRANSOPS

You can use GROUPTRANSOPS to tune the number of SQL operations in a GoldenGate transaction. As you saw in Figure 7-5, the GoldenGate Replicat groups together source transactions into a GoldenGate transaction. By default, the Replicat includes a minimum of 1,000 SQL operations in a transaction. By setting GROUPTRANSOPS higher, say to 2,000, you may get increased performance. In addition to having a larger transaction, a higher value for GROUPTRANSOPS reduces the number of checkpoints written to the GoldenGate checkpoint table. GROUPTRANSOPS can be set in your Replicat parameter file as shown in the following example:

```
GROUPTRANSOPS 2000
```

Be careful not to set GROUPTRANSOPS too high. Doing so can cause an increase in latency on the target because the target transaction size is larger on the target than the source.

Tuning Disk Storage

By its very nature as a data-replication product, GoldenGate generates a lot of disk I/O. Trails are written by the Local Extract, read and written by the data-pump Extract, and finally read by the Replicat. As such, to achieve the highest performance it's critical to place your trail files on the fastest possible disk storage. Here are some suggestions for tuning disk storage for GoldenGate to achieve the best performance:

- Place GoldenGate files on the fastest available storage and storage controller. Although NAS is acceptable for GoldenGate files, generally SAN storage has better performance than NAS due to the NAS network overhead. Storage technology is constantly changing, and performance should be evaluated at the time of your decision.

- Use RAID 0+1 rather than RAID 5. RAID 5 maintains parity information that isn't needed and slows down writing the trails.

- Always evaluate the performance of the disks used to store your trail files. For example, on Linux use the `IOSTAT` command to determine if any disk devices are a bottleneck.

- Use the `GROUPTRANSOPS` parameter as described in the last section to reduce I/O.

Tuning the Network

Depending on the number of data changes in your replication environment, the Extract could be sending large amounts of data over the network to be processed by the Replicat. Network performance between your source and target is critical to overall GoldenGate performance. As mentioned earlier, you can use tools such as the Windows System Monitor or the `netstat` command on Linux to gather network statistics. You can compare these to the baseline network statistics to determine if you're experiencing an ongoing performance problem or just a temporary spike.

In addition to server commands, you can also look at GoldenGate itself to see if network issues may be causing a performance bottleneck. Let's walk through an example of how to detect a network bottleneck using GoldenGate commands.

First let's run an `info` command on the Local Extract. A portion of the output is shown in the following example:

```
GGSCI (sourceserver) > info ext LHREMD1, showch 10
...
Write Checkpoint #1

  GGS Log Trail

  Current Checkpoint (current write position):
    Sequence #: 11
    RBA: 977
    Timestamp: 2011-01-28 23:19:46.828700
    Extract Trail: dirdat/l1
```

You should run the `info` command several times and compare the output, specifically the values for the Write Checkpoint. Look for the highest Write Checkpoint # in each command output and make sure the RBA and timestamp are increasing. Run the same commands for the data-pump Extracts.

If the Write Checkpoint values are increasing for the Local Extract and *not* for the data-pump Extract, then there is a network bottleneck for the data-pump Extract. The Local Extract is able to process data, but the data pump is bottlenecked. Eventually the data-pump Extract backs up with transactions due to the network bottleneck and runs out of internal memory and then abends.

You can also run commands on the Replicat to confirm there is a network bottleneck. The following example runs a `status` command on the Replicat as shown in the following example:

```
GGSCI (targetserver) > send replicat RHREMD1, status

Sending STATUS request to REPLICAT RHREMD1 ...
  Current status: At EOF
  Sequence #: 17
  RBA: 2852
  0 records in current transaction
```

In the example, the Replicat is in At EOF. If the Replicat is At EOF and the Local Extract is processing data, you know there is a bottleneck with the data pump and the network. The Local Extract is extracting changes, but there is nothing for the Replicat to process because of the network bottleneck. Keep in mind that the Replicat will continue processing normally for a while if there is any leftover data in the target trail file until it hits the end of file. Then it will stop processing because it isn't receiving data over the network in the target trail file from the data pump.

You can take several tuning approaches to help alleviate network performance issues. The first approach is to create parallel data pumps, as covered earlier in this chapter. Parallel data pumps alleviate any network bandwidth limitations caused by using a single data-pump process. Second, you can adjust some additional network tuning options on the RMTHOST parameter. You see those next.

Tuning the RMTHOST Parameter

The default GoldenGate TCP socket buffer size is 30,000 bytes. By increasing this buffer size, you can send larger packets of data over the network. The *Oracle GoldenGate Windows and UNIX Reference Guide* has a sample formula to help calculate the optimum TCP socket buffer size. You should also check your specific server limitations for maximum TCP buffer size. For example, on Linux you can check the following settings to determine the maximum TCP transmit and receive buffer sizes:

```
net.core.rmem_max = 262144
net.core.wmem_max = 262144
```

In this example, the transmit and receive buffers are set to 256KB. You can check with your server and network administrator to determine if these sizes can be adjusted higher, such as 4MB, to allow GoldenGate to take advantage of higher TCP buffer sizes. GoldenGate can utilize larger TCP buffer sizes if you add an option to the RMTHOST parameter as shown in the following example:

```
RmtHost targetserver, MgrPort 7809, TCPBUFSIZE 100000
```

This example customizes the TCP buffer size to 100,000 bytes in the data-pump Extract to try to improve performance by sending larger TCP packets. Another network tuning option of the RMTHOST parameter is the COMPRESS option, as shown in the following example:

```
RmtHost targetserver, MgrPort 7809, TCPBUFSIZE 100000, COMPRESS
```

Using COMPRESS, GoldenGate compresses outgoing blocks of data over the network and then decompresses the data before writing it to the trail. According to the GoldenGate Reference manual, compression ratios of 4:1 or greater are possible. Keep in mind, the compress and uncompress add some CPU overhead to your servers.

Tuning the Database

This book doesn't spend a great deal of time covering general database tuning, but it's safe to say a poorly tuned database will negatively impact GoldenGate performance. This is especially true on the Replicat side where GoldenGate is executing actual database DML statements to change the data. You should ensure that your database is tuned properly prior to turning on GoldenGate. There are a few major areas you can check to help ensure proper Replicat performance on the target database:

- Verify that the target tables used by GoldenGate have unique keys and SQL indexes are created on those keys.

- Verify that database optimizer statistics are kept up to date to ensure that the database chooses the most efficient SQL execution plans.

- Make sure the database tables that are the target of replication aren't overly fragmented. If so, they should be reorganized to eliminate the fragmentation.

- Run database performance reports such as AWR for Oracle database and verify there are no major performance issues.

Summary

This chapter covered a basic methodology for tuning GoldenGate replication. It reviewed capturing baselines of GoldenGate performance statistics to help you determine when you have a performance issue and how it can best be resolved. You then saw some specific approaches and examples of tuning GoldenGate by using strategies such as parallel processing groups and using GoldenGate parameters like BATCHSQL and GROUPTRANSOPS.

CHAPTER 8

Monitoring Oracle GoldenGate

GoldenGate has a lot of moving parts that depend on other systems to operate properly. The goal for replication is to replicate data from source to target in real time without losing any data. Every system is different and has different strengths and weaknesses. You can monitor the weak points, but sometimes you may also want to monitor the strong points even though they rarely break. As Murphy's Law says, "Anything that can go wrong, will go wrong." The cost of fixing a problem may be much more than the expense of implementing a good monitoring system. With a good monitoring system, you can reduce downtime due to errors, or even stop problems before they occur.

This chapter goes over some scenarios that illustrate what can go wrong in the GoldenGate data-propagation chain. Next, it discusses different ways to detect and identify errors. Finally, it presents some automated scripts that can make your life easier. This chapter teaches you how to identify issues and gives you some basic ideas on how to resolve them. To learn about advanced troubleshooting, fixing issues, and using tuning techniques, please refer the chapter 7, 11 and 14 of this book.

Designing a Monitoring Strategy

You need to master two factors in order to design a comprehensive monitoring strategy:

- *Internal factor:* You need to understand how GoldenGate works internally. You should have full control as a GoldenGate administrator. If something wrong within the GoldenGate system, you should be able to identify the issue and fix it yourself.

- *External factor:* These are the systems that GoldenGate depends on. In large organizations, you may not have full access to these systems, such as sophisticated network-, server-, and storage-monitoring tools and utilities. In some cases, you can't even access the database-monitoring tools if you aren't a DBA. But you don't need to have full access to these systems to monitor your GoldenGate processes. This chapter discusses the available monitoring techniques that are available to GoldenGate administrators.

In addition to these factors, you also need to identify all the possible ways that GoldenGate can break. The possible monitoring points for a simple GoldenGate configuration are shown in Figure 8-1; this chapter covers each of them. If you can manage a simple configuration, you can manage a complex configuration. The number of moving parts in the GoldenGate system doesn't matter—you just need to add more monitoring to each additional component. For example, with an active-active configuration, you need to replicate the monitoring activities on monitor points 1 to 7 in Figure 8-1 from the source side to the target side. You also need to do the same thing on the target side for monitor points 7 to 13. If you add an additional data-pump process, then you need to add a monitor to points 2, 3, 4, and 7 on the source side and the corresponding points at the target. However, this is the logical view. The actual number of scripts may vary. For example, one script may have a birds-eye view of GoldenGate's overall health.

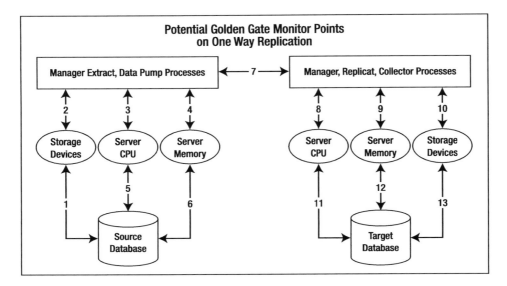

Figure 8-1. Potential GoldenGate monitor points

Each Extract process has a database connection querying the database dictionary to check if there is any change. If changes occur, extract process reads the online redo log to capture the changes and writes to the trail file. If the data isn't in the online redo log, it reads the archived log. If the data isn't in the archived log, extract process reads the alternative archived log if you specify ALTARCHIVELOGDEST <path name> in the Extract parameter files. If extract process still can't find the transaction with the correct Commit Sequence Number (CSN), extract process abends and tells you the missing file sequence number.

▓ **Note** The CSN is GoldenGate specific; each database system has its own way of tracking the commit sequence. Oracle uses the System Change Number (SCN), DB2 z/OS uses the relative byte address (RBA), MySQL uses LogNUm, and so forth.

Why Monitoring the Extract Is Important

In Oracle, the Extract relies on the Oracle redo log to work. Online redo logs are converted to archived logs after the last entry is written, for a database in archivelog mode. In some systems, the DBA may compress and move the archived logs to other locations that aren't accessible to GoldenGate. If the Extract is down for long period of time and the archived log isn't accessible, then you lose data. In mission-critical environments, you need to monitor your Extract process closely.

In normal database systems, GoldenGate trail files use only around 30% or less of the overall redo log file. The other 70% of the redo data are system-related logs that aren't needed for GoldenGate. So, for example, if you store the trail files for two weeks in case of a disaster, the total trail files size for two weeks is <daily total redo size> × 0.3 × 14. You need around four times the total daily redo size to store the entire two weeks of change-log data. Two weeks of outage is very rare on major database systems. Therefore, as long as the Extract process can generate the trail files, the Replicat will load them.

Getting the Maximum Threshold

It's important to get the maximum threshold for how much GoldenGate can transfer through the network. For example, if GoldenGate has to be down for 5 hours due to a scheduled outage, you need to know how long it will take GoldenGate to catch up to zero lag. To do this, you can stop the data pump for a few hours and then restart it. You can use the stats command at the GoldenGate Software Command Interface (GGSCI) prompt to calculate the number of operations. In addition, you can check the accumulated file size and consumption rates. You see how to do that later in this chapter.

Which Processes to Monitor in the GoldenGate Environment

This chapter uses Extract EXTGGS1, Data Pump DPGGS1, and Replicat REPGGS1 for demonstration purposes. It's a simple one-way extract. GoldenGate processes use CSN, seqno and RBA to connect and sequence each process together. CSN, seqno and RBA are the tools to identify the lag in GoldenGate Environments. If you know exactly where the lags are, then you can put more monitoring in that process.

As mentioned earlier, Oracle GoldenGate uses CSNs to track the commit order. Each database system has its own unique serial number; refer to the Oracle GoldenGate Administration Guide for a complete list of CSNs. The CSN is also associated with the timestamp.

■ **Note** In a Real Application Clusters (RAC) environment, it's very important to have all the clustered servers in the exact same timestamp. Otherwise, you get an "incompatible records with SCN mismatch error." If you get this error, either you lose the data or you need to use the Logdump utility to identify the problem records and patch the data manually.

In addition to the CSN, seqno also plays an important role in monitoring and troubleshooting. Seqno is the sequence number for the trail files; each type of trail file has its own sequence number. For example, seqno=100 in the Extract trail file may not be the same as sequence number 100 in the Replicat or data pump, even if they're in the same propagation process. The naming convention for the trail file is *aannnnnn*, where *aa* is two characters trail file prefix and the six *n*s are the seqno. If GoldenGate uses up all the available seqno values, it starts over from 000000. Technically, you can have a maximum of one million trail files. So, set up the trail file size properly if you need to keep a lot of trail files.

The last key metric is the redo log sequence number. Whenever you issue an `alter extract begin [now]|[timestamp]` command, GoldenGate searches the Oracle data dictionary to find out which redo log to begin reading from. If no timestamp is given, GoldenGate starts from the last checkpoint file. Therefore, it may take a while to start up an Extract, especially with the NODYNAMICRESOLUTION parameter.

Monitoring All Running Processes

The `info all` GGSCI prompt command gives you a good indicator of GoldenGate's overall health. As shown here, Lag should be 0 and the Time Since Chkpt should be less than 10 seconds on normal operations. If you have a long lag in your Extract, the value in the Lag column is large or doesn't decrease:

```
GGSCI  28> info all
Program        Status        Group        Lag              Time Since Chkpt
MANAGER        RUNNING
EXTRACT        RUNNING       DPGGS1       00:00:00         00:00:00
EXTRACT        RUNNING       EXTGGS1      00:00:00         00:00:04
REPLICAT       RUNNING       REPGGS1      00:00:00         00:00:09
```

Monitoring the Detail Extract

To understand the current status of the Extract, you can add detail to the info GGSIC command as follows:

```
GGSCI> Info extract extggs1, detail
EXTRACT      EXTGGS1    Last Started 2011-04-09 22:36    Status RUNNING
Checkpoint Lag         00:00:00 (updated 00:00:02 ago)
Log Read Checkpoint    Oracle Redo Logs
                       2011-04-10 00:16:47  Seqno 175, RBA 36263936
  Target Extract Trails:
  Remote Trail Name                             Seqno            RBA         Max MB
  C:\ggs\dirdat\C1                                9              2964          5

  Extract Source                       Begin              End

  C:\APP\ORADATA\ORCL\RED001.LOG   2011-04-09 22:02   2011-04-10 00:16
  C:\APP\ORADATA\ORCL\RED003.LOG   2011-04-09 20:14   2011-04-09 22:02
  C:\APP\ORADATA\ORCL\RED001.LOG   * Initialized *    2011-04-09 20:14

Current directory      C:\ggs

Report file            C:\ggs\dirrpt\EXTGGS1.rpt
Parameter file       C:\ggs\dirprm\EXTGGS1.prm
Checkpoint file      C:\ggs\dirchk\EXTGGS1.cpe
Process file         C:\ggs\dirpcs\EXTGGS1.pce
Error log            C:\ggs\ggserr.log
```

According to these results, Golden Gate is reading the redo log **seqno** 175. In RAC, you see the sequence number for each node. **Seqno** 9 is the remote trail file sequence number.

The **send** command gives you similar information about the source and target **seqno**s:

```
GGSCI  32> Send extract extggs1 status
Sending STATUS request to EXTRACT EXTGGS1 ...
EXTRACT EXTGGS1 (PID 7220)
  Current status: Recovery complete: At EOF

  Current read position:
  Sequence #: 175
  RBA: 36263936
  Timestamp: 2011-04-10 00:27:47.000000

  Current write position:
  Sequence #: 9
  RBA: 2964
  Timestamp: 2011-04-10 00:27:53.063000
  Extract Trail: C:\ggs\dirdat\C1
```

Checking the Current Oracle Online Redo Log

As we know from previous section that extract EXTGGS1 is reading the sequence# 175, and we would like to know if the sequence# 175 is the most current or not. The following query tells us which redo log file sequence# Oracle is processing.

```
SELECT
A.MEMBER,
        B.SEQUENCE#,
        B.STATUS,
        B.FIRST_CHANGE#,
        B.NEXT_CHANGE#,
        B.ARCHIVED
  FROM  V$LOGFILE A, V$LOG B
 WHERE  A.GROUP# = B.GROUP#
```

MEMBER		SEQUENCE#	STATUS	FIRST_CHANGE#	NEXT_CHANGE#
C:\ORCL\RED003.LOG	174		INACTIVE	6591047	6621440
C:\ORCL\RED002.LOG	173		INACTIVE	6560323	6591047
C:\ORCL\RED001.LOG	175		URRENT	6621440	
281474976710655					

first_change# and next_change# are the Oracle SCN numbers. The current redo log **sequence#** is 175. EXTGGS1 is also on sequence number 175. Both sequence# are 175 and they are in sync. So there is no lag in Golden Gate extract process. Redo logs with **sequence#** 174 and lower are in the archived log area.

Checking the Archived Log

To find out if GoldenGate is reading the online or archived redo log, you can use the following GGSCI command:

```
GGSCI> Info extract extggs1, detail
EXTRACT     EXTGGS1  Last Started 2011-04-09 22:36   Status RUNNING
Checkpoint Lag        00:00:00 (updated 00:00:02 ago)
Log Read Checkpoint  Oracle Redo Logs
                     2011-04-10 00:16:47  Seqno 175, RBA 36263936
```

Seqno is 175, because it's the current online redo log. If the extract isn't reading the online redo log and behind, then the seqno is less than 175. You can check which archived log it's reading as follows:

```
SELECT   SEQUENCE#,
         NAME,
         FIRST_CHANGE#,
         NEXT_CHANGE#
  FROM   V$ARCHIVED_LOG
```

SEQUENCE#	NAME		FIRST_CHANGE#	NEXT_CHANGE#
171	C:\ARC0000000171_0718807864.0001	6527997		6542114
172	C:\ARC0000000172_0718807864.0001	6542114		6560323
173	C:\ARC0000000173_0718807864.0001	6560323		6591047
174	C:\ARC0000000174_0718807864.0001	6591047		6621440

The default archived log naming convention includes the log sequence#. If the DBA changed the naming convention, you can use sequence# to find out which archived redo log file GoldenGate is reading. During normal operations, max(sequence#)+1 should be the current redo seqno—175 in this case. If not, the Extract process is behind. To determine whether the Extract is writing to the trail file, check the trail file size. In " Monitoring The Detail Extract" section, the trail file is c1000009, where 9 is the trail file seqno. The trail file RBA is 2964, so you can use info extract extggs1, detail a few times to check if the RBA increases. Or you can use ls -ls in Unix/Linux or dir in Windows a few times to check the trail file size.

Monitoring the GoldenGate Rate and Redo Log Consumption Rate

By default, the stats command lists all the tables that have transactions. You can limit the display using totalsonly, by table, and reportrate. You can also reset the stats.

```
GGSCI  30> stats extggs1
Sending STATS request to EXTRACT EXTGGS1 ...
Start of Statistics at 2011-04-10 00:05:46.
Output to C:\ggs\dirdat\C1:
Extracting from GGS.SOURCE_TABLE to GGS.SOURCE_TABLE:
*** Total statistics since 2011-04-09 22:36:18 ***
        Total inserts                    0.00
        Total updates                   12.00
        Total deletes                    0.00
        Total discards                   0.00
        Total operations                12.00
*** Daily statistics since 2011-04-10 00:00:00 ***
        No database operations have been performed.
*** Hourly statistics since 2011-04-10 00:00:00 ***
        No database operations have been performed.
```

```
*** Latest statistics since 2011-04-09 22:36:18 ***
        Total inserts                          0.00
        Total updates                         12.00
        Total deletes                          0.00
        Total discards                         0.00
        Total operations                      12.00
End of Statistics.
```

If you execute the following commands, they should give a similar number of operations if there is no special filter in the mappings:

```
On Source:
GGSCI> stats dpggs1 totalsonly *
GGSCI> stats extggs1 totalsonly *

On Target
GGSCI> stats repggs1 totalsonly *
```

If you see different numbers of operations, then there may be data lost or filtered in the process. For example, in one-way replication, all the stats from the Extract and Replicate side should match. If you have 10 records inserted into the source table but only 9 in target, there must be something wrong.

Monitoring Lags for Each Group

There are different ways to find out the lags in the GoldenGate process. All the approaches are similar, and you can use one or all of them to validate the lags.

Using getlag

The first approach uses the getlag command:

```
GGSCI> lag extract extggs1
```

Or

```
GGSCI> send extract extggs1, getlag

Sending GETLAG request to EXTRACT EXTGGS1 ...
Last record lag: 1 seconds.
```

You get one of the three statuses:

- "At EOF, no more records to process": There is no lag in the Extract, data pump, or Replicat. If the data still isn't replicating, check the trail file names or the database connection to make sure they're set up properly.

- "Waiting for data to process": In the Extract, Extract process is waiting for the redo log. In the data pump, Extract is waiting for the Extract trail files. In the Replicat, Replicate process is waiting for the Data Pump or Extract trail files. The lag may be the network or disk I/O issues.

- "Processing data": The Extract, data pump, or Replicat is busy grinding the data. One of these processes may be the bottleneck. It's normal if this status is temporary and goes away after a few seconds.

Using Write Checkpoint

The next approach uses the `Write Checkpoint #n` command to validate the lag:

```
GGSCI> info extract extggs1, showch 10

Write Checkpoint #1

  GGS Log Trail

  Current Checkpoint (current write position):
    Sequence #: 7
    RBA: 1411
    Timestamp: 2011-04-11 22:00:53.446000
Extract Trail: C:\ggs\dirdat\C2

Write Checkpoint #1

  GGS Log Trail

  Current Checkpoint (current write position):
    Sequence #: 6
    RBA: 4994
    Timestamp: 2011-04-10 22:51:25.477000
    Extract Trail: C:\ggs\dirdat\C2
```

Execute the above command on the data pump process, and compare the Sequence#, RBA, and timestamp. If we expect the extract process to capture the data, the sequence# and RBA should increase in Extract, Data Pump and Replicat processes. If the sequence# or RBA are stuck or increased slower than other process, then that process may have lag issue.

Using the Trail File Generation Rate

Another approach to monitor the lag is to note the current Sequence# and file size for the Extract, data pump, and Replicat processes. This chapter uses c1$nnnnnn$ for the data pump and c2$nnnnnnn$ for the Replicat (the six ns in c1 and c2 aren't the same—each has its own sequence number).

We can get the maximum sequence# for c1 and c2 by listing the directory files (`ls -l` in Linux/Unix or `dir` in Windows). The maximum sequence# is the current trail file for the process. For examples, Extract is writing the C1000011 file, but if the Data Pump process is reading anything other than C1000011 file, then we have lag in the Data Pump process. C1000011 is connected between Extract and Data Pump processes. Whereas C200008 is connected between Data Pump and Replicat processes.

Check the maximum Sequence# for each trail file as shown here:

```
GGSCI (STRICHCHUT61) 21> shell dir dirdat

Directory of C:\ggs\dirdat

04/12/2011  06:28 PM              994 C1000010
04/12/2011  06:28 PM              994 C1000011
04/12/2011  06:29 PM            1,411 C2000007
04/12/2011  06:29 PM            1,455 C2000008
```

The maximum Sequence# for c1 is 11 and for C2 is 8 as shown above.

To confirm if the extract is writing to the current trail file without any lag, we can use the following GGSCI command:

```
GGSCI> info extggs1, detail

EXTRACT     EXTGGS1   Last Started 2011-04-12 18:28   Status RUNNING
Checkpoint Lag        00:00:00 (updated 00:00:05 ago)
Log Read Checkpoint   Oracle Redo Logs
                      2011-04-12 19:13:40  Seqno 187, RBA 33210880

  Target Extract Trails:
  Remote Trail Name                          Seqno      RBA     Max MB
  C:\ggs\dirdat\C1                             11               994          5
```

The Extract is reading the redo log seqno 187. You can use the query in the "Checking the Current Oracle Online Redo Log" section of this chapter to find out if seqno 187 is current or old. If the current Oracle redo log seqno is 187, then there is no lag in the Extract. If it's larger than 187, then the lag is on the source database side and the Extract can't keep up with the redo log generation. This lag situation may be temporary—for example, during large updates. But if the lag persists, you need to tune the Extract. Also note that the extract is writing to seqno 11 for the trail file c1.

To confirm if the Data Pump is also reading the seqno 11, do the following GGSCI command:

```
GGSCI> info dpggs1, detail

EXTRACT     DPGGS1    Last Started 2011-04-12 18:29   Status RUNNING
Checkpoint Lag        00:00:00 (updated 00:00:04 ago)
Log Read Checkpoint   File c:\ggs\dirdat\c1000011
                      2011-04-12 18:28:41.860000  RBA 994


  Target Extract Trails:
  Remote Trail Name                          Seqno      RBA     Max MB
  C:\ggs\dirdat\C2                              8               1455         5
```

The data pump is also reading c1000011 (seqno 11), so there is no lag. If the data dump is reading a seqno less than 11, then the data pump can't keep up with the Extract. This may be due to a network issue, in which case you need to tune the Data Pump process. Note that the data pump is writing seqno 8 on remote trail file c2. To check the replicat is in-sync with the data dump, run the following GGSCI command:

```
GGSCI 22> info repggs1, detail

REPLICAT    REPGGS1    Last Started 2011-04-12 18:28    Status RUNNING
Checkpoint Lag         00:00:00 (updated 00:00:06 ago)
Log Read Checkpoint    File c:\ggs\dirdat\c2000008
                       2011-04-12 18:28:41.860000  RBA 1455
```

In this case, the Replicat is reading and processing seqno 8 on c2. The data pump is also writing seqno 8 on C2, so there is no lag. However, if that Replicat was reading a seqno less than 8, then there might be a database issue on the target database.

Recording the Lag Status in the ggserr.log File

You also can set the lag report frequency in the Manager parameter file:

```
LAGINFO[MINUTES|SECONDS|HOURS], example. LAGINFOSECONDS 30
LAGREPORT[MINUTES|HOURS], example LAGREPORTMINUTES 1
```

The Manager reports the lag information to the ggserr.log file every 30 seconds, and it checks the lag every minute. Check ggserr for the lag reports.

Viewing Event and Error Logs

The view reports <group_name> command shows the most recent errors and events occurring to groups:

```
GGSCI > view report extggs1
GGSCI > view report mgr
GGSCI >  view report repggs1
```

The detailed history is in ggserr.log. GoldenGate also logs errors in **/var/log/messages** and to the Event Log in Windows.

Automating Monitoring

Now that you know how to monitor GoldenGate processes manually, it's time to automate them. This section goes over a few monitoring scripts. All the scripts are scalable to multiple Extracts and Replicats. As a best practice, the monitoring scripts should be in different systems, because if the monitoring server is down, you don't get any alerts that are running on that server. With all your monitoring scripts in different places, you can endure any system outages without missing any alerts.

Checking GoldenGate Process Scripts

This monitoring script is low overhead; you can run it every 5 minutes to check whether any GoldenGate process is up. The script doesn't include a restart because most Manager parameters should include an auto-restart. Copy the block for each new process you want to monitor:

```
#!/bin/ksh

EMAIL_LIST="shingchung@aol.com 5555555555@vtext.com"

host=`hostname`
gghome=/ggs

check=`ps -ef|grep extggs1|grep -v "grep extggs1"|wc -l`;
check_num=`expr $check`

if [ $check_num -le 0 ]
then
echo "GoldenGate Extract EXTGGS1 is down on $host." > $gghome/extggs1.out
tail -200 $gghome/dirrpt/eextggs1.rpt >> $gghome/extggs1.out
    mailx -s "GoldenGate EXTGGS1 Down on $host" $EMAIL_LIST < $gghome/extggs1.out
fi

check=`ps -ef|grep dpggs1|grep -v "grep dpggs1"|wc -l`;
check_num=`expr $check`

if [ $check_num -le 0 ]
then
echo "GoldenGate Extract DPGGS1 is down on $host." > $gghome/dpggs1.out
    tail -200 $gghome/dirrpt/dpggs1.rpt >>$gghome/dpggs1.out
     mailx -s "GoldenGate Extract DPGGS1 Down on $host" $EMAIL_LIST < $gghome/dpggs1.out
fi
```

If there is any abend or even an inadvertent stop, you get an alert e-mail or page. If a network issue or temporary database issue causes an abend, a should fix it; then the alert will go away. However, in rare cases, if GoldenGate hangs, this script won't catch the error. You can use the lag-alert script in the next section to catch almost all GoldenGate issues.

Monitoring Lag Scripts

This lag-monitoring script reports the overall lag from the source database to target database. It's all on PL/SQL and is easy to port to other databases.

You must run this script on the target database. You can use a table with the most frequent transactions, or you can use a dummy table, source_table, and target_table to track the lag. If you use a dummy table, you can update the same column with a timestamp every second using dbms_job or a scheduled job. Then, calculate the time difference for the same table on the target side. The difference is the lag value.

You can use two different schedules for this script:

- Run GGS.GET_LAG every 5 seconds to update the LAG_HISTORY table.

- Run GGS.GET_LAG every hour to send information about the lag value to you, so you know the alert is running. If you don't get hourly information alert, then you know something is wrong.

This script is an independent monitoring process that doesn't tie to any GoldenGate process. So, it alerts us if any of the monitor points are broken in Figure 8-1. Some of the scenarios are as following:

- The GoldenGate administrator stops the Extract inadvertently, so GoldenGate is in the STOP state rather than ABEND.

- Someone deletes the Extract by mistake.

- The Extract process hangs.

- The source server goes down.

- Someone accidentally turns off the monitoring shell scripts on the source/target side.

If there are any issues with the CPU, memory, locks, and so on that cause the database to slow down, you get a high lag alert.

GG_LAG_HISOTRY table stores all the historical lag values. You can use this table for reporting and integrating with other monitoring tools and ETLs. Sample lag charts are shown in Figure 8-2 and Figure 8-3:

```
CREATE TABLE GGS.GG_LAG_HISTORY
(
  AUDIT_TIME  DATE,
  LAG         NUMBER
)

---- Dummy Source table. Map this table in the extract that you are monitoring
CREATE TABLE GGS.SOURCE_TABLE
(
  UPDATE_DATE  DATE,
  UPDATE_ID    NUMBER
)

---- Dummy Target table. Map this in the replicat that you are replicating
CREATE TABLE GGS.TARGET_TABLE
(
  UPDATE_DATE  DATE,
  UPDATE_ID    NUMBER
)

---- Schedule this to run every one or five seconds.
CREATE OR REPLACE PROCEDURE GGS.GET_LAG
IS
   L_MAX_TIME  DATE;
   L_LAG       NUMBER;
BEGIN

   SELECT  MAX (UPDATE_DATE) INTO L_MAX_TIME FROM TARGET_TABLE;
```

```
---- if target and source are in different timezone, add timezone offset value in this
calculation.
   SELECT   (SYSDATE - UPDATE_DATE) * 24 * 60 * 60
     INTO   L_LAG
     FROM   GGS.TARGET_TABLE;

   INSERT INTO GGS.GG_LAG_HISTORY (AUDIT_TIME, LAG)
     VALUES   (SYSDATE, L_LAG);

   COMMIT;

------ email alerts if the lag is more than 5 minutes.
   IF L_LAG > 300
   THEN

---- if you want Oracle to send email alert, you can use this.
      GGS.SEND_EMAIL ('shingchung@aol.com.com, 5555555555@vtext.com',
                     'Golden Gate Admin',
                     'ggs@somecompany.com',
                     'Golden Gate Data Is Behind',
                     'The Lag Is ' || L_LAG || ' Seconds');
   END IF;

---- if you want use kick this off from shell script, this dbms output will return the lag
value
   DBMS_OUTPUT.PUT_LINE (L_LAG);
EXCEPTION
   WHEN OTHERS
   THEN
      NULL;
END GET_LAG;
/

---- this is the send_email procedure for Oracle for your reference, you can use your own.
CREATE OR REPLACE PROCEDURE GGS.SEND_EMAIL (I_TO_EMAIL      IN VARCHAR2,
                                            I_FROM_NAME     IN VARCHAR2,
                                            I_FROM_EMAIL    IN VARCHAR2,
                                            I_SUBJECT       IN VARCHAR2,
                                            I_MESSEGE       IN VARCHAR2)
IS
   C                   UTL_SMTP.CONNECTION;
   L_EMAIL_START_POS   NUMBER (5) := 1;
   L_EMAIL_END_POS     NUMBER (5) := 0;
   L_EMAIL_CNT         NUMBER (5) := 0;
   L_EMAIL             VARCHAR2 (250);
   L_LAST_EMAIL_ADDR   BOOLEAN := FALSE;

   PROCEDURE SEND_HEADER (NAME IN VARCHAR2, HEADER IN VARCHAR2)
   AS
   BEGIN
      UTL_SMTP.WRITE_DATA (C, NAME || ': ' || HEADER || UTL_TCP.CRLF);
   END;
```

```
BEGIN
   C := UTL_SMTP.OPEN_CONNECTION ('your.mail.relay.server');
   UTL_SMTP.HELO (C, 'foo.com');
   UTL_SMTP.MAIL (C, I_FROM_EMAIL);

   LOOP
      L_EMAIL_CNT := L_EMAIL_CNT + 1;

      L_EMAIL_END_POS :=
         INSTR (STR1   => I_TO_EMAIL,
                STR2   => ',',
                POS    => 1,
                NTH    => L_EMAIL_CNT);

      L_LAST_EMAIL_ADDR := (L_EMAIL_END_POS <= 0);

      L_EMAIL_END_POS :=
         CASE
            WHEN (L_EMAIL_END_POS <= 0) THEN LENGTH (I_TO_EMAIL) + 1
            WHEN (L_EMAIL_START_POS = 0) THEN L_EMAIL_END_POS - 1
            ELSE L_EMAIL_END_POS
         END;

      L_EMAIL :=
         SUBSTR (STR1   => I_TO_EMAIL,
                 POS    => L_EMAIL_START_POS,
                 LEN    => (L_EMAIL_END_POS - L_EMAIL_START_POS));

      UTL_SMTP.RCPT (C, L_EMAIL);

      EXIT WHEN L_LAST_EMAIL_ADDR;

      L_EMAIL_START_POS := L_EMAIL_END_POS + 1;
   END LOOP;

   UTL_SMTP.OPEN_DATA (C);
   SEND_HEADER ('From', '"' || I_FROM_NAME || '" <' || I_FROM_EMAIL || '>');
   SEND_HEADER ('To', '"Recipient" <' || I_TO_EMAIL || '>');
   SEND_HEADER ('Subject', I_SUBJECT);
   UTL_SMTP.WRITE_DATA (C, UTL_TCP.CRLF || I_MESSEGE);
   UTL_SMTP.CLOSE_DATA (C);
   UTL_SMTP.QUIT (C);
EXCEPTION
   WHEN UTL_SMTP.TRANSIENT_ERROR OR UTL_SMTP.PERMANENT_ERROR
   THEN
      BEGIN
         UTL_SMTP.QUIT (C);
```

```
    EXCEPTION
        WHEN UTL_SMTP.TRANSIENT_ERROR OR UTL_SMTP.PERMANENT_ERROR
        THEN
            NULL;
    END;

    RAISE_APPLICATION_ERROR (
        -20000,
        'Failed: ' || SQLERRM
    );
END SEND_EMAIL;
/
```

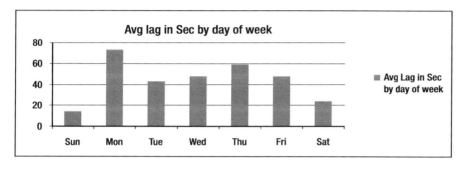

Figure 8-2. Average lag in seconds by day of week

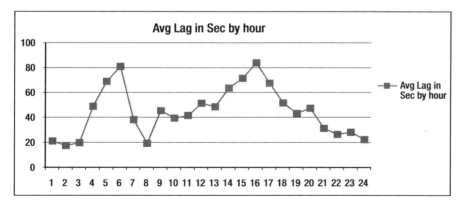

Figure 8-3. Average lag in seconds by hour

Checking Memory and CPU Scripts

If memory and CPU are the weakest links in your system, then this script will be handy to report memory and CPU usage every hour. It e-mails you the memory and CPU usage for all the GoldenGate Extract processes, as well as the total free memory. Note that **goldengate** is the Unix/Linux user id.

Here's the script:

```
#!/bin/ksh

EMAIL_LIST="shingchung@aol.com 5555555555@vtext.com"

host=`hostname`
cd /ggs/scripts
rm top.log
rm top.rpt
top -h -f top.log -n 50
cat top.log | grep extract > top.rpt
echo "" >> top.rpt
echo "Free Memory: " >> top.rpt
vmstat 1 2 | tail -1 | awk '{printf "%d%s\n", ($5*4)/1024, "MB" }' >> top.rpt

mailx -s "GoldenGate Memory Usage on $host" $EMAIL_LIST < /ggs/scripts/top.rpt

Output:
19   ?    14000 goldengate 152 20  2331M  1201M run    602:09 31.64 31.59 extract
10   ?    13655 goldengate 137 20 80912K 16432K sleep 1568:25  5.97  5.96 extract

Free Memory:
47610MB
```

The Extract process is using 31.59% of one CPU, and the data pump is using 5.96%. The Extract usually consumes more CPU than the data pump. Memory usage for the Extract is around 2331MB total and 1201MB in resident memory. The entire server memory is 47GB, so you still have plenty of memory free. The GoldenGate Extract process usually consumes 1% to 5% of overall CPU utilization.

Checking Disk Space

Even if disk space isn't an issue for you, it's nice have a script running that monitors it. You never know: your disk space space may fill up in the next few years without your noticing. You definitely need this script if trail file disk space is your weakest link. Many scripts are available online for various systems, so this section doesn't list one. Google "check disk space scripts" to get the correct scripts for you operating systems.

You can write as many monitoring scripts as you want, but you don't want to tax your systems. All the scripts in this chapter are lightweight, so they're safe to use.

Summary

This chapter has shown you how to set up a very good monitoring system for your Extract, data dump, and Replicat. If you have many other GoldenGate processes that need to monitor, then you just need to add them to your existing scripts. Figure 8-1 includes 13 links in the GoldenGate processes, but your configuration may have many more.

There are more ways that GoldenGate can break that you can imagine, but the automated PL/SQL lag-monitoring script presented in this chapter can notify you about issues, sometimes even before something major happens. It's an independent process as long as the target database is up. If the target database is down, you don't get the hourly lag status e-mail, so you know something is wrong. The alert can't tell you exactly what went wrong, but the other scripts in this chapter can pinpoint for you the exact issues.

This chapter also showed you how to monitor the health of your overall GoldenGate systems. Before you implement a GoldenGate monitoring process, it's important to know what can go wrong in your systems so you can identify problems before they get worse.

■ **Note** The Management Pack for GoldenGate (also called GoldenGate Director) can do some basic monitoring and alerts. Director also stores the lags and events information to its proprietary tables, so you can create reports from them. But use it at your own risk, because Oracle may change its table structures from version to version. See Chapter 10 for more information about Director.

CHAPTER 9

Oracle GoldenGate Veridata

GoldenGate Veridata is a high-performance cross-platform data comparison tool that supports high-volume compares while both source and target data are online and the data is being updated. Veridata three-tiered architecture spreads out the loads among different servers without compromising the performance of the source and target database systems.

Veridata uses compressed row hash data to do a comparison that reduces the CPU cycles and network bandwidth required for comparing the data,.but it's not merely a data comparison tool. Veridata can keep track of changing data and perform comparisons when the data is being updated—a feat impossible with any other tool today.

In this chapter, we will go over the key components of Veridata so you will learn why it is unique, and why no other product can compete with it right now. Then we will go over some of the key features and benefits and show how Veridata will work with your data projects and help your organization's efficiency. Once you understand what Veridata is and how it can help you, we will go through a quick tutorial on how to set it up. (It will literally take only a few minutes to set up a comparison job—that is how efficient this tool is.) Finally, we will go over tips and tricks to help you archive some complex data comparison scenarios.

Veridata Components

In order to get Veridata up and running, you need to set up five Veridata components, as shown in Figure 9-1.

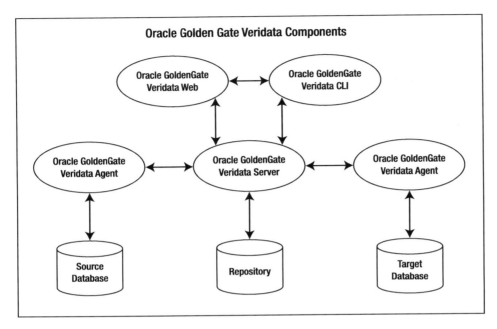

Figure 9-1. Oracle GoldenGate Veridata components

GoldenGate Veridata Server

Veridata Server is the key component of the entire Veridata system. Without it, the comparison will need to perform on either source or target databases, which will negatively impact the performance of the server. This is because any comparison jobs are both CPU and I/O intensive.

Veridata Server performs the following functions:

- Coordinates all aspect of the Oracle GoldenGate Veridata execution tasks with the agents.

- Sorts rows on Veridata Server. The default is to sort on the database that the agent is installed on.

- Compares the data collected from the GoldenGate Veridata Agents.

- Conducts the confirmation comparisons of out-of-sync data (to be explained later).

- Produces out-of-sync, confirmation, and performance reports.

GoldenGate Veridata Web

Oracle GoldenGate Web is a web-based client to the Veridata server. This is the tool that we will be using to configure most of the Veridata tasks. It performs the following functions:

- Configures all comparison objects and rules, including connections, groups, jobs, etc

- Starts and stops the comparison jobs

- Provides real-time status on the job status

- Reviews the comparisons and out-of-sync data reports

GoldenGate Veridata Repository

Veridata Repository stores all the configurations for all the comparison objects and rules. The metadata is stored as clear text in the database tables in the repository database, so you can query them to create your own custom reports. It also stores the job status, so you can integrate it with your ETL and monitoring tools seamlessly.

GoldenGate Veridata Agent, Java, and C-Code

Veridata Agent executes the SQL to fetch and return blocks of data to the Server to compare. It also extracts the out-of-sync rows detail to the Server for reporting purposes. Java agent doesn't require GoldenGate Manager, but C-code based agent requires GoldenGate Manager Process.

GoldenGate Veridata CLI (Vericom)

Vericom is a command-line interface to schedule the compare jobs. It can override some profiles settings, partition sql-predicates, shut down Veridata Server and generate/review the out-of-sync reports. However, it cannot configure the comparison settings and rules that only can be done on the Veridata Web client.

How Veridata Comparison Works

By default, Veridata comparison activities are divided into two steps: initial compares and confirmation compares. Confirmation compare is optional if the data is not expected to change during the compare or the data is filtered by the partition sql-predicates. Initial compare generates an Out-Of-Sync report (OOS). The Confirmed-Out-Of-Sync (COOS) reports are created during the confirmation compare process.

By default, Veridata compares rows literally (value-for-value) for all primary key columns. It uses a hash value for all non-key columns to compare. The row hash value is a compressed unique digital signature that is used to compare two source values. For example, a row length of 2000 bytes can be transposed to 12 bytes hashed value. It is not absolute, but the likelihood that two original values are identical is very high. This reduces the network traffic from Veridata Agent to Veridata Server. Comparison methods can be changed in the Column Mapping screen.

How Veridata Can Help You

You can use Veridata in so many different ways, it is impossible for me to list all of them here. The following are some of the key features and benefits:

- It works seamlessly with data replication tools, such as GoldenGate one-way replication and two-way synchronization. GoldenGate just captures and delivers the data, but it won't check the data for you unless you add some custom codes to do the validations. Veridata can do two-phase comparison that will report the data discrepancies on the bad data and any data that GoldenGate skips.

- Enhances enterprise data quality among all the systems, where bad data can lead to poor decision-making; failed service-level agreements; and ultimately, operational, financial, and legal risk. With Veridata validating all your business-critical data constantly, you can identify the bad data before business users report it. Veridata supports Oracle materialized views, views and Veridata specific partition that make it feasible to compare the data in different granularities and cardinalities.

- Reduces time in data comparison because of the high performance. Veridata optimizes the comparison in Extract layers in the Agent by using hashed values, then it compares the data in a separate server. So it removes the overhead from the source and target databases.

- It is non-intrusive so it enables real-time data comparisons with zero downtime on the changing data. We can compare the data between two OLTP systems while their data is changing. Veridata will use two-phase confirmation on the data synchronizations.

- Supports data or database migration projects in both initial-copy and real-time sync phases to ensure the data accuracy. We can use GoldenGate to do no-downtime migration, but with Veridata running on the background to cross-check the data between the source and migrated databases, we don't need to write expensive queries to do the data comparison during any phases of the migrations.

- Supports cross-database comparison between Oracle, SQL Server, Teradata, HP Enscribe, and HP SQL/MP databases.

- Easy to use. It can be used by both IT and business users. We can set up most of the compares without writing a single SQL statement.

- It is a standalone tool that is not dependent on Oracle GoldenGate. You don't need to install GoldenGate at all to run Veridata.

- It has role-based security to control access and protect sensitive data.

- Selective comparison compares selected columns. It can also do incremental compares with appropriate setup.

- It has a flexible command-line interface to automate and schedule compare jobs.

Setting Up the Veridata Compares

After Veridata is installed, you can use the following guide to use your own data or the data we use in this chapter. The high-level steps are as follows:

1. Create database connections, source and target.

2. Create group, a group of comparing pairs.

3. Create compare pairs, what tables to compare.

4. Create job, to run one or more groups.

5. Create profile (how you want it to run.) This is optional, as you can use the default profile.

6. Run job.

Creating Database Connections

After you log in to the GoldenGate Veridata Web, click the Connection Configuration on the left panel as shown in Figure 9-2, then fill in the following information for both source and target. Make sure GoldenGate Veridata agents are installed on both database instances.

You can either use the Wizard to set up the connection or use the setup screen as shown in Figure 9-2. Use defaults for other options for now.

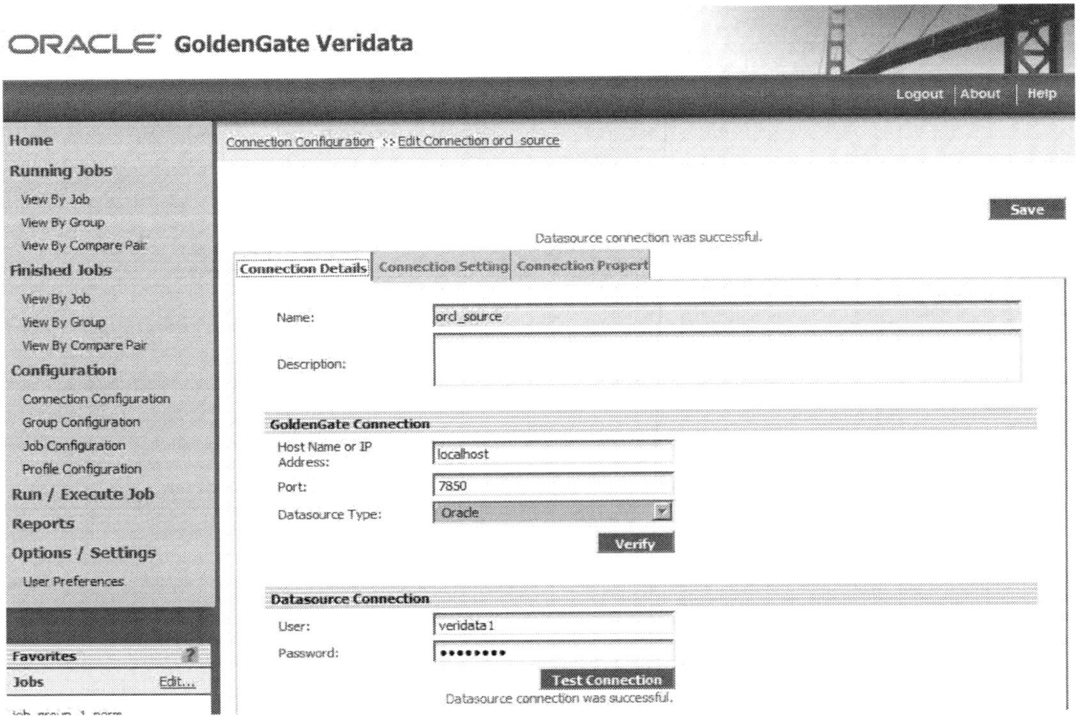

Figure 9-2. Connection configuration

Setting Up Tables and Data Scripts.

The following tables and data are used in this tutorial, so you can follow this guide. You can also use your own tables. I have created the table using **dba_objects** 50 times in the scripts. If your system is fast, you can add more loops in the code, so you can see the Running Jobs option in the left panel.

```
create table big_table_source as select 0 seqno, a.* from dba_objects a where 0=1;
create table big_table_target as select 0 seqno, a.* from dba_objects a where 0=1;
```

The following script populates the sample tables on the same database. If you want to test the comparison on different data, you have to copy the data to another database.

```
CREATE OR REPLACE PROCEDURE populate_big_table IS
BEGIN
    FOR i IN 1..50
```

```
    LOOP
        insert into big_source select i, a.* from dba_objects a;
        insert into big_target select i, a.* from dba_objects a;
        commit;
    END LOOP;
END populate_big_table;
```

Creating a Group

In Group Configuration, add the source and target connections to the group. One Group can have many compare pairs and one job has many groups. For example, you can break down the group by subject areas, or by schedules.

Creating Compare Pairs

GoldenGate Compare Pairs is what we need to compare. We can compare tables, materialized views, and views. This is the heart of Veridata, where the business rules are. It is part of the Group Configurations. You can follow the steps below to set up the tables that we want to compare.

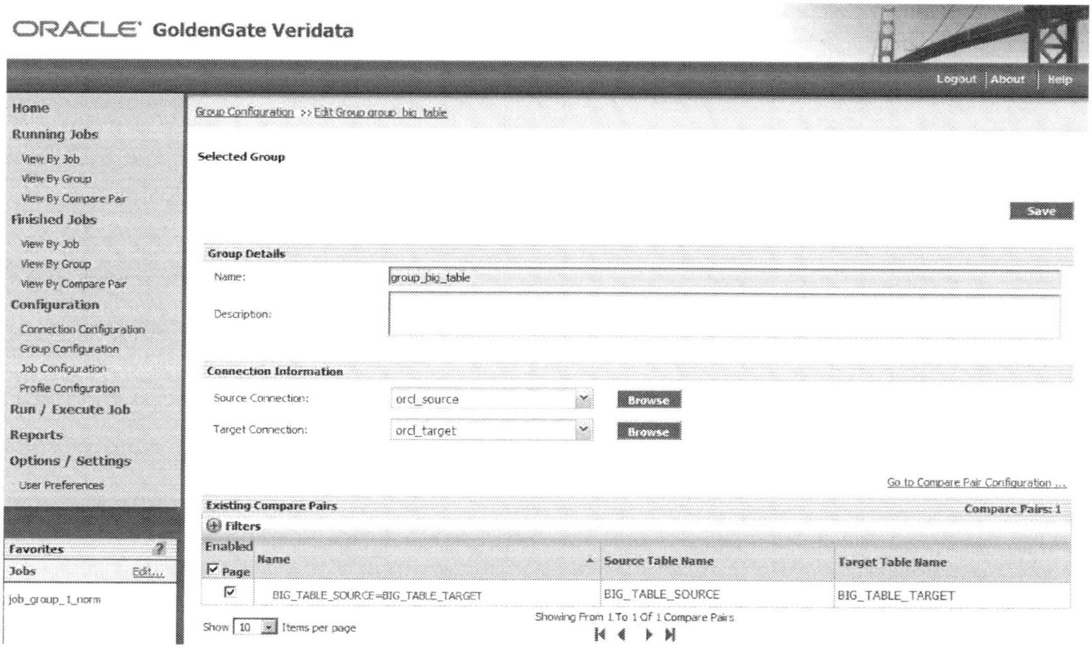

Figure 9-3. GoldenGate Group Configuration

Click the Go to Compare Pair Configuration . . . link on the GoldenGate Group Configuration screen as shown in Figure 9-3. It will take you to the Compare Pair Mapping screen as shown in Figure 9-4.

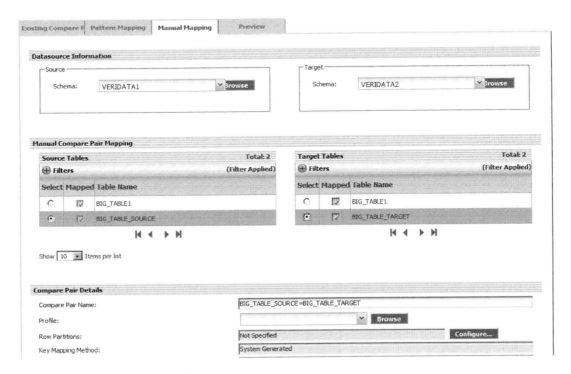

Figure 9-4. Compare Pair Mapping

In the Compare Pair Mapping screen, you can use Manual Mapping to add the compare pairs. After you pick up the compare pair, make sure your compare name is in the Compare Pair Detail section. In the example shown, BIG_TABLE_SOURCE=BIG_TABLE_TARGET is the compare pair name. Click the Preview tab to confirm the settings.

Creating a Job

Jobs are like shell scripts, they are used to run a series of compare groups. There is no built-in scheduler in Veridata, so you use the OS schedulers (crontab, Windows schedulers) to run "vericom" command-line jobs. A job name and a group are the only required parameters. You can check the group name big_group_table that you just created in the previous section.

Creating a Profile

Creating a profile is optional; you can use the default profile for now. We will go over this in detail later in the chapter.

Running the Veridata Job

You can run the compare job by clicking the Run/Execute job tab in the left panel on the Veridata Main screen. Or you can use the command `vericon.exe -job job_big_table`.

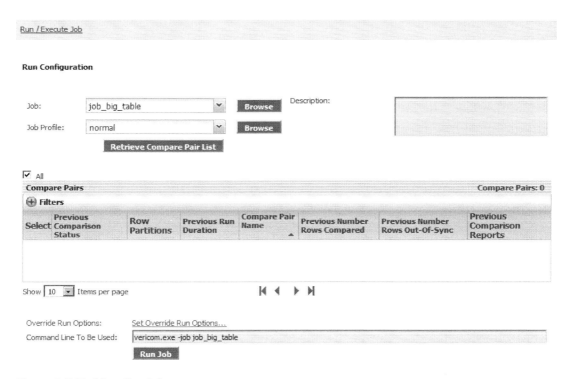

Figure 9-5. Veridata Run Job

The command line for this job is also shown in Figure 9-5, `vericon.exe -job job_big_table` for Windows. Click the Run Job button to run the job. The Run Job button text will change to Stop Job if it is running. Click it if you want to stop the job. You can also go to the Running Jobs or Finished Jobs panels to check the status. If you get any error, you can drill down the group and compare pairs to get the detail error messages.

Improving Performance and Reducing Overhead

Veridata processes can be very CPU intensive, and sometimes I/O intensive. If you need Veridata to do a lot of work with a minimum footprint, you should make every effort to reduce the system utilization to help the performance. Because the default options are not necessarily the best options, there are a few tricks that can improve performance and reduce unnecessary overhead.

Excluding Columns

In Column Mapping, you can use User Defined to remove the column(s) from the mapping. The removed columns can be added back later on. The primary keys can't be removed from the mapping as Veridata uses them to compare. By default, Veridata queries every column in both source and target to compare.

Tuning Profiles Settings

There are two types of sorting methods: database sorting and NSort on the Veridata Server. If database servers have spare CPU or IO, then use the default option of "sort on database". If the database is a revenue-generating environment that needs every single resource possible to get high Service Level Agreement (SLA), then we can use the "sort on server" option. Please note, Veridata server is also doing actual compares and other tasks; if it peaks out 100% CPU during sort, you may wish to sort the data on the database server or add more CPUs to the Veridata Server.

Disabling the Confirm Out of Sync Step

If you don't expect the data to change during the compare, such as daily/weekly/monthly ETL, filtered data via partitioning, or running the compare right after all the data is copied, you can disable the Confirm-Out-Of-Sync step in the profile settings.

Increasing the Number of Threads

You can increase the number of threads on Veridata servers. The default number of CPUs is four. Since all comparisons take place on the server side, Veridata compares are quite CPU intensive. Verify the CPU usage during the compares before you increase the number of threads. This can be set in both the Initial Compares and Confirmation Compares profile settings.

Compares Methods

Using hash to compare is generally faster. Hash is the default, but if you have to use literally to get 100% accuracy, you can change the compare method in the Column Mapping. Literal comparison is performed value for value, as opposed to a comparison that uses a hash.

Right Trim on Character Fields

By default, Veridata has RTRIM on character fields on, so your queries look like the following example. You can turn RTRIM off in the Edit Database Connection setting, Truncate Trailing Spaces When Comparing Values. This reduces some CPU cycles to trim all the varchar columns in every single row.

```
SELECT    "SEQNO",
          RTRIM ("OWNER"),
          RTRIM ("OBJECT_NAME"),
          RTRIM ("SUBOBJECT_NAME"),
          "OBJECT_ID",
          "DATA_OBJECT_ID",
          RTRIM ("OBJECT_TYPE"),
          TO_CHAR ("CREATED", 'yyyy-MM-DD:hh24:mi:ss'),
          TO_CHAR ("LAST_DDL_TIME", 'yyyy-MM-DD:hh24:mi:ss'),
          RTRIM ("TIMESTAMP"),
          RTRIM ("STATUS"),
          RTRIM ("TEMPORARY"),
          RTRIM ("GENERATED"),
          RTRIM ("SECONDARY"),
          "NAMESPACE",
          RTRIM ("EDITION_NAME")
   FROM   "VERIDATA2"."BIG_TABLE_TARGET" X
```

Comparing Incremental Data for Large Tables

If you have a table with billions of rows, you cannot afford to do a full table scan every time you need to compare. Instead, you can use row partition features to compare (Veridata row partition, not the database partition). This requires nothing more than adding a sql-predicate to the WHERE clause which, if added correctly, will make a big difference in terms of performance. For example, you can add SEQNO=1 to both the source and target row partition in the Compare Pair Configuration Screen, and the Veridata will generate the SQL as follows:

```
SELECT    "SEQNO",
          "OWNER",
          "OBJECT_NAME",
          "SUBOBJECT_NAME",
          "OBJECT_ID",
          "DATA_OBJECT_ID",
          "OBJECT_TYPE",
          TO_CHAR ("CREATED", 'yyyy-MM-DD:hh24:mi:ss'),
          TO_CHAR ("LAST_DDL_TIME", 'yyyy-MM-DD:hh24:mi:ss'),
          "TIMESTAMP",
          "STATUS",
          "TEMPORARY",
          "GENERATED",
          "SECONDARY",
          "NAMESPACE",
          "EDITION_NAME"
   FROM   "VERIDATA2"."BIG_TABLE_TARGET" X
  WHERE   SEQNO = 1
```

If you need to compare the data replicated in one day—for example, change_date is the column that you use to track the change—then you can put this to the sql-predicate statement in both source and target.

```
Change_date between sysdate-1 and sysdate
```

Veridata will compare the data that has changed since yesterday.

Comparing GoldenGate Real-Time Replication Data

If there is no timestamp in your table, then the confirm out-of-sync option is the only option to make sure the data is consistent. There are three statuses for confirmation:

- In-flight: row was out-of-sync in the initial compares step, but it has changed. Veridata cannot confirm it is in-sync yet.

- In-sync: row was out-of-sync in the initial compares step; it is in-sync now.

- Persistently out of sync: row was out-of-sync in the initial compares step, but is still out-of-sync after the confirmation step.

By default, the initial compares and confirmation steps are running in parallel. It waits for 60 seconds between two steps. This value can be changed in the profile setting.

Comparing Different Column Types and Compare Formats

You can override the default Column Mapping name, type, and even format. In Compare Pair Configuration, click the column name hyperlink; you will see the dialog in Figure 9-6. You can type over the Source Column name, Source Datatype and their compare formats. This is useful if source and target have different column names and even different data types, although they are actually the same data.

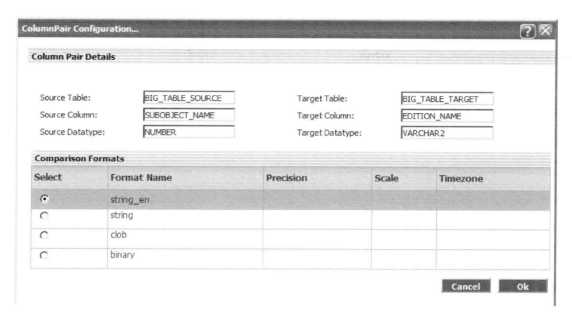

Figure 9-6. Change default data type and compare format

Using Performance Statistics

Veridata keeps a few performance statistics for each run; they are in the Finished Job panel as shown in Figure 9-7. You can use these statistics to prepare for the production run; for example, to calculate the run time for each job and conduct performance tunings.

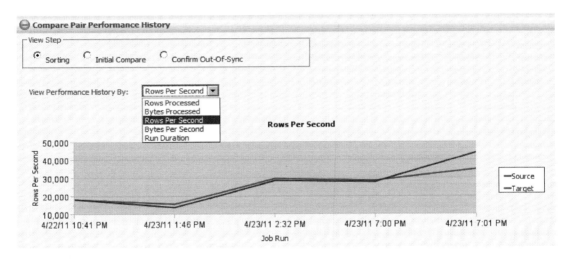

Compare Pair Performance

	Sorting (Source)	Sorting (Target)	Initial Compare	Confirm Out-Of-Sync
Start Time:	4/23/11 7:01:09 PM	4/23/11 7:01:09 PM	4/23/11 7:01:08 PM	4/23/11 7:01:09 PM
Run Duration:	00:00:02	00:00:02	00:00:03	00:00:02
Rows Processed:	73236	73236	73236	0
Rows Per Second:	44224	34974	28070	0
Bytes Processed:	2332796	2332796	2332796	0
Bytes Per Second:	1408693	1114038	894134	0

Figure 9-7. Performance statistics

You also can view detail performance in the Compare Pair Reports in the same screen by clicking the Report link. The following are the sample Compare Pair Reports:

```
Processing first rowhash block from source at 2011-04-23 19:01:09.
Processing first rowhash block from target at 2011-04-23 19:01:10.

Performance Statistics for source Rowhash at 2011-04-23 19:01:10.

                rows: 73236
     duration (secs): 00:00:01
            rows/sec: 73236.00
           row bytes: 7937097
       row bytes/sec: 7937097
           bytes/row: 108
        rh bytes/row: 4
         rows skipped: 333760
```

```
                     blocks skipped: 0
                     hash comp rate: 0.04
                    total comp rate: 0.02
                  pct time fetching: 0.00
                   pct time waiting: 0.00
               time until first row: 00:00:00
                           ipc msgs: 12
                          ipc bytes: 2337393
                          bytes/msg: 194782
               compressed bytes/msg: 72710
                          bytes/sec: 2337393
               compressed bytes/sec: 872521
               msg compression ratio: 0.37
```

```
NSORT statistics:
Nsort version 3.4.29 (Windows-x86 32-bit) using 49M of memory out of 50M
Pointer sort performed Sat Apr 23 19:01:08 2011
              Input Phase        Output Phase        Overall
Elapsed      2.03                 0.08                2.11
I/O Busy     2.02   100%          0.01   100%         2.03
Action  User  Sys Busy      User  Sys Busy      User  Sys Busy
main    0.00  0.00  0%      0.00  0.00  0%      0.00  0.00  0%
   1    0.14  0.00  7%      0.00  0.00  0%      0.14  0.00  7%
   2    0.12  0.00  6%      0.02  0.00 25%      0.14  0.00  7%
All     0.26  0.00 13%      0.02  0.00 25%      0.28  0.00 13%
      Majflt    Minflt   Sort Procs Aio Procs/QueueSize RegionKB
        0/0          0            2      0/0                 512
File Name                    I/O Mode Busy   Wait MB/sec  Xfers      Bytes    Records
Input Reads
  <release records>          buffered 100%   1.08  1.08      9    2186324      73236
Output Writes
  <return records>           buffered 100%   0.00 218.63     9    2186324      73236
```

Using Vericom Command Line

Vericom command-line scripts are usually used to automate the scheduled jobs. It can be used to override the settings in groups, compare pairs, and profiles. For example, you can override the sql-predicates with system dates to compare the most recent data only. Set up number of threads depending on the day or night jobs.

By default, Vericom will run the job in the background and it will not wait for the job to finish before returning the prompt.

```
C:\Veridata\server\bin>vericom -j job_big_table
Connecting to: localhost:4150
Run ID: (1035, 0, 0)
```

The exit code will be zero if the job started successfully, but it will not tell you if any compares fail.

If you want to kick off the job to capture the detail messages and status, you can use either –w or –wp arguments. –wp <number> is poll interval in minutes.

```
C:\Veridata\server\bin>vericom -j job_big_table -w
Connecting to: localhost:4150
Run ID: (1035, 0, 0)
                              Job Start Time: 2011-05-01 22:12:57
                              Job Stop Time: 2011-05-01 22:13:02
                        Job Report Filename: C:\00001035\job_big_table.rpt
                     Number of Compare Pairs: 1
         Number of Compare Pairs With Errors: 0
           Number of Compare Pairs With OOS: 0
         Number of Compare Pairs With No OOS: 1
          Number of Compare Pairs Cancelled: 0
                       Job Completion Status: IN SYNC
```

You can also redirect the output to a file and email to the monitoring team. The –w or –wp arguments will return the correct Exit codes.

```
There are six exit statues from the GoldenGate manuals.


0: The Vericom command finished successfully.  If –w or –wp was not specified, the exit status
is 0 if the job started successfully.  The actual compare errors will not be captured.
1: Invalid vericom syntax was used.
2: Vericom could not find the connection information by looking in the veridata.loc or
veridata.cfg, and the connection parameter "{ -url | -u } <url>" is not specified with the
command arguments.
3: Syntax is correct, but missing required flags.  For example, if –j or –c is specified, then
-g <group> input is required.
4: Job ran successfully, but the compare status has something other than in-sync.
5: Communication error with Oracle Veridata Server.
```

For a full list of the Vericom command arguments, type vericom –helprun.

Setting Up Role-Based Security

Veridata role-based security is very easy to set up. It already defines a fixed number of roles. You just need to add users or groups to the pre-defined roles, then Veridata will apply the security for you.

To configure the security role, use the following link to get to the Tomcat Web Server Administration Tool screen as shown in Figure 9-8: http://<hostname>:<port>/admin.

The default Apache Tomcat Web Server port is 8830. To change the default port, modify the server.xml file in the <Veridata_install_dir>/server/web/conf directory. Search for 8830 and replace it with another port number.

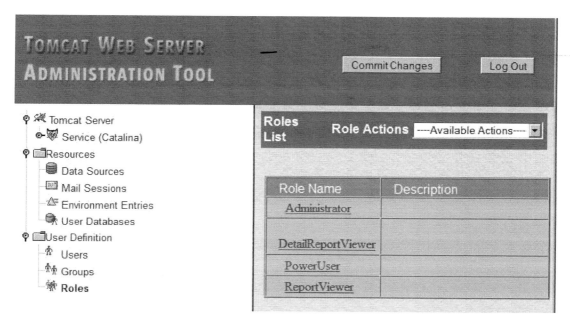

Figure 9-8. User definition roles in Tomcat Web Server Administration Tool

Here are the descriptions of the role names:

- *Administrator:* This is the admin id that you use for the login initially. This role can perform all functions.

- *DetailReportView:* This is the ReportViewer role, but it can also view the out-of-sync report information through the Web interface or at the file level. Some business-sensitive information may be in the detail reports.

- *PowerUser:* As with the admin role, you can do everything except any configuration function on the server side.

- *ReportViewer:* With this role, you only can view the reports, jobs, and configurations.

Summary

Oracle GoldenGate Veridata is a comparison tool that enables the comparison to be performed on changing data, something that is impossible with any other tool. It has very good security built-in, so it can be used by both IT and business users to protect business-sensitive data.

Veridata can be used in both the command-line and Web-based client. It is flexible enough to integrate with the existing Extract Transform and Load (ETL) and monitoring processes.

The performance of Veridata is impressive; it has the right architecture to compare data between two databases with "compressed" row hash values. With proper setup, there is no other data-comparison tool that can perform better than Veridata.

CHAPTER 10

GoldenGate Director

Oracle GoldenGate Director is a multi-tiered GUI application that enables the development and monitoring of almost all Oracle GoldenGate processes. With Director, you don't need to remember the parameter and argument syntax. In parameter files, the order of the codes is important. Director takes care of the order for you. However, you always can use Param File Editor to overwrite parameters manually. It also offers context-sensitive help that gives you high-level assistance on what the parameters do.

In order to administer Oracle GoldenGate, you have to open many SSH windows for each server on which GoldenGate is running. With Director, you no longer need to log in to all the servers. You only need to log in to the Director Client; then you can administer all the Oracle GoldenGate servers that are set up in the Director repository. GoldenGate developers/administrators don't even need to know the UNIX/Windows login. Not having to log in to each system is a very nice feature if your GoldenGate servers are on different platforms and databases—Director handles the database versions and platform-specific commands and parameters for you.

The GoldenGate Software Command Interface (GGSCI) command line doesn't have an automated monitoring and alert feature. Director displays the near real-time lag on each process. You can also set up lag and abend reports in a few minutes without writing any custom scripts.

With all these features, Director enables rapid development, a faster learning curve, and quicker testing for most Oracle GoldenGate tasks. It only takes two minutes to set up an initial load task and about five minutes to set up a simple Extract and Replicat.

This chapter goes over the key components the Director. Then you walk through the process of setting up the initial load, one-way replication, and the data-pump process. At the end, the chapter discusses some of Director's advanced features.

Director Components

Director consists of five components, as shown in Figure 10-1. They are GoldenGate GGSCI instances that have Manager processes running, Director Administrator that is used to configure the GoldenGate Director, Director Server/database that manages all the jobs, Director Web that is used to do some simple monitoring and administrations, and lastly, Desktop Client that is used to do all the Director tasks.

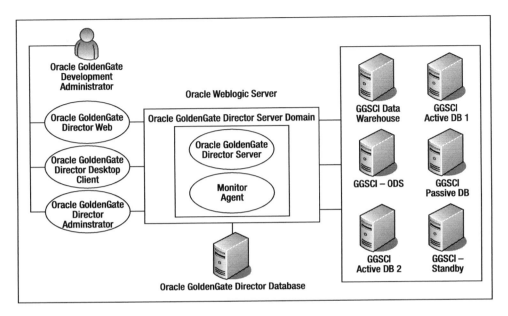

Figure 10-1. Director components

GoldenGate GGSCI Instances

GoldenGate director can link to many Manager processes or referred data source in the Director Client application. The Manager IP address and port number are the only required parameters required for Director Server to connect to the GGSCI instances.

Director Administrator

Director Administrator is used to set up all the GGSCI instance configurations. All of this information is stored in the Director repository database.

Director Server and Database

Director Server runs as a WebLogic domain. There is no need to run the default WebLogic domain when you start up Director Server. However, you need to install the WebLogic server components. Director Monitor Agent is part of Director Server, so you don't need to do anything during the installation process. Director Repository database stores all the configurations and the statistics in clear text format, so we can query the tables for our ad-hoc reporting.

Director Web

Director Web monitors and controls the Oracle GoldenGate Extract and Replicat processes. It's usually used by the production support team that is monitoring the software. Director Web allows you to start and stop the process; but you can't change the parameter files, so you can't do advanced programming with Director Web. It has a limited GGSCI interface that you can use to manage the Extract and Replicat processes. Refer to the Oracle GoldenGate Administrator's Guide for the supported GGSCI commands.

To use Director Web, type this URL in your web browser:

`http:/dirhost.abc.com:7001/acon`

Change `dirhost.abc.com` to your Director Server IP or hostname. 7001 is default WebLogic port; to change the default port to something else, you need to change the `config.xml` file in the Director domain:

```
<listen-port>80</listen-port>
<listen-port-enabled>true</listen-port-enabled>
```

With Director Web, you can even administer and monitor Oracle GoldenGate tasks from any compatible browser, including Blackberry, iPhone, and iPad, as shown in Figure 10-2.

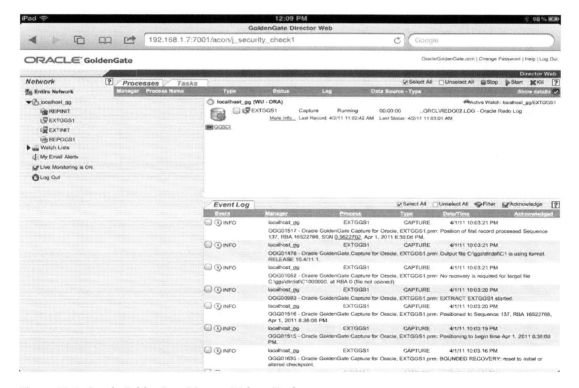

Figure 10-2. Oracle GoldenGate Director Web on iPad

Director Client

On the desktop, Director Client can create/change/delete the parameter and trail files. It also displays online help for the available Oracle GoldenGate parameters.

Before using the Director desktop client or web application, you have to set up the Manager process in a GGSCI instance and start it—you can't do anything without Manager started and running. Both Director Web and Director Client depend on the Manager process to control the Extract and Replicat. Therefore, you can't modify the Manager parameter files using either Director Client or Web.

You use the Director Client in this book. Anything you can do in Director Web, you also can do in Director Client. Their interfaces are similar.

This chapter shows you how to set up some basic and advanced Oracle GoldenGate mappings using Director Client on the desktop. You skip some Oracle GoldenGate concepts because they're covered in previous chapters, the Administrator's Guide, the Reference Guides, and Director Online Help.

Director Client is a GUI application. This chapter includes a number of screenshots so you can be sure you're on the same page as you follow along with the examples. In Director Client, the same menu bar or button may behave differently depending on which object you've highlighted. For example, the View Detail menu item displays different dialogs when you highlight Extract Object, Data Source, and Trail Files.

It's important to follow the steps at the beginning of the chapter; you skip some basic instructions later. When you're familiar with the Director interfaces, some tasks are easier and faster than the GGSCI alone. With Oracle GoldenGate Manager running, you don't even need to touch vi or Notepad to perform most common development tasks.

Setting Up the Data Source

Before you use the Director application, you have to set up the data source using Oracle Golden Gate Director Admin Tool. Make sure Director Server is already running, and then follow these steps:

1. Enter the Username and Password, as shown in Figure 10-3. The default is admin for both Username and Password.

Figure 10-3. Director login screen

2. From the drop-down menu, choose the server name with the TCP port number.

3. Click Login. The Account page appears.

4. On the Account page, create a new user or use the admin ID.

5. Click the Monitor Agent tab, and confirm that you're monitoring your data source.

There are only two roles in Director Client: Owner and Observer. You can define them on the Data Source tab. In addition, user activities are logged in the `access.log` file under the Director WebLogic domain.

Owner has full control of this data source. If you leave the Owner field blank, then all users can see and access the processes associated with this data source. If the Host Is Observable option is selected, all non-owners are in read-only mode for this data source.

Director stores user-specific configurations by user. So if you share the same user id, you see the exact same screen that other users see, such as diagrams and alerts.

Go ahead and create a data source that has a manager already running. In Director terms, a data source is also referred to as a *Manager process*. It is the exact same Manager process that Golden Gate uses to manage all the extracts and replicats. Note that you must create a Manager parameter file with a required port number in order for the desktop client to work. Use Check Connection to confirm if is the manager is running. You can't create a Manager parameter file using Director Client. You can run GGSCI in Director Client, but it doesn't support the `Edit` command. For a list of nonsupported features in the GGSCI tab in one of the Director dialogs, refer to the Director Administrator's Guide.

On the Monitor Agent tab, be sure to turn on monitoring for your data source.

Modifying the Manager Parameter file

Now you can launch the Director Client. From the menu bar, select File ➤ Login, enter **admin/admin** if you want to use the default password, or enter the login you created in the Oracle GDSC Admin Tool. Click the Data Source tab, and then drag the data source you created in the Admin Tool to the diagram area. Now, you should see a Data Source icon as shown in Figure 10-4.

Modifying the Parameter File Using the Built-in Editor

Right-click the data source icon in the diagram panel, and select Advanced ➤ Edit Param File as shown in Figure 10-4. You have full control of the parameter file in this built-in editor. You'll usually use it to edit parameters that haven't been implemented in the Director GUI.

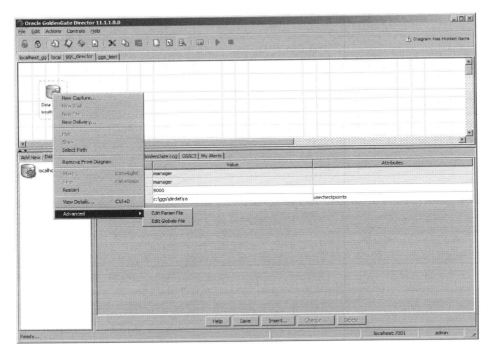

Figure 10-4. Editing the Manager parameter file

Modifying the Parameter File Using the GUI

You also can modify the Manager parameter file using the Director interface. For example, to add the
purgeoldextracts parameter to the parameter file, highlight the data source and then click the Insert
button. The dialog shown in Figure 10-5 opens. It's a very nice feature that this dialog shows all the
available Manager parameters and attributes along with their online help.

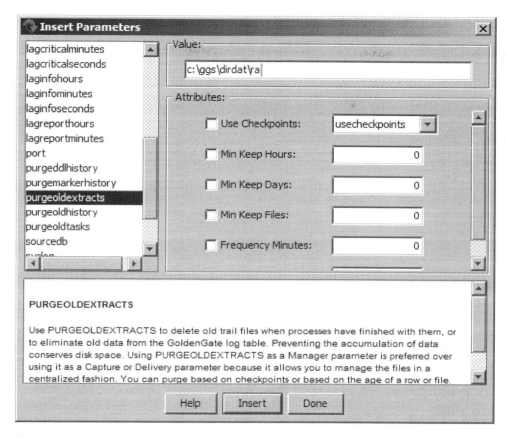

Figure 10-5. Inserting a parameter into the Manager parameter file

Select `purgeoldextracts` from the list at left, and enter your `dirdat` full path with a two-character trail-file prefix. Then click Insert. You can add other parameters if you wish, or click the Done button if you're finished.

Right-click the data source, and choose Restart to refresh the Manager. You can also go to GGSCI and enter `refresh mgr`.

Next, you walk through several tasks using Director Client.

Setting Up the Initial Load

The Oracle GoldenGate Initial Load task is very easy to set up in Director. It has a menu item to automate this; you only need to map the table(s).

Adding an Initial Load Task

Click the data source and choose Actions ➤ Add New ➤ Initial Load Task, as shown in Figure 10-6.

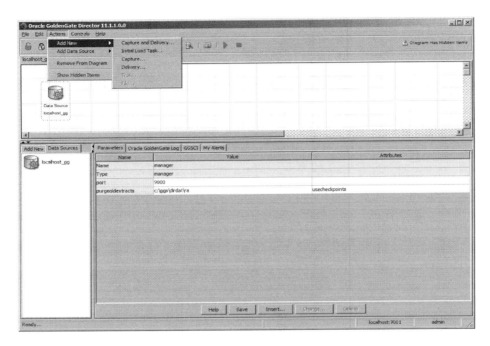

Figure 10-6. Choosing Initial Load Task

You can fill in the Capture Name and Delivery Name in the Initial Load Task dialog. Make sure the source and target database logins are correct. Click OK. Director creates all the necessary files for you, as shown in Figure 10-7. Next, you tell Oracle GoldenGate what tables you need to replicate with the initial load.

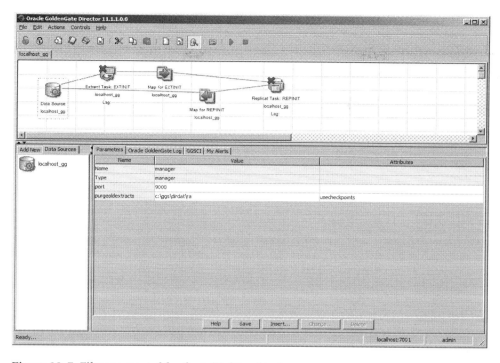

Figure 10-7. Files are created for the Initial Load task.

Mappings tell Oracle GoldenGate what you need to replicate over to the target database. So, you need to create mapping rules. The guidelines for creating mapping rules are as follows:

- When configuring a mapping statement for a `Capture` object, don't specify target tables or column mapping.

- When configuring a mapping statement for a `Delivery` object, specify the source and target tables. If needed, map source columns to target columns and specify column-conversion functions.

On the diagram, click Map for EXTINIT and then click the Insert button at the bottom. The Insert New Mapping dialog opens. For now, use the Mapping Type value Table, as shown in the Figure 10-8. Enter the table name in the Table Name text box. Click Insert for each new mapping.

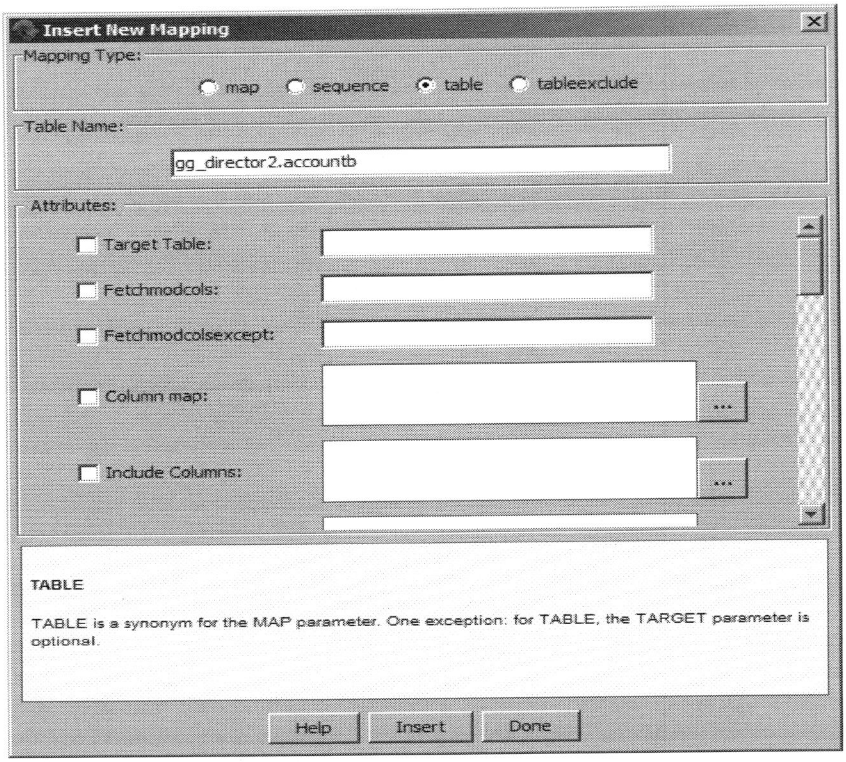

Figure 10-8. Insert New Mapping dialog for the Extract

Your mapped tables are checked on the first column of the Parameters tab as shown in Figure 10-9. If you don't see them, click the Show Tables button. You also can select tables in the table list panel, as shown in the Figure 10-9.

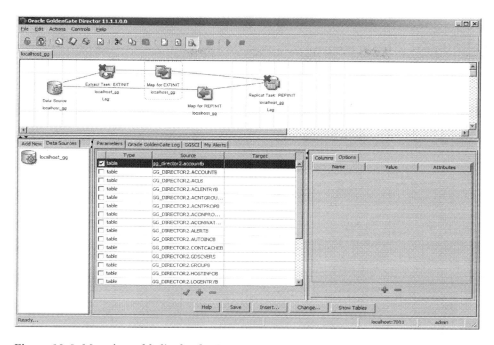

Figure 10-9. Mapping table list for the Extract

To view or edit your Extract parameter file, right-click Extract for EXTINIT and choose Advanced ➤ Edit Param. The dialog shown in Figure 10-10 opens.

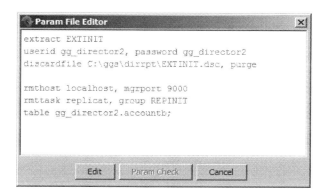

Figure 10-10. It's good practice to validate the parameter file before running it.

Do the same map for Map for REPINIT. Highlight the mapped table, and then click Change. Enter the Target table name in the Attributes box as shown in Figure 10-8.

Now, right-click the EXTINIT Extract, and choose Start as shown in Figure 10-11. Doing so spawns a GGSCI process to start the Extract. Note that in Windows Director, the spawned GGSCI process window sometimes doesn't exit properly; if this happens, go to the spawned GGSCI window and type Exit. Or, you can start EXTINIT in GGSCI. The diagram refreshes the status in real time.

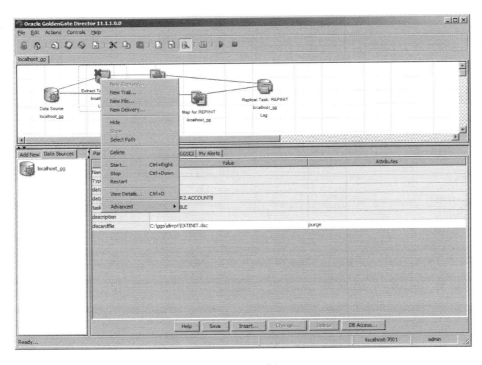

Figure 10-11. Start the Extract from the Extract object.

Creating a One-Way Replication

When you create an Extract for the first time, you need to do the following database tasks that Director Client can't do for you:

- Enable Supplemental Logging Minimum at the database level on the source database

- Grant the proper privileges for Oracle GoldenGate users on the source and target

If you want to log additional column change data, you need to add trandata for the Extract tables. To do so, right-click the data source again, and choose View Details. The dialog shown in Figure 10-12 opens. Click the Tran/Redo Log Data tab, and then click Get Info. Director inserts default login information; if you need other schema, change the login information in the Database Access section and click Get Info to refresh the table list. Highlight the tables, and click the Add Trandata (you can hold the Shift key to select multiple tables).

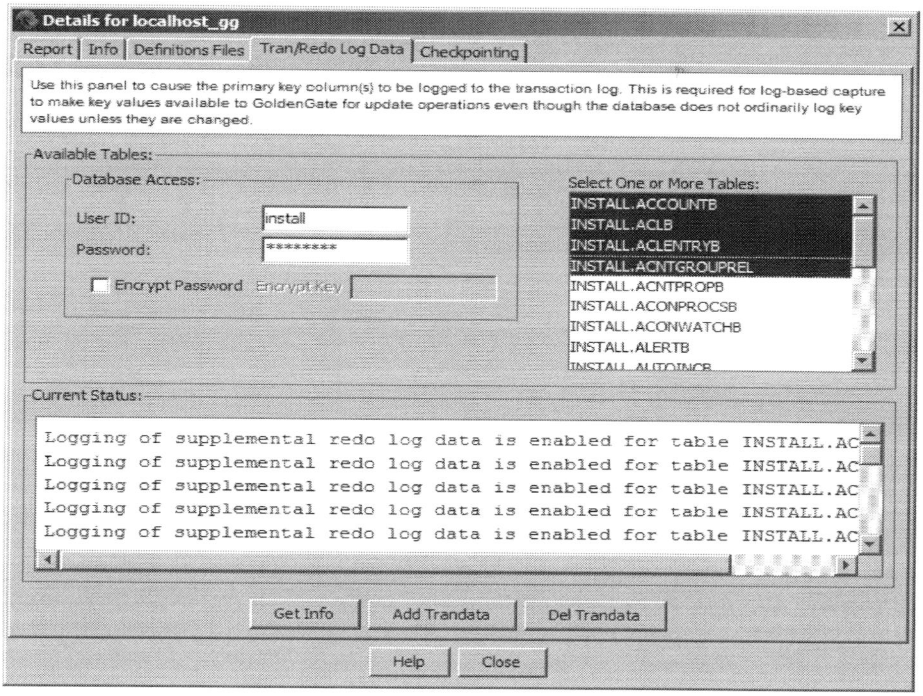

Figure 10-12. Adding trandata.

After you click Add Trandata, you have the option to choose the trandata columns. If you want to capture all columns, select all the columns and click OK.

Now you can create the Extract. Right-click the data source on which you want the Extract to run, and select New Capture. The only required field is Capture Name; all the other fields are filled by Director. Enter the Extract name **EXTGGS1**. Change the database access information to your own.

If your capture is on Oracle Real Application Clusters (RAC), you need to alter the Extract with the threads attribute as shown here in GGSCI (**4** indicates four-node RAC):

```
GGSCI> alter extract extggs1, translog, threads 4, begin now
EXTRACT altered.
```

When the Extract EXTGGS1 has been created, right-click the EXTGGS1 icon in the diagram and select New Trail. Enter the trail-file options shown in Figure 10-13, and then click OK. The diagram in your panel should look like the one in the Figure 10-14.

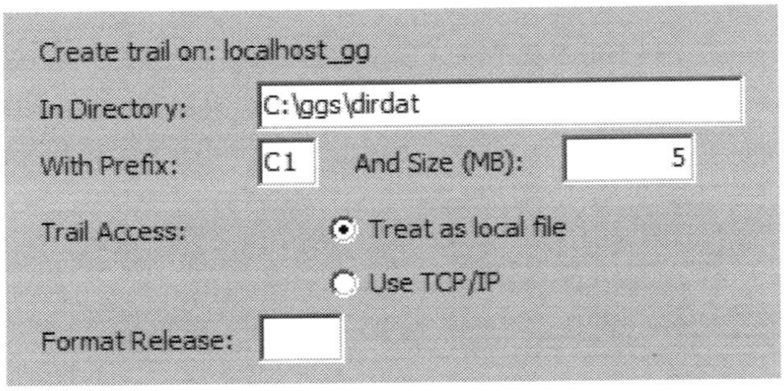

Figure 10-13. *Add trail-file options.*

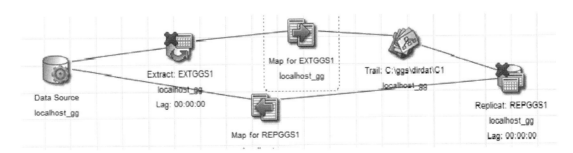

Figure 10-14. *Complete Extract tasks diagram*

Right-click the Trail icon, and select New Delivery. Use REPGGS1 as the Replicat name, and enter the full path for the `dirdat` directory. Click OK. You now have a total of six icons in your diagram, as shown in Figure 10-15.

Figure 10-15. Complate Extract and Relplicat diagram

Similar to the initial load mapping, add the table in which you want to replicate using the Map icons. Finally, check your Extract and Replicat parameter files using Param File Editor. Make sure your parameter files are similar to Figure 10-16 and Figure 10-17.

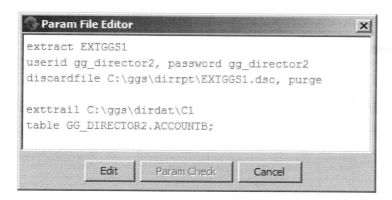

Figure 10-16. Extract parameter file

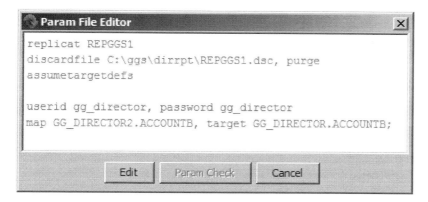

Figure 10-17. Replicat parameter file

In GGSCI, type info all to make sure Director has created two groups for you:

```
GGSCI> info all
Program      Status      Group      Lag          Time Since Chkpt

MANAGER      RUNNING
EXTRACT      STOPPED     EXTGGS1    00:00:00      01:18:10
REPLICAT     STOPPED     REPGGS1    00:00:00      01:12:13
```

When everything is set, you can start the extract and replicat from the Director Extract and Replicat icons or GGSCI.

After you start the Extract and Replicat, the Xs on them should be gone. The lines between the icons change from grey to green. The lag values are also displayed on the icons. You can go to the GGSCI tab to check their status, as shown in Figure 10-18. Click the Trail icon; it also shows the current relative byte address (RBA) and seqno. Feel free to add a new table to the Extract and Replicat; make sure you restart them after any changes.

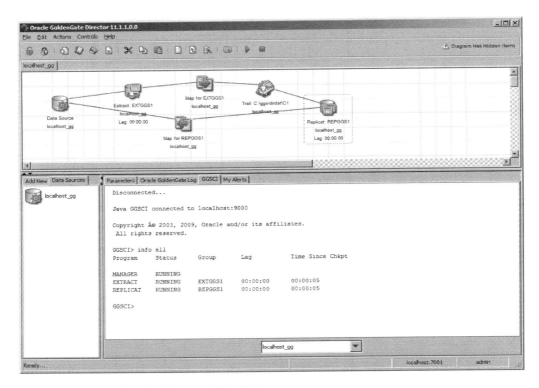

Figure 10-18. Running the Extract and Replicat

Adding a Data Pump Process

It's a best practice to use an Oracle GoldenGate Data Pump process when two systems aren't on the same server, so the GoldenGate process can survive a long outage without losing data. To add a Data Pump process, add a new Capture from the data source, and name it DPGGS1. Click OK. Then, add a trail file from the Extract DPGGS1 object. The prefix for the data-pump trail file is C2, as shown in Figure 10-19. Trail Access is TCP/IP now, because Data Pump process sends the trail files directly to the server at the Replicat side.

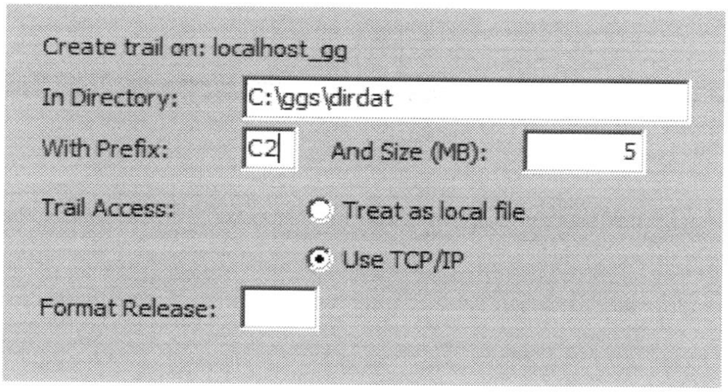

Figure 10-19. Adding a trail file for the Data Pump process

Using the Param File Editor, remove the login information, because you don't need it for this data pump, and add the **passthru** parameter as shown in Figure 10-20. You can also add the mapping table here or use the Map for DPGGS1 parameter interface to add it.

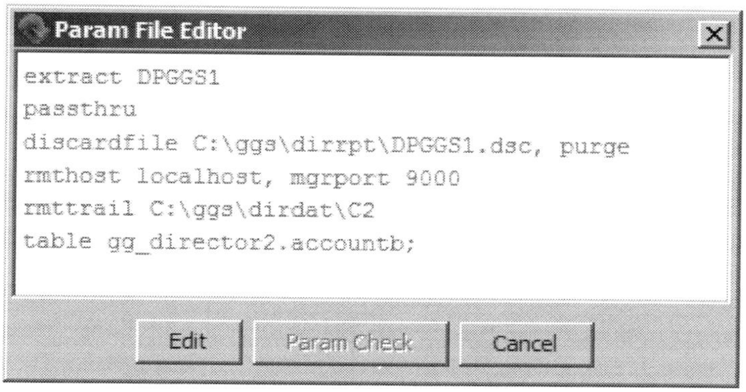

Figure 10-20. Data pump parameter file

Stop the Extract EXTGGS1, wait for the lag to become zero, and then stop the Replicat REPGGS1. In GGSCI, change the Extract/Replicat to point to the new trail files, as shown here:

```
GGSCI> alter extract dpggs1, exttrailsource c:\ggs\dirdat\c1
EXTRACT altered.

GGSCI> alter replicat repggs1, exttrail c:\ggs\dirdat\c2
REPLICAT altered.
```

Note that the **exttrail** path must exactly match in both the Replicat and Extract. For example, .\dirdat\c1 isn't equal to c:\ggs|dirdat\c1 from Director's perspective. However, the Oracle GoldenGate processes treat them the same and run them fine—you just don't get the correct diagram, as shown in Figure 10-21.

Figure 10-21. Complete flow with the Data Pump process

Start the Extract, data pump, and Replicat. You may need to restart the Oracle GoldenGate d client in order to see the diagram with the proper green lines. The Refresh Diagram feature doesn't work sometimes.

Now that everything is running, it's a good time to check out the View Detail features for the Extract, Replicat, and data source icons. Right-click each icon, and select View Detail. Doing so executes some GGSCI commands for you, such as `View report <group name>`, `info <group name>`, `lag extract <group name>`, `send <group name>`, and so on.

Additional Director Features and Tricks

There are many other Director features that aren't covered in the previous sections. This section goes over some key features and tricks. After reading this section, you'll know what Director can do for you compared to the Oracle GoldenGate GGSCI command line.

Alter Extract or Replicat RUN Options

Director allows you to alter the Extract/Replicat RUN options. For example, suppose you want to reset the Extract begin timestamp or Replicat seqno/RBA. To do so, click the Extract/Replicat object in the diagram, and choose Controls ➤ Run Options. The Extract/Replicat must be stopped in order for you to adjust these options. It's important to understand the process before doing this in production, or the data will be lost if you skip the records inadvertently.

Changing the Trail-File Size

If Oracle GoldenGate generates too many trail files, it's difficult to maintain them. A trail file that's too big is also risky: if a large trail file is corrupted, then you lose a lot of data. You need to monitor and adjust the trail-file size if the source activity changes and affects the trail-file generation rate. To change the trail-file size, click the Trail object in the diagram, and choose Controls ➤ Run Options. Then you can enter the new trail file size.

Extracting Tranlogoptions

By default, Director doesn't include `tranlogoptions`. The `tranlogoptions` parameter controls the way Oracle GoldenGate interacts with the transaction logs; it's database specific. To add `tranlogoptions`, select it in the list of parameters shown in Figure 10-22, and then click Insert. To get to the following dialog, click on the Insert button on the Parameter tab on any mapping icons.

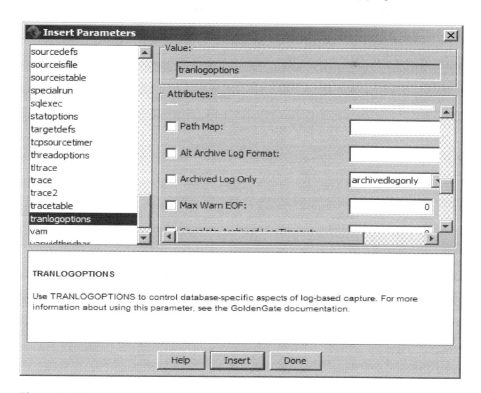

Figure 10-22. Extract tranlogoptions *parameter*

Director doesn't validate the parameters. It appends the attributes to a single tranlogoptions line and doesn't "dedupe" for you. You can insert one tranlogoptions item per line, as shown here:

```
TRANLOGOPTIONS ASMUSER SYS@ASM, ASMPASSWORD AEBIZD,ENCRYPTKEY DEFAULT
TRANLOGOPTIONS ALTARCHIVELOGDEST /ggs/gg_archive
TRANLOGOPTIONS CONVERTUCS2CLOBS
```

Generating Definition Files

Generating definition files is similar to adding trandata options. Without Director, you need to use the DEFGEN utility to create a definition file. To create a definition file in Director, select the data source object in the diagram, and choose Control ➤ View Details. Then, click the Definitions Files tab, as shown in Figure 10-23.

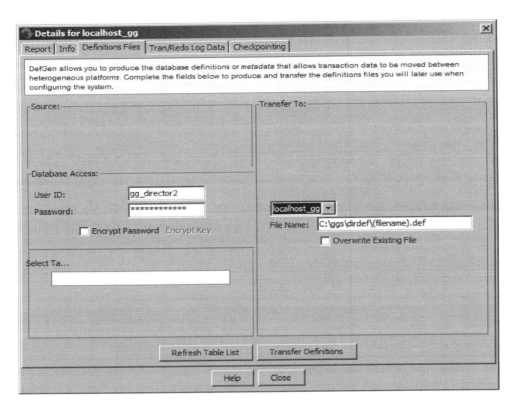

Figure 10-23. Sourcedef and Targetdef file generation

Enter the Database Access information for each table you need to add to the source/target definition files. Select one or more tables in the Select Table box, and click Transfer Definitions when you're finished. The tables automatically transfer to the target/source location via the Manager process. You may have more than one definition files for each schema on either the source or target; if so, concatenate the files, or append them to the existing **sourcedef** file, as shown in Figure 10-24.

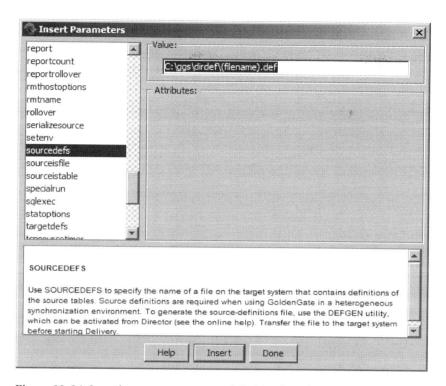

Figure 10-24. Inserting a source or target definition into the parameter file

Be sure to add the **sourcedef/targetdef** file to the Extract or Replicat parameter file. Use the Insert Parameter option on the Parameters tab in the Extract or Replicat to do this.

Finding Parameters or Attributes in Director

Director doesn't implement all the parameters in its GUI interface, including TRANSMEMORY and many others. You have to use Edit Param feature to add these parameters manually. In some cases, attributes are also missing, such as FETCHOPTIONS NOUSESNAPSHOT. To remedy this situation, you can add FETCHOPTIONS and manually enter NOUSESNAPSHOT in the text box.

Oracle GoldenGate also compresses parameters. The nocompressupdates parameter doesn't appear in the list, but if you choose compressupdates, you can then pick nocompressupdates in the drop-down list, as shown in Figure 10-25.

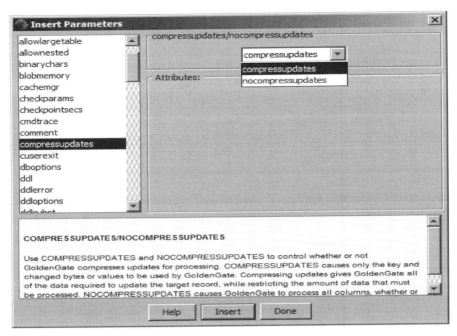

Figure 10-25. Nocompressupdates is in the drop-down list instead of the parameter list panel.

As you can see in Figure 10-25, the compressdeletes parameter isn't in the list; neither is nocompressdeletes. These are important parameters if you need to get full values of the deleted rows in the trail file. You have to add them using the Edit Param feature.

Advanced Mapping

Select the Map for EXTGGS1 icon in the diagram, and then click the Change button on the parameter tab or Insert if you need to add a new mapping; the dialog shown in Figure 10-26 opens. Note that if you change the Mapping Type in the Change Mapping dialog, *all* attributes will disappear from the dialog; they're still in the parameters file, but you have to reopen this dialog to get them to reappear.

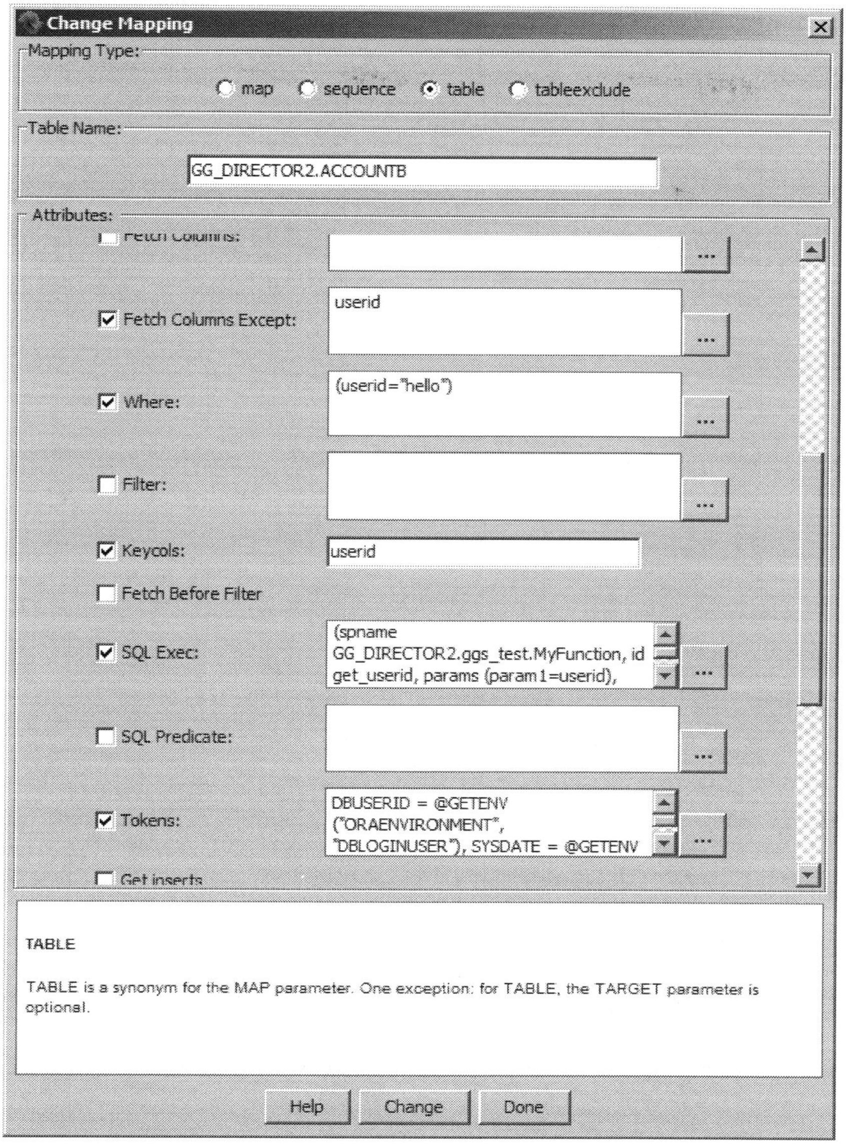

Figure 10-26. Mapping Type has a lot of attributes.

Figure 10-27 shows the SQL Exec parameter editor. Without the Director Client interface, it is very difficult to debug the SQL Exec statement and lead to many syntax errors. Because there is no good IDE for editing parameter files, you have to use vi or another generic text editor.

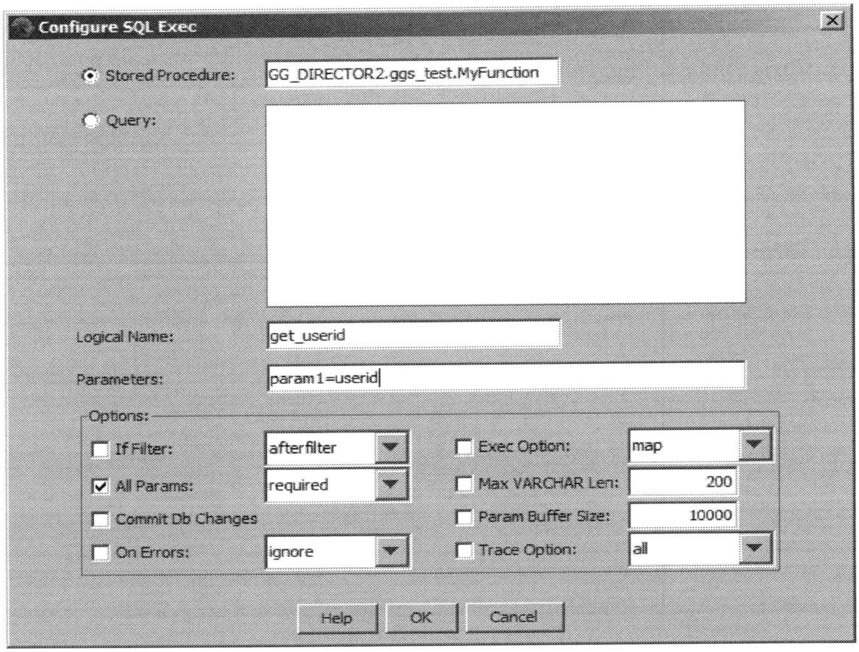

Figure 10-27. SQL Exec editor for queries and PL/SQL

Director creates the following parameter code for you automatically after you click on the Ok button. Without Director Client, you have to type this word by word in a text editor in the exact same syntax.

```
extract EXTGGS1
userid gg_director2, password gg_director2
discardfile C:\ggs\dirrpt\EXTGGS1.dsc, purge

exttrail C:\ggs\dirdat\C1
table GG_DIRECTOR2.ACCOUNTB, colmap (usedefaults,
phone=@strext(phone,2,6)), fetchcolsexcept (userid), where (userid="hello"),
keycols (userid), sqlexec (spname GG_DIRECTOR2.ggs_test.MyFunction, id get_userid,
 params (param1=userid), allparams required), tokens (DBUSERID = @GETENV ("ORAENVIRONMENT",
"DBLOGINUSER"), SYSDATE = @GETENV ("ORATRANSACTION", "TIMESTAMP"), OPERATION =
@GETENV("GGHEADER","OPTYPE"));
```

Alerts

Oracle GoldenGate doesn't have any built-in alerts. If anything fails or hangs, you won't know it if you aren't watching the system. You have to write alert scripts manually, as discussed in Chapter 8, or you can use Director. With Director, it's very easy to set up an alert. To do so, click the My Alerts tab on the main screen.

There are only two types of alerts: Checkpoint Lag and Event Text in the `ggserr.log` file. Let's look at two examples.

First, suppose you want an Event Text alert to check for any message containing *ABEND*. Such messages should also appear in `/var/log/messages` and the Windows Event log. The "AbendAlert" alert entry should be similar to Figure 10-28.

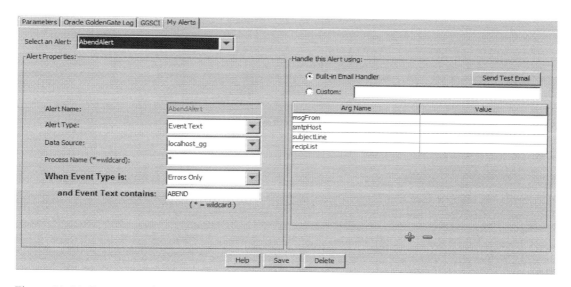

Figure 10-28. Event Text alert

Here are the steps to add this alert:

1. In the Alert Type drop-down list, choose Event Text.

2. In the Data Source drop-down list, choose `localhost_gg` or your data source that has the Manager process running.

3. In the Process Name text box, enter * for all processes. Or, to use one process, type its name, such as EXTGGS1.

4. In the When Event Type Is drop-down list, choose Errors Only. You're creating an *ABEND* alert, and abend is an error.

5. In the And Event Text Contains text box, enter **ABEND**. This is the actual text that appears in the `ggserr.log` and `/var/log/` messages.

6. In the msgFrom Value field, enter anything you want, so you know who sent the alert.

7. In the smtphost field, enter any SMTP mail-relay server.

8. In the subjectline field, enter something like EXTGGS1 **has abended**.

9. In the reciplist field, enter the e-mail addresses of the alert recipients.

Next, let's set up a Lag alert. To do so, enter the information shown in Figure 10-29.

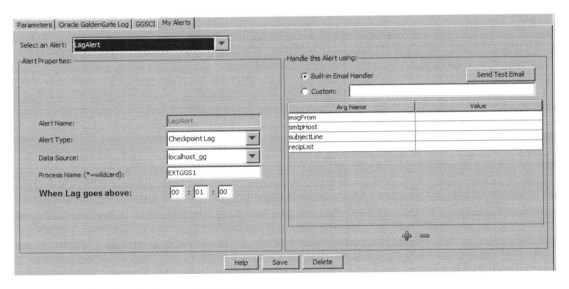

Figure 10-29. Lag alert for Extract EXTGGS1

Director doesn't need a server login because it handles all the requests via the Manager process on the server side. So if the Manager is down, you don't get any alerts. Refer to the chapter 8 for more advanced topics.

Summary

By now, you should be familiar with the Director processes. Director is a cross-platform tool, so you can use it for other databases and platforms with some minor changes. The differences are handled by Director behind the scenes.

It's out of this chapter's scope to go over every scenario, but you should be able to use Director to do the following additional tasks:

- Perform DDL synchronization with the DDL and DDLOPTIONS parameters

- Perform Active-Active synchronization with collision handling using the IGNOREREPLICATES, GETAPPLOPS, and TRANLOGOPTIONS EXCLUDEUSER parameters

- Change log captures with INSERTALLRECORDS and GETUPDATEBEFORES

- Troubleshoot and fix most common Oracle GoldenGate errors using Director Client

CHAPTER 11

Troubleshooting Oracle GoldenGate

As database professionals, one of the most difficult aspects of working with Oracle GoldenGate is how to troubleshoot and resolve errors that occur throughout the lifecycle of the implementation. Due to the nature of Oracle GoldenGate functionality and operations as enterprise software, it involves all layers of the technology stack from source to target database to network issues and more. The goal of this chapter is to provide you with the best possible overall framework to identify and resolve problems that occur within the Oracle GoldenGate ecosystem.

Common Problems and Solutions

In order to equip you with the best possible approach to solving issues that arise with Oracle GoldenGate, you look first into the most commonly found problems by using a holistic approach to troubleshooting Oracle GoldenGate environments. Because Oracle GoldenGate touches multiple areas including database, network, storage, and operating systems, the chapter in turn addresses these areas as related to Oracle GoldenGate problem resolution. In preparation for this discussion, it's useful to take a visual approach to Oracle GoldenGate root-cause analysis, as shown in Figure 11-1.

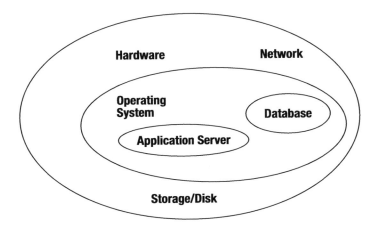

Figure 11-1. Holistic approach to troubleshooting Oracle Goldengate software

This chapter examines the following areas that can cause grief in Oracle GoldenGate environments:

- Process failures

- Trail-file issues

- Synchronization problems

- Startup problems on source and target systems

- Database configuration and availability issues

As part of your journey into troubleshooting Oracle GoldenGate, this chapter provides tips and techniques you can use to trace and identify the source of problems so you can quickly solve them. Let's get started!

Oracle GoldenGate Process Failures

The first type of problem you may encounter within Oracle GoldenGate environments are process failures. These may occur on the source, on the target, or on both environments for one or more of the Oracle GoldenGate processes.

Recall from earlier chapters that an Oracle GoldenGate environment consists of many different background processes on the source and target database systems, such as Extract, Data Pump, Replicat, Collector, and Manager processes. If any of these critical processes fail, then replication activities will most likely come to a screeching halt, thus impacting data integrity and the operation of real-time data transfer between your Oracle GoldenGate environments.

This section looks first into process failures that occur during normal Oracle GoldenGate operations as well as methods to resolve these types of process failures. The preliminary task to perform if you find an Oracle GoldenGate process failure is to investigate the details by using the GoldenGate Software Command Interface (GGSCI) command INFO ALL:

```
C:\ggs_src>ggsci
Oracle GoldenGate Command Interpreter for Oracle
Version 11.1.1.0.0 Build 078
Windows (optimized), Oracle 11 on Jul 28 2010 17:20:29
Copyright (C) 1995, 2010, Oracle and/or its affiliates. All rights reserve
GGSCI (oracledba) 1> info all
Program     Status      Group       Lag             Time Since Chkpt
MANAGER     STOPPED
```

In many cases, the Manager process fails when network issues occur on either the source or target environment for Oracle GoldenGate. You should check to make sure the Manager process is up and running. If the Manager process isn't running, then you need to restart it by executing the following command from within GGSCI:

```
GGSCI> START MANAGER
```

To verify that Manager has started successfully, issue the Oracle GoldenGate GGSCI command again after you start it. The following example makes sure Manager has started correctly and without errors:

```
GGSCI (oracledba) 7> start manager
Manager started.
GGSCI (oracledba) 8> info all
Program     Status      Group       Lag             Time Since Chkpt
MANAGER     RUNNING
```

As one of the key Oracle GoldenGate processes, the Manager process abends or fails if network ports are blocked by a firewall. You can check by using the `ping` command to verify whether there is a network problem with ports. You should work closely with your network or system administrator to ensure that the ports allocated by the Manager process are open and available so that Manager can communicate with both the source and target systems for Oracle GoldenGate.

Oracle GoldenGate Extract Process Failures

Oracle GoldenGate Extract process failures can occur either on the source systems or on the intermediate systems that use a data pump Extract process. Because the Extract process communicates with the source database, Manager process, and target Replicat processes, if there is a failure with these Oracle GoldenGate processes, then Extract either hangs or abends and fail. When you're dealing with an Extract failure, you should first run the Oracle GoldenGate GGSCI `VIEW REPORT` command to examine the current status of your Oracle GoldenGate environment. If the Extract process fails on the source system, run the following command:

```
GGSCI> VIEW REPORT <extract name>
```

Examine the output from the `VIEW REPORT` command in GGSCI; the details provide clues to further investigation for resolving the Extract failure. After you've resolved the issue, you need to restart the Extract process by executing the GGSCI `START EXTRACT <extract name>` command. Issue the command with the `DETAIL` option, as shown here:

```
GGSCI> START EXTRACT <extract name>, DETAIL
```

Now, let's look with an example of an Extract process failing on an Oracle 11g source database server. To view a report from GoldenGate, execute the command GGSCI to enter the GoldenGate command-line interface, and then enter VIEW REPORT EATAA, which references the name of the sample Extract process group:

```
GGSCI (oracledba) 3> view report eataa
************************************************************************
                    Oracle GoldenGate Capture for Oracle
                        Version 11.1.1.0.0 Build 078
            Windows (optimized), Oracle 11 on Jul 28 2010 18:00:34

Copyright (C) 1995, 2010, Oracle and/or its affiliates. All rights reserved.
                        Starting at 2011-03-14 00:00:32
************************************************************************
Operating System Version:
Microsoft Windows Vista Business Edition, on x86
Version 6.0 (Build 6002: Service Pack 2)
Process id: 2524
Description:
************************************************************************
**              Running with the following parameters                **
************************************************************************
--Example Extract Parameter File
SOURCEISTABLE
2011-03-14 00:00:33  INFO    OGG-01017  Wildcard resolution set to IMMEDIATE bec
ause SOURCEISTABLE is used.
USERID ggs, PASSWORD *****
Source Context :
  SourceModule            : [ggdb.ora.sess]
  SourceID                : [../gglib/ggdbora/ocisess.c]
  SourceFunction          : [OCISESS_try]
  SourceLine              : [498]
2011-03-14 00:00:33  ERROR   OGG-00664  OCI Error during OCIServerAttach (status
 = 12560-ORA-12560: TNS:protocol adapter error).
2011-03-14 00:00:33  ERROR   OGG-01668  PROCESS ABENDING.
```

In this case, Extract fails to run due to an Oracle protocol network error on the source database server. The network error is caused by a failed Oracle 11g network listener (TNS) failing to start correctly. You troubleshoot the error by examining the listener.ora and tnsnames.ora network configuration and correcting any errors. Then, restart both the Oracle listener and GoldenGate processes. By correcting the source Oracle 11g listener protocol error, you can successfully restart the Extract process.

Another useful way to investigate Extract failure problems is to run the GGSCI command INFO <extract name>, DETAIL to obtain a listing of the current Extract file locations for additional analysis:

```
GGSCI (oracledba) 26> info extora, detail
EXTRACT    EXTORA    Initialized   2011-03-13 23:45   Status STOPPED
Checkpoint Lag       00:00:00 (updated 00:22:24 ago)
Log Read Checkpoint  Oracle Redo Logs
                     2011-03-13 23:45:30  Seqno 0, RBA 0
  Target Extract Trails:
  Remote Trail Name                              Seqno      RBA    Max MB
  AA                                                 0        0        10
```

```
Extract Source                          Begin           End
Not Available                           * Initialized * 2011-03-13 23:45
Current directory   C:\ggs_src
Report file         C:\ggs_src\dirrpt\EXTORA.rpt
Parameter file      C:\ggs_src\dirprm\EXTORA.prm
Checkpoint file     C:\ggs_src\dirchk\EXTORA.cpe
Process file        C:\ggs_src\dirpcs\EXTORA.pce
Error log           C:\ggs_src\ggserr.log
```

Next, let's look at more difficult situations that occur when an Oracle GoldenGate process fails without providing you with a report.

Oracle GoldenGate Process Failures Without Report Diagnostics

If an Oracle GoldenGate process fails before first writing out a report file to standard screen output, you can run it from the operating system's command shell (not GGSCI) to send process information to the terminal. To investigate, you can issue the startup by using the syntax <process> paramfile <path name>.prm at the operating-system level where <process> indicates either the Extract or Replicat process for Oracle GoldenGate and paramfile is the fully qualified file name of the parameter file for the Extract or Replicat. Here's an example:

```
C:\ggs_src>extract paramfile C:\ggs_src\dirprm\extora.prm
Version 6.0 (Build 6002: Service Pack 2)
Process id: 6056
Description:
2011-03-14 00:19:46  ERROR   OGG-00664  OCI Error beginning session (status = 10
17-ORA-01017: invalid username/password; logon denied).
2011-03-14 00:19:46  ERROR   OGG-01668  PROCESS ABENDING.
```

On UNIX and Linux platforms, you need to look for a core dump file located under the Oracle GoldenGate home directory where you've installed the Oracle GoldenGate software.

Oracle GoldenGate Trail File Problems

Recall from earlier chapters that Oracle GoldenGate process groups write and read data to special flat files called *trail files* on the source and target systems. Failure in processing these trail files halts correct operations of the Oracle GoldenGate software. This section looks at the following problems that can occur with trail files:

- Trail files that don't empty

- Trail files that don't roll over

- Trail file purging issues

Trail Files that Don't Empty

Sometimes you encounter a problem with trail files that don't empty and remain full of data. You should check to identify whether the trail file in question is a local or remote trail file. If the problem is with a local trail file that fails to empty, check for TCP/IP network latency issues between the source, intermediate, and target systems. If the remote trail file on the target system fails to empty on a regular basis, check to see if your Replicat process groups are available, running, and processing data from the remote trail files.

If the Replicat processes are running correctly without errors, the cause may be large transactions being processed by the Replicat on the target system. In this case, you can split up the tables and partition them to break out the large transactions into multiple trail files with additional Replicat process groups to process the transactions in parallel. To do so, use the Oracle GoldenGate Replicat parameter FILTER option with the @RANGE function in the MAP statement for the Replicat.

Trail Files that Don't Roll Over

Another issue that plagues Oracle GoldenGate trail-file operations occurs when a trail file fails to roll over to a new trail file after it fills up completely. One thing to check here is the maximum file size for the trail file in question. You can check this using Oracle GoldenGate GGSCI command INFO EXTTRAIL * or INFO RMTTRAIL * as shown in the following example:

```
GGSCI (oracledba) 1> info exttrail *
       Extract Trail: AA
             Extract: EXTORA
               Seqno: 0
                 RBA: 0
           File Size: 10M
```

You can locate this information by examining the File Size field. To change the trail-file size with Oracle GoldenGate, issue the Oracle GoldenGate GGSCI command ALTER EXTTRAIL or ALTER RMTTRAIL with the MEGABYTES option, as shown here:

```
GGSCI (oracledba) 3> alter exttrail aa megabytes 20, extract extora
EXTTRAIL altered.
GGSCI (oracledba) 4> info exttrail *
       Extract Trail: AA
             Extract: EXTORA
               Seqno: 0
                 RBA: 0
           File Size: 20M
```

Trail File Purging Issues

Trail files sometimes aren't purged correctly, thus causing errors during processing of data between the source and target database environments. Probably the most common source of failed purging operations with trail files occurs due to failure to use PURGEOLDEXTRACTS to manage the trail files in use by Oracle GoldenGate. You should add this parameter to the Manager parameter file to prevent old trail files from accumulating too fast and thus causing problems with your Oracle GoldenGate configuration. Keep in mind that you must grant the Oracle GoldenGate Manager user account the correct level of access permissions to read from and write to the trail files and file systems when using this.

Another cause of trail-file purging issues is an obsolete Replicat group that may still be referencing the old trail file. Oracle GoldenGate trail files aren't purged if other processes still read them. If an old Replicat group is referencing a trail file, you use the DELETE REPLICAT command from GGSCI to delete the obsolete Replicat process group so that the checkpoint records are deleted, thereby allowing the Manager process to purge the trail files. Keep in mind that if a checkpoint table is still used for the

Replicat group, you need to log into the target database with the DBLOGIN command before removing the checkpoint from the table and Replicat deletion. You can use the following syntax to perform this task:

```
DBLOGIN USERID , PASSWORD <pw>
DELETE REPLICAT <group>
```

Trail Files that Purge Too Soon

Another painful situation with trail files occurs when the trail files are purged too soon. This causes errors due to missing data between the source and target systems. One root cause to check for to solve this problem is multiple Replicats and data pumps reading from the same trail file.

Also check to see if you're using the PURGEOLDEXTRACTS parameter details. The key thing is to realize that you should only use this parameter as a Manager parameter—you shouldn't use PURGEOLDEXTRACTS as an Extract or Replicat parameter. When you use PURGEOLDEXTRACTS as a Manager parameter, you can use the option USECHECKPOINTS to defer purging of the trail file until all of the Oracle GoldenGate processes have finished processing data for the trail file. In addition, you can use the MIN option to store the trail file for a set period of time. Whenever you use the MIN option, you must also set the MAX option for PURGEOLDEXTRACTS to denote the maximum amount of time to keep the trail file.

Oracle GoldenGate Error Log Analysis

Fortunately, Oracle GoldenGate is a well instrumented software product that provides a superb error log file that contains details for all aspects of replication operations on both source and target systems. If an error occurs during GoldenGate processing, it's imperative that you review the Oracle GoldenGate error logs located under the source and target base installation directories. On Linux and UNIX systems, you can use the tail command to examine the last few error messages contained in the error log file for Oracle GoldenGate.

Let's look at the error log file for the Oracle 11g GoldenGate and Oracle 11g Windows source system. The file is called ggserr.log; you can open it with a text editor such as vi or Emacs on Linux and UNIX or Notepad on Windows platforms. In addition, you can view the error log file with the GGSCI command VIEW GGSEVT as shown here:

```
Oracle:  PROCESS ABENDING.
2011-03-14 00:19:46  INFO    OGG-00992  Oracle GoldenGate Capture for Oracle, extora.prm:
EXTRACT starting.
2011-03-14 00:19:46  INFO    OGG-01017  Oracle GoldenGate Capture for Oracle, extora.prm:
Wildcard resolution set to IMMEDIATE because SOURCEISTABLE is used.
2011-03-14 00:19:46  ERROR   OGG-00664  Oracle GoldenGate Capture for Oracle, extora.prm:  OCI
Error beginning session (status = 1017-ORA-01017: invalid username/password; logon denied).
2011-03-14 00:19:46  ERROR   OGG-01668  Oracle GoldenGate Capture for Oracle, extora.prm:
PROCESS ABENDING.
```

Understanding the Oracle GoldenGate Discard File

Recall from earlier chapters that Oracle GoldenGate creates a discard file whenever the DISCARDFILE parameter is used by either the Extract or Replicat. If there is a problem during processing of data from the source or target environments by either the Replicat or Extract, then the rejected records are dumped into the discard file. You should review the contents of the discard file on both the source and target database environments on a regular basis as part of your due diligence to catch data issues encountered by Oracle GoldenGate.

The discard file contains all column-level details for database operations that Oracle GoldenGate processes couldn't process successfully. Each discard file contains the following useful details:

- Database error message for the process, such as ORA-00100 for "No Data Found" with Oracle 11g

- The trail file sequence number for record(s) that the Extract or Replicat attempted to be processed

- The relative byte address of the record in the trail file

- Details of the discarded record that the Extract or Replicat attempted to process

Typically, a discard file is used by the Replicat to log operations that couldn't be reconstructed or applied, but you may find one useful for the Extract as well. Check the discard error for messages such as ORA-1403 or duplicate and/or rejected records. Here is a sample Oracle GoldenGate discard file:

```
ORA-20017:  repora 724935
ORA-06512: at "HR.REPORAINSERT", line 41
ORA-04088: error during execution of trigger 'HR.REPORA_INSERT'
Operation failed at seqno 15 rba 28483311
Problem replicating HR.EMP to HR.TRGTREP
Error occurred with insert record (target format)...
*
A_TIMESTAMP = 2011-03-09 11:28:11
OK = 1.0000
NOTOK = -1.0000
```

Discard records provide useful clues for issues that occur during processing so you can identify and solve the root cause quickly.

Discard File Not Created

Sometimes you may encounter the frustrating issue that Oracle GoldenGate fails to create a discard file. One common cause is that the discard file's location wasn't provided in the parameter file for use with the DISCARDFILE parameter. GoldenGate doesn't create a discard file by default, so you need to give a file name and location of the discard file—otherwise it won't be created.

A second cause of missing discard files occurs when the DISCARDFILE parameter doesn't reference the correct directory on the file system. You need to verify that sufficient read and write access permissions are granted for the discard file and the directory that contains the discard file. In addition, make sure the user who accesses the discard file has the required security permissions to access, read, and write to and from the file location.

Discard File Is Too Big

Keep in mind that Oracle GoldenGate constantly writes to the discard file as processing takes place. If the discard file isn't given sufficient disk space on the file system where it lives, then you may have errors with processing it. One recommendation is to adjust the size of the discard file by using the following parameters:

- **DISCARDROLLOVER**: Specifies the parameters for aging of the discard file.

- **MAXDISCARDRECS**: Limits the total number of errors written out to the discard file.

- **PURGE** *option for* **DISCARDFILE**: Purges the discard file before writing out new information

- **MEGABYTES** *option for* **DISCARDFILE**: Sets the maximum size of the discard file. The default size of the discard file is 1MB.

Can't Open the Discard File

Oracle GoldenGate processes for the Extract and Replicat use the discard file during operational activities. If there is an error in the location of the discard file, the Extract or Replicat process will fail in GoldenGate, as shown in the following error:

```
2011-03-16 00:54:08  ERROR   OGG-01091  Unable to open file "c:\win11trgt\dirrpt\report.dsc"
(error 3, The system cannot find the path specified.).
2011-03-16 00:54:08  ERROR   OGG-01668  PROCESS ABENDING.
```

Check the read and write permissions of the DISCARDFILE parameter you've configured in the Extract and Replicat parameter file to ensure that the directory exists and has the correct permissions granted.

Using Trace Commands with Oracle GoldenGate

Oracle GoldenGate provides several useful parameters that you can use to trace processes that fail within the Oracle GoldenGate environment. This section shows you how to use these tracing tools to identify root cause of failures in Oracle GoldenGate. The following tracing tools are discussed along with an example that showcases how to run TRACE:

- TLTRACE

- TRACE

- TRACE2

■ **Note** If you require the use of tracing in Oracle GoldenGate, you should first contact Oracle GoldenGate support while investigating failures within the Oracle GoldenGate environment so you can best deploy these tracing commands without adversely affecting your configuration.

Oracle GoldenGate Process Tracing with TLTRACE

The TLTRACE parameter allows you to run a trace for database transaction log activity. You can run a trace to show either basic or detailed information about records being processed. To enable a TLTRACE session, you need to add this parameter to the Extract or Replicat parameter file and restart the process.

Using TRACE Parameters with Oracle GoldenGate

The TRACE and TRACE2 parameters allow you to grab all details regarding Extract and Replicat processing. The TRACE parameter provides detailed processing information for Oracle GoldenGate processes. In contrast, you use the TRACE2 parameter to identify database code segments where either the Extract or Replicat is taking the most time to process.

Troubleshooting Case Study with Oracle GoldenGate

Let's walk through a case study that shows how to use GGSCI commands and the error log to understand why a process failed in an Oracle database environment. First you use the STATUS EXTRACT command, which returns the following:

```
GGSCI (ggs_src) 20> status extract extora
EXTRACT EXTORA: ABENDED
```

Next, use the VIEW GGSEVT command to drill deeper into the issue with the failed Extract process:

```
GGSCI (ggs_src) 22> view ggsevt
2011-03-11 10:28:11 GGS INFO 399 GoldenGate Command Interpreter
for Oracle: GGSCI command (admin): start extract ggext.
2011-03-11 10:38:15 GGS INFO 301 GoldenGate Manager for Oracle,
mgr.prm: Command received from GGSCI on host oracledba(START
EXTRACT GGEXT).
2011-03-11 10:40:02 GGS INFO 310 GoldenGate Capture for Oracle,
ggext.prm: EXTRACT EXTORA starting.
2011-03-11 10:41:11 GGS ERROR 501 GoldenGate Capture for Oracle,
extora.prm: Extract read, error 13 (Permission denied) opening redo
log C:\oracle\arch\0001_0000000568.arc for sequence
258.
2011-03-11 10:43:22 GGS ERROR 190 GoldenGate Capture for Oracle,
extora.prm: PROCESS ABENDING.
```

In this failure, error message 501 indicates that the Extract user doesn't have the correct permissions to read the redo logs on the source Oracle database. To fix this issue, you grant read and write permissions on the source Oracle database so the Extract process can retrieve the redo log files. After you've granted these read and write permissions to the Extract user, you need to stop the Manager process and exit GGSCI. Log out from the terminal session you have open, and restart the Oracle GoldenGate processes.

Oracle GoldenGate Configuration Issues

Oracle GoldenGate configuration issues pose challenges because once the environment has been installed and configured, if the original DBA has left the company, the new DBA team doesn't always have documentation from the past DBA to help them understand the configuration they've inherited. Configuration issues fall into the following areas:

- Incorrect software version installed for Oracle GoldenGate

- Database configuration issues on the source and/or target with Oracle GoldenGate

- Oracle GoldenGate parameter file configuration issues

- Operating system configuration issues

- Network configuration issues

Incorrect Software Versions with Oracle GoldenGate

Installing the wrong version and platform release for Oracle GoldenGate causes failures within the source and target environments. Oracle provides a unique build for the GoldenGate software based on platform, database, and version (32-bit versus 64-bit) that requires the correct version to be installed for your platform. For instance, you can't install 64-bit Oracle GoldenGate Linux software on an IBM AIX platform, or you'll receive errors.

The build name contains the operating system version, database version, GoldenGate release number, and GoldenGate build number, as shown in the following example for Oracle on Solaris:

```
ggs_Solaris_sparc_ora10g_64bit_v11_1_1_0_0_078.tar
```

To find out the GoldenGate version, change to the GoldenGate home directory and issue the GGSCI -v command from the operating system terminal shell window:

```
C:\ggs_src>ggsci -v
Oracle GoldenGate Command Interpreter for Oracle
Version 11.1.1.0.0 Build 078
Windows (optimized), Oracle 11 on Jul 28 2010 17:20:29
Copyright (C) 1995, 2010, Oracle and/or its affiliates. All rights reserved.
```

Database Availability Issues

If the source and target database environments aren't online and running correctly, Oracle GoldenGate processing fails because the Extract and Replicat processes frequently log in to the database environments to access redo log files for processing data-replication activities. You can check whether the database and listener are online by using the LSNRCTL and TNSPING commands for Oracle from an operating system shell window:

```
C:\ggs_src>lsnrctl status
LSNRCTL for 32-bit Windows: Version 11.2.0.1.0 - Production on 14-MAR-2011 01:53
Connecting to (DESCRIPTION=(ADDRESS=(PROTOCOL=IPC)(KEY=EXTPROC1521)))
STATUS of the LISTENER
----------------------
Listening Endpoints Summary...
  (DESCRIPTION=(ADDRESS=(PROTOCOL=ipc)(PIPENAME=\\.\pipe\EXTPROC1521ipc)))
  (DESCRIPTION=(ADDRESS=(PROTOCOL=tcp)(HOST=oracledba)(PORT=1521)))
Services Summary...
Service "CLRExtProc" has 1 instance(s).
  Instance "CLRExtProc", status UNKNOWN, has 1 handler(s) for this service...
Service "win11src" has 1 instance(s).
  Instance "win11src", status READY, has 1 handler(s) for this service...
The command completed successfully
C:\ggs_src>tnsping win11src
TNS Ping Utility for 32-bit Windows: Version 11.2.0.1.0 - Production on 14-MAR-2
```

```
Used parameter files:
C:\winora11g2\product\11.2.0\dbhome_1\network\admin\sqlnet.ora
Used TNSNAMES adapter to resolve the alias
Attempting to contact (DESCRIPTION = (ADDRESS = (PROTOCOL = TCP)(HOST = oracledb
a)(PORT = 1521)) (CONNECT_DATA = (SERVER = DEDICATED) (SERVICE_NAME = win11src))
)OK (80 msec)
```

On quick way to verify that the database is online is to use the UNIX or Linux command `ps -ef|grep smon` or, even better, to log on to Oracle SQL*PLUS as the Oracle GoldenGate user for the Extract and Replicat, as shown here:

```
C:\ggs_src>sqlplus ggs/ggs@win11src
SQL*Plus: Release 11.2.0.1.0 Production on Mon Mar 14 01:59:23 2011
Copyright (c) 1982, 2010, Oracle. All rights reserved.
Connected to:
Oracle Database 11g Enterprise Edition Release 11.2.0.1.0 - Production
With the Partitioning, OLAP, Data Mining and Real Application Testing options
SQL> select count(*) from hr.employees;
  COUNT(*)
----------
       107
```

You also need to check to verify that the Manager process is online and running as well as perform the previous checks for the source and target databases. Without access to the database systems and the Manager process, the Extract and Replicat will fail to run successfully.

Missing Oracle GoldenGate Process Groups

One common issue that plagues Oracle GoldenGate environments is missing process groups. As a starting point in troubleshooting such issues, you should execute the GGSCI INFO ALL command to view all of the current processes and groups on the system. The Extract group name may have been spelled incorrectly either when the group was created or when the START command was issued for the Oracle GoldenGate process.

Missing Oracle GoldenGate Trail Files

Often, Oracle GoldenGate environments have Extract parameter files or obey files that create Extract process groups that reference non-existent or missing trail files. Without a valid trail file, an Extract can't write out data captured from the online redo log files in the source database. Furthermore, the Replicat process will abend and fail because it can't read from the remote trail file. Without trail files, the Extract can't write the initial checkpoint and the Replicat has no available data source to read. You can issue the GGSCI command INFO EXTRACT <group> or the INFO REPLICAT <group> command with the DETAIL option to verify whether the trail file exists. In addition, after you identify the trail file, you can use the GGSCI command INFO EXTTRAIL <trail file name> to drill down further:

```
GGSCI (oracledba) 3> info extract extora detail
EXTRACT    EXTORA    Initialized    2011-03-13 23:45    Status STOPPED
Checkpoint Lag        00:00:00 (updated 02:24:26 ago)
Log Read Checkpoint  Oracle Redo Logs
                     2011-03-13 23:45:30  Seqno 0, RBA 0
```

```
Target Extract Trails:
Remote Trail Name                          Seqno        RBA      Max MB
AA                                           0            0        10

GGSCI (oracledba) 5> info exttrail aa

        Extract Trail: AA
              Extract: EXTORA
                Seqno: 0
                  RBA: 0
            File Size: 10M
```

Oracle GoldenGate Parameter File Configuration Issues

Oracle GoldenGate relies on parameter files to store and manage process operations for core functionality with the Extract for source data capture, the Manager process for network communication and interprocess operations, and the Replicat for target apply processing on the source system. If these parameter files aren't set up correctly or are unavailable, then Oracle GoldenGate processing will fail.

The first scenario involving parameter file configuration issues is to check whether the parameter file is located in the correct directory. By default, parameters are stored in the dirprm subdirectory after Oracle GoldenGate has been installed. You need to verify that the parameter files for the Extract and Replicat are in this directory and that these parameter files have the same name as the process group for Oracle GoldenGate. In the event that the parameter file is missing or not in this directory, perform a search to locate the correct parameter file. If you don't remember where you placed the configuration parameter file for the process group, you can use the GGSCI command INFO EXTRACT <group>, DETAIL to locate the correct file. If you want to store the parameter file in a different filesystem and directory, then you need to use the PARAMS argument with the ADD EXTRACT command in GGSCI when you add the new Extract; or, if you've already created the Extract group, you can use the GGSCI command ALTER EXTRACT to change the parameter file location.

Another issue that poses problem with parameter configurations is related to file access permissions. If the process group read and write permissions aren't granted correctly at either the operating system level or the database level, then failures will occur when the Extract or Replicat process attempts to access the database on either the source or target system. In addition, if the file permissions aren't set correctly, then errors will occur as well during Oracle GoldenGate operations. For Windows, you can check the permissions with the Windows Explorer graphical interface. On Linux and UNIX platforms, use the ls -l command to check the status for read, write, and execute permissions. You can use the chmod and chown UNIX and Linux commands to grant the required file system permissions to the Oracle GoldenGate parameter files as necessary.

A third configuration issue that occurs with Oracle GoldenGate process group parameter file configurations takes place when the required parameters are missing for either the Extract or Replicat. This is often the case when new users perform Oracle GoldenGate configuration without sufficient knowledge of the product. The following parameters are required for an Extract:

```
EXTRACT <group name>
USERID <ID>, PASSWORD <pw>
RMTHOST <hostname>, MGRPORT <port>
RMTTRAIL <trail name> | EXTTRAIL <trail name> |
RMTFILE <filename> | EXTFILE <filename>
TABLE <source table>;
```

A Replicat requires the following parameters to perform online change synchronization:

```
REPLICAT <group name>
SOURCEDEFS <file name> | ASSUMETARGETDEFS
USERID <ID>, PASSWORD <pw>
MAP <source table>, TARGET <target table>;
```

If the configuration parameters for the Extract and Replicat are listed in wrong order, then processing fails. Oracle GoldenGate parameters are processed in the exact order listed in a parameter file. Much like grammar rules in foreign languages, you must use the correct order and syntax for parameter files. Let's look at some key examples. The parameter RMTHOST must precede the RMTTRAIL parameter. The parameter TABLE or MAP must be listed after global and all the specific parameters that apply to it.

Syntax errors with parameter files are another source of mischief. Oracle GoldenGate reports syntax problems in the process report, and these often appear as "bad parameter" errors. One way to mitigate these syntax errors (which can be tricky to isolate in a parameter file) is to use the CHECKPARAMS parameter to verify syntax. Like a spell checker, CHECKPARAMS verifies the syntax whenever the Oracle GoldenGate process starts. It writes results to the report file and then stops the process.

▓ **Note** After using the CHECKPARAMS parameter and resolving syntax errors, remove the parameter from the process group parameter file. Otherwise, the process won't restart!

Some common syntax errors that occur in parameter files for Extracts and Replicats include the following:

- The Extract TABLE parameter or Replicat MAP parameter isn't terminated with a semicolon.

- Commas aren't followed by a space in parameter files.

- Missing commas, quotes, or parentheses in nested clauses exist, such as a COLMAP.

Operating System Configuration Issues with Oracle GoldenGate

Oracle GoldenGate relies on the operating system platform to perform replication activities on a real-time basis. All the core processes for Oracle GoldenGate operate as system background processes—either as Linux/Windows daemon processes or as Windows services for Windows. If there is a hiccup at the operating system level, Oracle GoldenGate processes fail. Let's take a closer look at some common operating system issues that cause failures in Oracle GoldenGate and how you can resolve them.

First are configurations for the operating system that are missing system libraries. In the case of UNIX and Linux operating systems, if you see errors in Oracle GoldenGate that complain about a missing library, you should issue the env command from a shell window to check the settings for the LD_LIBRARY_PATH and PATH variables to ensure that they're correctly set. If these variables are incorrect, rectify the situation and set these values to the correct path in the .profile startup file in the Oracle GoldenGate home directory.

The error report may also display a message that the function stack needs to be increased. To increase the memory allocated for the stack, you can use the FUNCTIONSTACKSIZE parameter.

■ **Note** Be careful with the FUNCTIONSTACKSIZE parameter, because it may adversely affect Oracle GoldenGate performance. Be sure to first test it in a nonproduction environment when you make changes.

File-access problems can also cause failures at the operating system level. Both Extract and Replicat user accounts at the operating system level required full read and write permissions for all files in the Oracle GoldenGate directory. If you receive the error message "Bad parameter:Group name invalid," it indicates that the process can't open the checkpoint file. You should execute the GGSCI command INFO * to view the group name and then issue the command VIEW PARAMS <group> to make sure the group name from the GGSCI output for the INFO * command matches the one in the EXTRACT or REPLICAT parameter.

Finally, check the values for the key operating system environment variables for the database installed on the source and target systems. For instance, with Oracle, make sure you check that the ORACLE_SID and ORACLE_HOME system variables are set to the correct instance name in the GoldenGate user profile. You can use the env|grep ORA command in Linux and UNIX to check that these Oracle environment variables are set to the correct values.

Network Configuration Issues with Oracle GoldenGate

Oracle GoldenGate relies heavily on network operations to ensure data transfer and communications between source, intermediary, and target systems as part of its real-time data-replication functionality. Latency issues and network outages adversely affect Oracle GoldenGate environments. As such, it's paramount that Oracle GoldenGate administrators develop a close partnership with the system administrator and network operations team to ensure maximum uptime and performance for the Oracle GoldenGate environment. Network problems with Oracle GoldenGate fall into the following categories:

- Network access and connectivity
- Network latency
- Network availability and stability
- Network data-transfer issues

Let's look into each of these key areas how to resolve issues. One of the first errors I experienced years ago when I was a newbie to Oracle GoldenGate was a connection that refused errors that I noticed in the Extract report file. Typically, whenever you receive a common TCP/IP error such as "4127 connection refused." it indicates that the target Manager or Server isn't running, or that the Extract process is pointing to the wrong TCP/IP address or Manager port number. The report for the Extract shows an error in GGSCI similar to this:

ERROR: sending message to EXTRACT EATAA (TCP/IP error: Connection reset).

You can use the GGSCI command INFO MGR to identify the port number in use by the target Manager.

Another item to check the Extract parameter RMTHOST to ensure that MGRPORT is using the same port number as shown in the GGSCI INFO MGR command. If you used a host name, be sure to check that the server's domain name server (DNS) can resolve it. If an IP address was used, make sure to verify that it's correct. You can issue the IFCONFIG command for Linux or UNIX and the Windows IPCONFIG command to verify an IP address from the OS command shell. In addition, you should test network connectivity between the source and target systems by using the PING <host name> command. You can display the network routing table by using the NETSTAT command to check for routing access between source and target.

Another common network error that occurs with Oracle GoldenGate appears when the Extract returns the error "No Dynamic ports available." This means the target Manager process was unable to obtain a port on which to communicate with the source Manager. The Manager process looks for a port in the list specified with the DYNAMICPORTLIST parameter. However, if the DYNAMICPORTLIST parameter isn't specified, Manager then looks for the next available port higher than the one on which it's running. One issue when using the DYNAMICPORTLIST parameter for Manager is that there may not be enough numbers specified or freely available for use. Frequently, orphan processes occupy the ports desired by Manager. You should either kill the zombie processes that occupy these ports or investigate ports that can be reserved for use with Oracle GoldenGate. My Oracle Support Note 966097.1 (http://support.oracle.com) has additional troubleshooting tips for network analysis with Oracle GoldenGate.

Network Data-Transfer Issues

Sometimes, network latency issues cause a lag in data transfer by the Extract from the source system to the target system. You can identify the latency issue by viewing the Extract checkpoint in the trail with the INFO EXTRACT, SHOWCH GGSCI command, as shown in this example:

```
INFO EXTRACT <group>, SHOWCH

GGSCI (oracledba) 13> info extract eataa,showch
EXTRACT    EATAA    Initialized    2011-03-16 00:50    Status STOPPED
Checkpoint Lag           00:00:00 (updated 00:17:15 ago)
Log Read Checkpoint    Oracle Redo Logs
                       2011-03-16 00:50:47   Seqno 0, RBA 0


Current Checkpoint Detail:
Read Checkpoint #1
  Oracle Redo Log
  Startup Checkpoint (starting position in the data source):
    Sequence #: 0
    RBA: 0
    Timestamp: 2011-03-16 00:50:47.000000
    Redo File:
Recovery Checkpoint (position of oldest unprocessed transaction in the data so
urce):
    Sequence #: 0
    RBA: 0
    Timestamp: 2011-03-16 00:50:47.000000
    Redo File:

  Current Checkpoint (position of last record read in the data source):
    Sequence #: 0
    RBA: 0
    Timestamp: 2011-03-16 00:50:47.000000
    Redo File:
```

```
Write Checkpoint #1
  GGS Log Trail
  Current Checkpoint (current write position):
    Sequence #: 0
    RBA: 0
    Timestamp: 2011-03-16 00:53:45.022000
    Extract Trail: AA
Header:
  Version = 2
  Record Source = U
  Type = 4
  # Input Checkpoints = 1
  # Output Checkpoints = 1

File Information:
  Block Size = 2048
  Max Blocks = 100
  Record Length = 2048
  Current Offset = 0

Configuration:
  Data Source = 3
  Transaction Integrity = 1
  Task Type = 0

Status:
  Start Time = 2011-03-16 00:50:47
  Last Update Time = 2011-03-16 00:50:47
  Stop Status = G
  Last Result = 0
```

The statistic to look for is Write Checkpoint, an example of which is shown here:

```
Write Checkpoint #1
  GGS Log Trail
  Current Checkpoint (current write position):
    Sequence #: 0
    RBA: 0
    Timestamp: 2011-03-16 00:53:45.022000
    Extract Trail: AA
```

If the number of write checkpoints isn't increasing in Oracle GoldenGate, it means the Extract process is unable to send data across the network to the trail file. If you're using a data-pump Extract on the source system, then issuing the GGSCI command INFO EXTRACT for both Extract processes will show that the primary Extract's checkpoints are moving, because it's able to write to the local trail; however, the data-pump checkpoints aren't incremented, thus showing the network latency issue. When you encounter this latency issue, contact and work with your local system administrator or network operations team to remediate the network slowness. Further analysis can be performed by issue the INFO EXTRACT and INFO REPLICAT commands from within the GGSCI interface, with the DETAIL option:

```
INFO EXTRACT <group>, DETAIL
INFO REPLICAT <group>, DETAIL
```

Given that the Replicat process groups are up and running without any system issues in terms of access to reading from and writing to the trail files, the next step is to compare the Extract write point with the Replicat read point by reviewing the following statistics output from the GGSCI INFO EXTRACT command:

```
Remote Trail Name Seqno RBA  Max   MB
c:\ggs_src\dirdat\aa    1   251   50
```

Compare this to the report from the GGSCI command INFO REPLICAT:

```
Log Read Checkpoint File C:\ggs_trgt\DIRDAT\AA000001
2011-03-13 22:41:58.000000 RBA 2142225
```

Whenever you see that the Extract checkpoints aren't being incremented, INFO REPLICAT may show continued processing by indicating that the read relative byte address (RBA) is increasing up until the last record has been written to the trail file. It then stops moving because no more records are sent across the network and written out to the trail file. Meanwhile, back on the source system, the data-pump Extract process is unable to move data to the target and soon fails in an abend condition as it runs out of memory for processing data. However, the primary Extract process group continues to run because it writes out to the local trail file. Eventually, it reaches the last trail file in the series; and when it can't checkpoint, it fails and abends.

This proves the point that it's very important to resolve network issues as soon as possible to prevent the Extract process from falling too far behind in the transaction logs, because you don't want data to be out of sync. You should monitor the network between the source and target environments by using a network diagnostic tool such as HP OpenView or Tivoli as well as communicating these issues to your network administrator to verify that the network is in a healthy condition and latency issues have been minimized as much as possible. After you've verified that network performance is sufficient, check to see if the Extract process bandwidth is saturated. You may need to split the processing between multiple Extract process groups to remediate network performance issues. Multiple data pumps may also benefit environments without large bandwidth resources. This reduces the chance of an Extract failing if the network is unreliable and experiences periodic spikes or failures. You should group together tables with referential integrity to one another into the same Extract process group. You can also tune memory usage by the Extract in the event that the network latency issue has been addressed.

Oracle Database Issues with GoldenGate

In an ideal world, this book would cover the database configuration issues for each platform that supports Oracle GoldenGate. Because the details are beyond the scope of this book, I encourage you to consult the platform-related Oracle GoldenGate documentation for third-party RDBMS platforms online at http://download.oracle.com/docs/cd/E18101_01/index.htm. Oracle database-related issues that cause errors with the Oracle GoldenGate operations include the following:

- Extract process can't read or access the online redo logs or Oracle database archive log files

- Missing Oracle database archive logs

- Out of sync Oracle database issues

- Extract and Replicat failures with Oracle source and target database environments

- Data pump errors

Extract Can't Access Oracle Database Archive and Redo Logs

In the event that the Extract process can't find the requested archive or online redo log file on the source Oracle database, it waits. For instance, you may encounter error messages from within Oracle GoldenGate such as this:

```
2011-03-16 00:51:55  ERROR   OGG-00446  Error 5 (Access is denied.) opening log file
C:\WINORA11G2\ORADATA\WIN11SRC\REDO01.LOG for sequence 16. Not able to establish initial
position for begin time 2011-03-16 00:50:47.
2011-03-16 00:51:55  ERROR   OGG-01668  PROCESS ABENDING.
```

You can find out the log file that the Extract is looking for by issuing the GGSCI VIEW REPORT <group> command. Your best bet to resolve missing archive logs with the Extract is to restore the missing archive log files and then restart the Extract group. To avoid these errors, you should maintain sufficient archive logs available to the Extract until the data contained in these logs has been processed.

A second issue with Extracts and Oracle database archive log files occurs whenever the archive logs aren't stored in the default Oracle location. In this case, you can use the Extract parameter ALTARCHIVELOGDEST <path name> to use another location for the archive logs that the Extract needs for processing. One key way you can identify a missing archive log issue is that when this occurs, the Extract startup process runs slowly and appears to be in a hang condition as it looks back for the archive log sequences to find the specific logs that it requires. The Extract must search through all past logs if it was restarted while a database transaction was opened, thus creating the requirement to search and go back to past operations until a commit was received because only committed transactions are recorded by Oracle GoldenGate. In-flight transactions aren't captured and also aren't recorded in the Oracle database archive logs. It can take hours or even days for the Extract to search through the Oracle database archive logs to locate the requested log file. If the Extract fails to locate the archive log, it abends and fails.

You should run a query against the V$TRANSACTION dynamic performance view on the source Oracle database to ensure that no open transactions are present. You should also run the GGSCI SEND EXTRACT command on a regular basis to view and manage long-running transactions. One way to set a threshold for long-running Oracle database transactions is to use the parameter WARNLOGTRANS to identify long-running transactions in Oracle GoldenGate. In the event that your Oracle database online redo logs have dumped their current data to the archive logs and you can't restore the necessary archive logs, you must resynchronize both the source and target database environments.

Extract Failure Conditions Due to Oracle Source Database Issues

As mentioned earlier, Extracts must have read access to log in to the source Oracle database to read data from the online redo log files. Check the permissions for the Extract user account provided in the parameter file if you experience errors during operation. You can verify this by using the DBLOGIN command to check for permission and read-access issues. Another root cause of this issue is the disk-full condition for the source Oracle database file system.

Once you've resolved the read and login issues on the source Oracle database, you need to stop both the Manager and Extract processes with Oracle GoldenGate. Exit the GGSCI interface for Oracle GoldenGate, and then restart the Manager and Extract process groups on the source system.

Data-Pump Errors

Recall from earlier chapters that you can use a special Extract process group called a data pump on an intermediate system to enhance performance and availability with processing. One common problem occurs when you use the PASSTHRU parameter and try to use data transformations. This causes the data pump to fail because the PASSTHRU parameter isn't supported with Oracle GoldenGate. For the data pump pass-through mode with Oracle GoldenGate, both source and target table names and structures must be the same, and no filtering operations can be performed on the data.

Another thing to check for in the data-pump parameter file when you use the PASSTHRU parameter is whether you're using the USERID or SOURCEDB parameter. If the source system doesn't contain a database, these parameters shouldn't be used. If you're using pass-through for some tables and normal processing for other tables, then for normal processing of these tables, the system must have a database. In addition, you need to specify the database login parameters with Oracle GoldenGate as well as use a source definitions file if any filtering is performed. Furthermore, you need to use a target definitions file for any column mapping or conversion operations.

Replicat Errors on the Oracle Database Target System

The Oracle Replicat performs the critical task of reading data from the remote trail files on the target database system. It uses SQL statements to apply the transactions to the target database system. The following issues can occur with Replicat processing and cause failures in Oracle GoldenGate:

- The Replicat hangs or fails to process data against the target Oracle database.

- The Replicat abends and fails on the target database system.

- Large transactions cause the Replicat to fail.

Let's look into each of these issues with Replicats and how to resolve them.

Replicat Hangs on the Target System

Sometimes the Replicat process stalls and doesn't continue to process data from the remote trail file on the target system. If this issue occurs, check the status of the Replicat process group by issuing the GGSCI command INFO REPLICAT and noting the trail file name as well as the checkpoint information.

Make sure you verify that the Replicat is reading data from the same trail file the Extract process group is writing to. If you discover that this isn't the case, then you need to rectify the situation by executing the GGSCI command ALTER REPLICAT <group>, EXTTRAIL <trail file name>. Then, to verify that everything is correct, issue the GGSCI command INFO RMTTRAIL * on the target system. In the event that the trail file wasn't created, you can create a new trail file by executing the GGSCI command ADD EXTTRAIL <trail file name>, EXTRACT <group> on the source system.

Replicat Experiences an Abend Failure on the Target System

Recall from earlier chapters that Replicat processes live on the target database system and use a special database table called the *checkpoint table*. If this table is accidentally deleted or corrupted, Replicat processing fails. One indication of this is the abend condition shown here:

```
2011-03-16 01:13:58  ERROR   OGG-00446  Checkpoint table GGS.CHECKPOINT does not exist. Please
create the table or recreate the REPORA group using the correct table.
2011-03-16 01:13:58  ERROR   OGG-01668  PROCESS ABENDING.
```

You may also see errors on the source system with the Extract such as GGS error 516, "Extract read, No data found selecting position from checkpoint table."

The solution to corrupted checkpoint errors is to drop and re-create the checkpoint table on the target system for the Replicat or to use the convchk utility and then restart the Replicat. My Oracle Support Note 965703.1 (http://support.oracle.com) has tips on using the convchk utility.

The syntax for the convchk utility is

```
convchk <replicat group> <schema>.<checkpoint table name>
```

Let's look at how to use the convchk utility to repair a corrupted checkpoint table for Oracle GoldenGate with a Replicat on Windows. You run this from a Windows or UNIX/Linux shell prompt window and not from within the GGSCI interface:

```
C:\ggs_trgt>convchk repora ggs.checkpoint
**********************************************************************
              Oracle GoldenGate Checkpoint Conversion Utility
                     Version 11.1.1.0.0 Build 078
              Windows (optimized) on Jul 28 2010 17:43:24
Copyright (C) 1995, 2010, Oracle and/or its affiliates. All rights reserved.
                     Starting at 2011-03-16 01:23:18
**********************************************************************
Operating System Version:
Microsoft Windows Vista Business Edition, on x86
Version 6.0 (Build 6002: Service Pack 2)
Process id: 4880
Opening existing checkpoint file C:\ggs_trgt\dirchk\REPORA.cpr for group REPORA.
Checkpoint C:\ggs_trgt\dirchk\REPORA.cpr backed up to
C:\ggs_trgt\dirchk\REPORA.cpr.1300252998.bak.
Updating checkpoint table in 8.0.2-compatible checkpoint file.
Successfully converted checkpoint to 8.0.2-compatible format.
Checkpoint conversion successful for group REPORA.
```

Once you've fixed the checkpoint table for the Replicat, you should be able to start the Replicat without errors as shown here:

```
GGSCI (oracledba) 14>  info repora, detail
REPLICAT   REPORA    Last Started 2011-03-16 01:29   Status RUNNING
Checkpoint Lag        00:00:00 (updated 00:00:07 ago)
Log Read Checkpoint   File c:\ggs_src\trails\aa000000
                      First Record  RBA 0
    Extract Source                      Begin            End
    c:\ggs_src\trails\aa000000          * Initialized *  First Record
    c:\ggs_src\trails\aa000000          * Initialized *  First Record
Current directory     C:\ggs_trgt
Report file           C:\ggs_trgt\dirrpt\REPORA.rpt
Parameter file        C:\ggs_trgt\dirprm\REPORA.prm
Checkpoint file       C:\ggs_trgt\dirchk\REPORA.cpr
Checkpoint table      GGS.CHECKPOINT
Process file          C:\ggs_trgt\dirpcs\REPORA.pcr
Error log             C:\ggs_trgt\ggserr.log
```

▓ **Note** The convchk utility causes the checkpoint file to become the new master for Replicat checkpoints. The Replicat resynchronizes the truncated checkpoint table with data from the checkpoint file.

Replicat Fails on Large Transactions

If the target system can't support large transactions, the Replicat process groups will fail with an out-of-memory condition. To solve this error, you can set the MAXTRANSOPS parameter to split up the Replicat transactions into smaller transactions or use multiple Replicat groups to process these in parallel.

Incompatible Record Errors with a Replicat

One common problem during Replicat processing on the target system occurs when incompatible records bring the Replicat to its knees and failure. In the GGSCI logs, you see an error similar to the following:

```
2011-03-09 11:00:22 GGS ERROR 509 GoldenGate Delivery for Oracle, REPORA.prm: Extract read,
Incompatible record in C:\GGS_TRGT\DIRDAT\AA000000, rba 5466 (getting header).
```

This occurs if the data gets corrupted in transit from the source system to the target system. Another cause is a data format that isn't compatible with Replicat processing. If you use the FORMATASCII, FORMATSQL, or FORMATXML parameter for the Extract during the initial load, it will cause the failure to occur.

Incompatible-record errors with the Replicat also occur due to misconfiguration of trail files that are sent from the source to the target system when the Extract is configured to overwrite an existing trail file. For instance, if you have two Extract processes writing to the same trail file, they will overwrite the one the Replicat is looking to use, thus causing an incompatible-record error.

The Replicat needs complete records to apply the data successfully from the trail file to the target system. Sometimes the Extract and Replicat groups are dropped and rebuilt with the exact same trail-file name. This causes the Extract process to begin writing again at the first part of the same trail file, causing issues with stepping on the trail file.

You can use the Logdump utility to investigate error 509 conditions with Oracle and GoldenGate. In the event that you can't salvage the data, the best solution is to resynchronize the target database with a new initial load and to add new trail files correctly to avoid future issues.

Data-Synchronization Issues

As much as you might like Oracle GoldenGate to automate the data-verification process, it doesn't perform these checks. However, you can implement conflict-resolution scripts and programs to check for data synchronization between source and target systems. Oracle GoldenGate performs basic checks by matching target rows from the source and target database primary key and unique-key columns, or substitute key columns if you define these with the KEYCOLS option for the TABLE and MAP statements in the Extract and Replicat.

You should perform out-of-sync data checks on a regular basis as part of your database administration duties for Oracle GoldenGate to remediate synchronization issues. Veridata provides a suite of tools to check for data-synchronization issues with Oracle GoldenGate environments.

What causes data-synchronization issues, you may ask? There are several key factors:

- Tables missing key constraints
- Character-set configuration issues
- Column-missing errors
- Fetch failures on source and target tables

Tables Missing Key Constraints

Oracle GoldenGate relies on table-key constraints to map source-to-target DDL and DML activities. Without these keys, Oracle GoldenGate uses all of the table columns as a key value. This may cause multiple rows of the table to be updated if they contain identical data. One way to address this issue to avoid data duplication is to set the KEYCOLS option for the TABLE and MAP statements in the Extract and Replicat parameter files along with the LIMITROWS option to prevent multiple rows from being updated.

Character Set Configuration Issues

Because Oracle GoldenGate uses the database character set to perform data-synchronization tasks, you need to make sure the Oracle source and target character sets are the same to avoid synchronization errors. If they're different, then errors will result. You can check the character sets by looking at the NLS_LANG environment variable on both the source and target Oracle database systems. The source NLS_LANG value must be set to the same exact character set as the target system. In addition, the target Oracle database character set needs to be set as a superset of the source Oracle database system.

Missing-Column Errors

If columns are found to be missing between source and target, Oracle GoldenGate won't replicate data correctly. This has its root cause in two areas. The first case arises if supplemental data hasn't been enabled on the source and target Oracle database environments correctly. For Oracle, you use the ADD TRANDATA command to add the required supplemental log data either at the database level or on a table-by-table basis.

Another cause of missing-column errors occurs when the KEYCOLS parameter is used to perform column-mapping transformations from the source to target environments. If there is a mismatch in source-to-target key-column mapping, errors occur. You need to make sure you include either an existing key or a unique column in the KEYCOLS definition to resolve this error.

Filters and functions used in Extract and Replicat parameter files also cause these errors in the event that the correct existing key column isn't specified and found between the source and target mapping transformations given in the Extract and Replicat parameter files.

Fetch Failures

Database fetch failures cause data-synchronization errors if source-row data is deleted during Oracle GoldenGate processing. Another root cause of fetch failures occurs when undo retention for the Oracle source and target environments expires. This causes the mandatory read-consistent image of the data that the Extract process is looking for to disappear, with the end result that the Oracle Snapshot Too Old message is displayed. You can resolve this issue by adding the `FETCHOPTIONS NOUSESNAPSHOT` parameter to the Extract process group configuration. This parameter makes the Extract fetch data from the table instead of going to the undo tablespace.

After you've verified that Oracle GoldenGate has processed the record, you need to remove `FETCHOPTIONS` so the Extract returns to fetching data from the undo tablespace. You should also increase the amount of time that Oracle maintains data in the undo tablespace on the source and target Oracle databases.

Summary

This chapter provided you with tips and techniques for how to troubleshoot Oracle GoldenGate issues from a holistic perspective. You learned how to identify and resolve common issues that cause failures with Oracle GoldenGate processing due to database, operating system, and network configuration setups. In addition, the chapter discussed ways to enable tracing of the Oracle GoldenGate environment to isolate the root cause of operational issues. For more information, see My Oracle Support at `http://support.oracle.com`.

CHAPTER 12

Disaster Recovery Replication

There are many strategies available for maintaining a disaster recovery database. These range from simply keeping backup copies of the database at an offsite location to database-level replication and even storage mirroring. This chapter will give you a good understanding of how to set up up the GoldenGate replication solution for maintaining a disaster recovery database. The major advantage of using GoldenGate for disaster recovery replication is that it can become your organization's universal database disaster recovery solution. GoldenGate works across many different databases and platforms. Using GoldenGate, you can develop standard disaster recovery processes and implement them across your organization, regardless of the specific DBMS being used.

Earlier in Chapter 4 you set up basic replication. In this chapter you'll build on that basic configuration and implement a specific replication configuration for disaster recovery purposes. In many ways, the GoldenGate configuration for disaster recovery is similar to basic replication, with a few enhancements. This chapter will cover setting up and configuring GoldenGate replication for disaster recovery. We'll cover how to handle both planned and unplanned outage scenarios and how you can use GoldenGate to minimize downtime.

Prerequisites

You need to have the following prerequisites in place before you can start setting up replication for disaster recovery:

- The GoldenGate software installed on the source and target servers as described in Chapter 2

- The GoldenGate database User ID created on the source and target databases

- The server name or IP address of the target database server

- The GoldenGate Manager process up and running on the source and the target

- TCP/IP network connectivity open from the source server to the target server's GoldenGate manager port and vice versa

- An understanding of the business and technical replication requirements for the disaster recovery replication

There are a few additional prerequisites that are important for disaster recovery replication:

- Backups of your GoldenGate software files and working directories on the source and target servers

- SQL scripts to grant any necessary object privileges required by your application during a switchover or failover

- Processes and scripts to move your application and users from the source to the target server and back again

First, let's review the requirements for disaster recovery replication. Understanding the requirements is probably the single most important factor in the success of any replication project.

Requirements

You need to gain a solid understanding of the specific requirements which will drive the disaster recovery replication technical design. Here are some of the typical requirements and considerations for disaster recovery replication. We'll refer to the source database you are replicating from as the primary database and the remote target database as the standby or disaster recovery database. The primary database, also know as the trusted source, is the active database where the application programs connect under normal circumstances.

Once you define your requirements, you will need to ensure that you can meet these requirements using Oracle GoldenGate disaster recovery replication.

- Keep the standby database synchronized with the primary database.

- The primary database will be actively processing changes. For the purposes of this chapter, we will assume the standby database will be used for read-only queries; however, remember that with GoldenGate you could allow writes to the standby database in a bidirectional configuration. If you allow writes to the standby then you need to handle any data conflicts, as discussed in Chapter 5.

- To allow for the fastest recovery time, typically you will want the database structures and data in the standby database to be identical to the primary database. However, by using GoldenGate you have the flexibility to allow differences in your primary and standby databases. For example, you may decide you only want to keep a critical subset of your data for disaster recovery purposes rather than the entire database. You can do this with GoldenGate filtering as covered in Chapter 5. For Oracle databases, you can also use the GoldenGate DDL replication feature to keep the database tables synchronized as well as the data.

- Usually you will want the data in the primary database to be kept current with the disaster recovery site to within at most a few seconds of difference in case of failover. For example, if you were processing financial transactions, any lag differences between the primary and the standby data could be costly. This will vary depending on your particular application. For some applications you may be able to tolerate the standby lagging behind the primary database for a period of time. Also, there may be some databases which do not need to be kept current and only need to be refreshed periodically. In that case, you can still set up the same GoldenGate configuration we will cover in this chapter, but only turn it on as needed.

- Fast switchover from the primary database to the standby disaster recovery database for both planned and unplanned outages.

- After failover or switchover to the standby database, the database roles are reversed and it becomes the primary database. As needed, the database roles can be reversed back to their original configuration at a later time.

- After failover or switchover, changes to the standby database must be captured to allow for synchronization when the primary database is returned to the configuration.

In this chapter, we will show how you can meet these requirements using GoldenGate. For the examples, we will use the HR schema as in the earlier chapters.

Disaster Recovery Replication Topology

The underlying topology for disaster recovery is one-way replication, with some enhancements to support disaster recovery, as shown in Figure 12-1. You may remember from Chapter 3, that one-way replication is the simplest topology and is often used for reporting or query offloading purposes. In our case, the one-way replication topology will be used for disaster recovery purposes. Data is replicated from a single source database, the primary, to a single target database, the standby, in only one direction. Changes to database data are only made at the primary database and then replicated to the standby database.

For disaster recovery, a few enhancements are needed to the basic one-way replication topology. The primary database normally handles application activity except in the event of a switchover or failover. We will refer to a switchover as a planned outage for things like software maintenance. A failover is an unplanned outage where the primary database is totally lost for some period of time. During a switchover or failover the standby database will become the primary database.

In order to meet the disaster recovery requirements we covered in the last section, you'll have to ensure you can quickly and accurately switch the application activity from the primary database to the standby database and back. Also, you must capture any database changes made on the standby database to resynchronize with the primary database once it comes back online. We've indicated that with a dotted line in our illustration in Figure 12-1.

Figure 12-1. Disaster recovery replication topology

Now let's look at how to implement the disaster recovery replication requirements and topology using GoldenGate.

Setup

Once the prerequisites are complete, setting up disaster recovery replication from source to target can be accomplished in two parts and seven total steps, as shown in Figures 12-2 and 12-3.

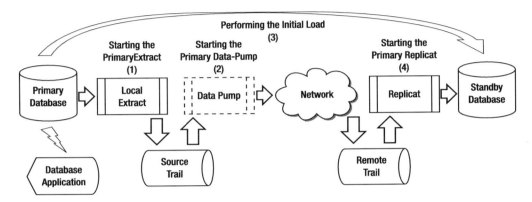

Figure 12-2. Disaster recovery replication setup, part 1

The steps are similar to setting up basic one-way replication, which we covered in Chapter 4.

Part 1 includes the first four steps for setting up replication from the primary database to the standby database. These four steps include initially loading the data and then keeping the data synchronized after the initial load. Since we already covered these steps and concepts in Chapter 4, we won't cover them again here. In the following sections in this chapter we'll provide the GoldenGate parameter files and only explain the new concepts for disaster recovery where applicable.

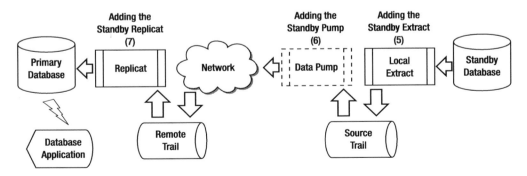

Figure 12-3. Disaster recovery reverse replication setup, part 2

Part 2, as shown in Figure 12-3, includes the last three steps for configuring replication back from the standby database to the primary, should it be needed. You will configure, but not start, the replication back from the standby database to the primary database. The three steps for setting up replication from the standby database to the primary database include setting up and configuring the Local Extract, data-pump Extract, and Replicat. These Extracts and Replicats will be used later in switchover and failover scenarios. The steps in Figure 12-3 are described as follows:

1. Add the standby Extract. Configure and add the standby Extract to be prepared to capture database changes in the event of a switchover or failover. If there is an outage, the standby Local Extract will already be in place and ready to start capturing changes.

2. Add the standby data-pump Extract. Configure and add the standby data pump to be prepared to capture changes from the standby database in the event of an outage on the primary database.

3. Add the standby Replicat. Configure and add the standby Replicat to be prepared to begin applying changes back to the primary database if there is an outage.

Let's look at each of the disaster recovery replication steps, beginnning with configuring the Local Extract in the next section.

Configuring the Local Extract for Disaster Recovery

Let's begin by configuring the Local Extract. In order to do this, you will first need to create a parameter file for the Extract. Remember, we're configuring the Local Extract to capture all the SQL DML changes from the primary database HR schema for replication to the standby database HR schema. We will keep an exact copy of the database data synchronized so it can be used for switchover or failover.

Let's take a look at the parameters for the Local Extract on the primary server as shown in the following example. Since we used LHREMD1 in an earlier chapter, let's name the disaster recovery Local Extract LHREMP2.

```
GGSCI (primaryserver) 1> edit params LHREMP2

Extract LHREMP2


-----------------------------------------------------------------
-- Local extract for HR schema
-----------------------------------------------------------------

USERID GGER, PASSWORD userpw

ExtTrail dirdat/l3

ReportCount Every 10000 Records, Rate
Report at 00:30

DiscardFile dirrpt/LHREMP2.dsc, Append
DiscardRollover at 02:00

Table HR.*;
```

These parameters should look familiar as we covered them all in Chapters 4 and 5. The next step is to add the Extract to the GoldenGate configuration. You should pick a new unused trail file name. In this example, you can use trail file l3 for the Local Extract trail, since trail files l1 and l2 were used in previous examples. You can add the extract using the following commands from GGSCI:

```
GGSCI (primaryserver) > ADD EXTRACT LHREMP2, TRANLOG, BEGIN NOW
GGSCI (primaryserver) > ADD EXTTRAIL dirdat/l3, EXTRACT LHREMP2, MEGABYTES 100
```

After adding the Extract, you need to start it to begin capturing changes as shown in the following example:

```
GGSCI (primaryserver) > START EXTRACT LHREMP2
```

You should make sure the Extract is running properly after it is started. If you see a status of STOPPED or ABENDED there may be a problem. You should see a status of RUNNING and the RBA value increasing if you are processing data. You can use the INFO command and verify the status of the Local Extract LHREMP2:

```
GGSCI (primaryserver) 2> INFO EXTRACT LHREMP2
```

If the Extract is not running, you can review the GoldenGate error log file and try to resolve the problem. You should also run the stats command as shown here for LHREMP2:

```
GGSCI (primaryserver) 2> STATS EXT LHREMP2
```

You're now finished starting the Local Extract, so let's move on to the next step: starting the data-pump Extract.

Configuring the Data Pump for Disaster Recovery

Now that the Local Extract is started, you can proceed with configuring, adding, and starting the data pump for disaster recovery. In our example, you configure the data pump to read the l3 trail file written out by the Local Extract named LHREMP2 and pump it over the TCP/IP network to the target standby server to trail l4 to be processed by the Replicat. One consideration for disaster recovery is you may be sending your trail files over long distances to the remote standby site. You should verify you have the network capacity and performance to support your GoldenGate disaster recovery network requirements. If needed, you can tune the GoldenGate parameters for the network which we reviewed in Chapter 7.

From GGSCI, let's edit the parameters for the data pump as shown in this example:

```
GGSCI (primaryserver) 1> edit params PHREMP2

Extract PHREMP2


-----------------------------------------------------------------
-- Data-pump Extract for HR schema
-----------------------------------------------------------------


PassThru

ReportCount Every 10000 Records, Rate
Report at 00:30
```

```
DiscardFile dirrpt/PHREMP2.dsc, Append
DiscardRollover at 02:00

RmtHost standbyserver, MgrPort 7809
RmtTrail dirdat/l4

Table HR.* ;
```

Now that you've set up the disaster recovery data-pump Extract configuration parameters, the next step is to add the data-pump Extract group on the primary server. You can do that using the commands shown in the following example:

```
GGSCI (primaryserver) > ADD EXTRACT PHREMP2, EXTTRAILSOURCE dirdat/l3
GGSCI (primaryserver) > ADD RMTTRAIL dirdat/l4, EXTRACT PHREMP2, MEGABYTES 100
```

After adding the data-pump Extract, you can start it to begin processing records from the source trail file as shown in this example:

```
GGSCI (primaryserver) > START EXTRACT PHREMP2
```

Once the data-pump Extract has started, you can verify it is running using the same INFO EXTRACT command that you used for the Local Extract. You should also run the STATS command on the data-pump Extract to make sure it is processing changes.

Now that the Local Extract and data-pump Extract for disaster recovery are started, you can begin the initial data load. You learned about the different methods for initially loading data in Chapter 4. These methods will also work fine for the initial data load for your disaster recovery replication. You can use either GoldenGate itself, or the DBMS vendor load utilities to do the initial data load. Please refer to Chapter 4 for more details on the initial load process.

Configuring the Replicat for Disaster Recovery

After the initial data load, you can start the Replicat to apply the changes that have been captured by the Extract while the load was running. If needed, turn on the HANDLECOLLISIONS parameter to resolve any errors with missing or duplicate data. It will take some time for the Replicat to catch up with applying all the changes made during the load, particularly for a large database with heavy change volume and a long load time.

Once the initial data load changes have been applied by the Replicat and there is no GoldenGate lag left, the primary and standby databases will be fully synchronized. At this point, the Local and data-pump Extracts and Replicat can continue to run and keep the databases synchronized in real time with the ongoing changes.

Before starting to configure the Replicat, you should go back and double-check the GoldenGate prerequisites have been met on the target standby server. We covered those at the beginning of the chapter in the section "Prerequisites." Once you have confirmed the prerequisites are met, let's begin configuring the Replicat. Remember, you're configuring the Replicat to apply all the DML changes from the HR schema based on our disaster recovery requirements to replicate all the data. If you wanted to filter or transform data you could also do that here by adding the appropriate parameters.

Since you already used RHREMP1 for a Replicat name earlier, you can name this replicat RHREMP2. Let's begin by taking a look at the Replicat parameters for RHREMP2 on the standby server.

```
GGSCI (standbyserver) 1> edit params RHREMP2

Replicat RHREMP2

---------------------------------------------------------------------
-- Replicat for HR Schema
---------------------------------------------------------------------

USERID GGER, PASSWORD userpw

ReportCount Every 10000 Records, Rate
Report at 00:30

DiscardFile dirrpt/RHREMP2.dsc, Append
DiscardRollover at 02:00

-- HandleCollisions should be turned off after the initial load synchronization.
HandleCollisions

AssumeTargetDefs

Map HR.*, Target HR.* ;
```

Now that you've set up the Replicat configuration parameters, the next step is to add the Replicat group. In the following example you are adding the RHREMP2 replicat to the GoldenGate configuration. The Replicat will process the l4 trail which was pumped over by the disaster recovery data pump.

```
GGSCI (standbyserver) > ADD REPLICAT RHREMP2, EXTTRAIL dirdat/l4
```

Now let's start the RHREMP2 replicat.

```
GGSCI (standbyserver) > START REPLICAT RHREMP2
```

Once the Replicat has started, you can verify it is running using the INFO REPLICAT command. You should see a Status of RUNNING. If you see a Status of STOPPED or ABENDED there may be a problem.

Let's do an INFO command on our Replicat RHREMP1 to check the status as follows:

```
GGSCI (standbyserver) 2> INFO REPLICAT RHREMP2
```

You should also run the STATS command on your Replicat to make sure it is processing changes as in the following example for Replicat RHREMP2:

```
GGSCI (standbyserver) 2> STATS REP RHREMP2
```

Next, let's add the GoldenGate processes for the replication from the standby database back to the primary database.

Configuring the Standby Extract

Once Part 1 of your disaster recovery replication is complete and you are successfully replicating from the primary database to the standby database, the next part is to add the standby Extract. The standby Extract is similar to the primary Extract except it will be used to extract data to replicate from the standby database back to the primary database if needed. For now you're only *adding* the Extract. Later you'll *start* it during switchover and failover activities.

Let's begin by configuring the parameter file for the standby Local Extract. In our example you're configuring the Local Extract to capture all the SQL DML changes from the sample HR schema on the standby database. Since you've already used trails l3 and l4, let's use trails l5 and l6 for replication from the standby database back to the primary database.

Let's start by taking a look at the parameters for the Local Extract on the standby server.

```
GGSCI (standbyserver) 1> edit params LHREMP3

Extract LHREMP3

------------------------------------------------------------------
-- Local extract for HR schema
------------------------------------------------------------------

USERID GGER, PASSWORD userpw

ExtTrail dirdat/l5

ReportCount Every 10000 Records, Rate
Report at 00:30

DiscardFile dirrpt/LHREMP3.dsc, Append
DiscardRollover at 02:00

Table HR.*;
```

Next you will add the standby Extract to the GoldenGate configuration so you will be ready to start it later during a database switchover or failover. You can do that using the following commands from GGSCI:

```
GGSCI (standbyserver) > ADD EXTRACT LHREMP3, TRANLOG, BEGIN NOW
GGSCI (standbyserver) > ADD EXTTRAIL dirdat/l5, EXTRACT LHREMP3, MEGABYTES 100
```

Next, let's configure the standby data pump.

Configuring the Standby Data Pump

Now that the standby Local Extract is added, you can proceed with configuring and adding the standby data pump. The standby data pump is similar to the primary data pump except it will be used to pump the trails back from the standby database to the primary database if needed. In our example, you'll configure the data pump to read the l5 trail file written out by the standby Local Extract named LHREMP3 and pump it over the TCP/IP network to the target server to be processed by the standby Replicat.

From GGSCI, let's edit the parameters for our data pump as shown in this example.

```
GGSCI (standbyserver) 1> edit params PHREMP3

Extract PHREMP3

-------------------------------------------------------------------
-- Data-pump Extract for HR schema
-------------------------------------------------------------------

PassThru

ReportCount Every 10000 Records, Rate
Report at 00:30

DiscardFile dirrpt/PHREMP3.dsc, Append
DiscardRollover at 02:00

RmtHost standbyserver, MgrPort 7809
RmtTrail dirdat/l6

Table HR.* ;
```

Since you've reviewed these parameters previously in Chapters 4 and 5, let's proceed with adding the data pump. You can add the data-pump Extract using the commands shown in the following example.

```
GGSCI (standbyserver) > ADD EXTRACT PHREMP3, EXTTRAILSOURCE dirdat/l5
GGSCI (standbyserver) > ADD RMTTRAIL dirdat/l6, EXTRACT PHREMP3, MEGABYTES 100
```

You won't be starting the data pump until later, so let's move on to configuring the standby Replicat.

Configuring the Standby Replicat

Next you should add a standby Replicat which will be ready to apply any changes back to your primary database after a failover or switchover. This is similar to the primary replicat but will be used to replicate back to the primary database from the standby database. By adding it now before it is needed you will be ready to start it in the event of an outage.

First create a parameter file for Replicat RHREMP3 as shown in the following example:

```
GGSCI (primaryserver) 1> edit params RHREMP3

Replicat RHREMP3

-------------------------------------------------------------------
-- Replicat for HR Schema
-------------------------------------------------------------------

USERID GGER, PASSWORD userpw
```

```
ReportCount Every 10000 Records, Rate
Report at 00:30

DiscardFile dirrpt/RHREMP3.dsc, Append
DiscardRollover at 02:00

-- HandleCollisions should be turned off after the initial load synchronization.
HandleCollisions

AssumeTargetDefs

Map HR.*, Target HR.* ;
```

The next step is to add the standby Replicat group. In the following example you are adding the RHREMP3 replicat to the GoldenGate configuration.

```
GGSCI (primaryserver) > ADD REPLICAT RHREMP3, EXTTRAIL dirdat/l6
```

Remember you won't be starting the standby Replicat until a switchover or failover. You are now finished with the initial setup for the disaster recovery replication. All of the steps you have completed so far are in preparation for a potential switchover or failover situation. You are now prepared to perform a planned switchover or an unplanned failover to your standby database.

Performing a Planned Switchover

Even though you are preparing your environment for a complete unplanned disaster recovery scenario, there are many situations where you may need to bring down your primary database for a planned outage. Using GoldenGate replication, you can reduce these planned outage times to the bare minimum of switching your applications from the primary database to the standby database without losing any data during the process. You can have your application processing against the standby database while the primary database is down for maintenance and then switch back to the primary database after the maintenance is complete.

In our example, let's assume you need to apply a database software patch to the primary database which normally requires a four-hour outage. Now let's go through the steps using GoldenGate replication and keep the application outage window as short as possible. To keep it simple, we've divided the planned switchover steps into five parts, each with several steps. Let's begin with Part 1, as shown in Figure 12-4.

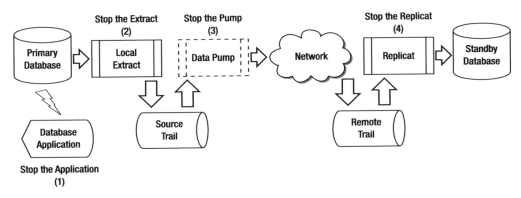

Figure 12-4. Disaster recovery planned switchover, part 1

Following are descriptions for the steps in Part 1, as shown in Figure 12-4.

1. Stop the application connected to the primary database.

2. After verifying there is no lag, stop the Local Extract as shown in the following
    example:

    ```
    GGSCI (primaryserver) > LAG EXTRACT LHREMD2
    Sending GETLAG request to EXTRACT LHREMD2 ...
    Last record lag: 10 seconds.
    At EOF, no more records to process.
    GGSCI (primaryserver) > STOP EXTRACT LHREMD2
    ```

3. After verifying there is no lag, stop the data-pump Extract as shown in the
    following example:

    ```
    GGSCI (primaryserver) > LAG EXTRACT PHREMD2
    Sending GETLAG request to EXTRACT PHREMD2 ...
    Last record lag: 6 seconds.
    At EOF, no more records to process.
    GGSCI (primaryserver) > STOP EXTRACT PHREMD2
    ```

4. After verifying there are no more records to process, stop the Replicat as
    shown in the following example:

    ```
    GGSCI (standbyserver) > LAG REPLICAT RHREMD2
    Sending GETLAG request to REPLICAT RHREMD2 ...
    Last record lag: 7 seconds.
    At EOF, no more records to process.
    GGSCI (standbyserver) > STOP REPLICAT RHREMD2
    ```

Now you've completed part 1 of the switchover process. The primary database is no longer being
used by the application and the replication from the primary database to the standby database is
stopped. Now you can proceed to part 2, as shown in Figure 12-4, and start the standby Extract and
switch the application to use the standby database.

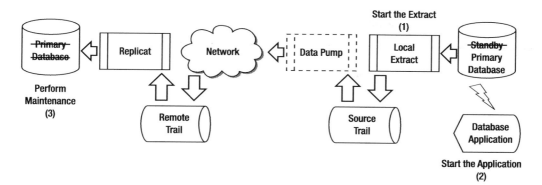

Figure 12-5. Disaster recovery planned switchover part 2

Following are descriptions for the steps in part 2 as shown in Figure 12-5.

1. To begin capturing changes in preparation for the application switchover, alter the Local Extract for the standby database to begin capturing changes now and then start it as follows:

    ```
    GGSCI (standbyserver) > ALTER EXTRACT LHREMD3. BEGIN NOW
    GGSCI (standbyserver) > START EXTRACT LHREMD3
    ```

2. Prepare the standby database for the application and start the application connected to the standby database. In preparation, you may need to grant some SQL permissions to your application users on the standby database. Also remember to enable any triggers or cascade delete constraints you may have stopped while the standby was the replication target.

3. At this time you should perform any maintenance required on the primary database while there are no applications connected. In the example, we are going to bring down the primary database and apply a database patch.

After completing part 2, you should be done with your database maintenance and ready to switch the databases back to their original configuration. In order to do that, you must apply any changes made to the standby database, while it was functioning as the primary database, back to the original primary database. Those steps are shown in Figure 12-6.

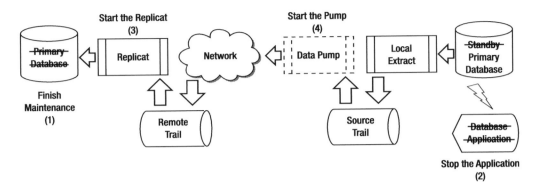

Figure 12-6. Disaster recovery planned switchover, part 3

Now let's review each of the steps in part 3, as shown in Figure 12-6.

1. First you need to complete any maintenance activities on the primary database. Until the maintenance is successfully completed, the standby database will act as the primary. Make sure to disable any triggers or cascade delete constraints on the primary before processing the GoldenGate changes from the standby.

2. Stop the application running against the standby database. At this time be sure to leave the Local Extract running so it can capture any remaining database transactions.

3. Start the the Replicat on the primary database to prepare to process the changes that were made on the standby database as shown in the following example:

   ```
   GGSCI (primaryserver) > START REPLICAT RHREMD3
   ```

4. Start the data-pump Extract on the standby to send change transactions to be processed by the Replicat on the primary as shown in the following example:

   ```
   GGSCI (standbyserver) > START EXTRACT PHREMD3
   ```

In part 3 you finished your database maintenance and then processed all the changes that were made to the standby database while it was acting as the primary database. Next you need to turn off the replication from the standby database to the primary database in part 4 as shown in Figure 12-7.

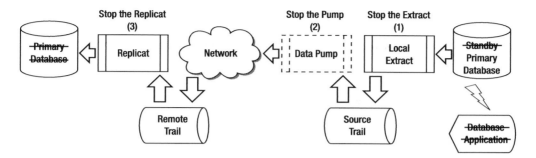

Figure 12-7. Disaster recovery planned switchover, part 4

Following are the descriptions of the steps for part 4 from Figure 12-7.

1. After verifying there is no lag, stop the Local Extract on the standby database as shown in the following example:

    ```
    GGSCI (standbyserver) > LAG EXTRACT LHREMD3
    Sending GETLAG request to EXTRACT LHREMD3 ...
    Last record lag: 5 seconds.
    At EOF, no more records to process.
    GGSCI (standbyserver) > STOP EXTRACT LHREMD3
    ```

2. After verifying there is no lag, stop the data-pump Extract on the standby database as shown in the following example:

    ```
    GGSCI (standbyserver) > LAG EXTRACT PHREMD3
    Sending GETLAG request to EXTRACT PHREMD3 ...
    Last record lag: 4 seconds.
    At EOF, no more records to process.
    GGSCI (standbyserver) > STOP EXTRACT PHREMD3
    ```

3. After verifying there are no more records to process, stop the Replicat on the primary database as shown in the following example:

    ```
    GGSCI (primaryserver) > LAG REPLICAT RHREMD3
    Sending GETLAG request to REPLICAT RHREMD3 ...
    Last record lag: 6 seconds.
    At EOF, no more records to process.
    GGSCI (primaryserver) > STOP REPLICAT RHREMD3
    ```

Now that the replication from the standby to the primary is complete and stopped, you can proceed with restarting the original replication from the primary database to the standby database in part 5, as shown in Figure 12-8.

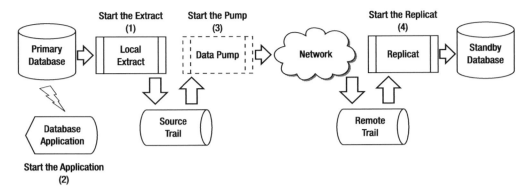

Figure 12-8. Disaster recovery planned switchover, part 5

The steps for Part 5, as shown in Figure 12-8, are as follows:

1. To being capturing changes in preparation for the application switchover back to the primary database, alter the Local Extract for the primary database to begin capturing changes beginning *now* and then start the Extract as follows:

    ```
    GGSCI (primaryserver) > ALTER EXTRACT LHREMD2, BEGIN NOW
    GGSCI (primaryserver) > START EXTRACT LHREMD2
    ```

2. Prepare the primary database for the application and start the application connected to the primary database. In preparation, you may need to grant some SQL permissions to your application users. Also remember to enable any triggers or cascade delete constraints you may have stopped while the primary database was the replication target.

3. Start the data-pump Extract on the primary database as shown in the following example:

    ```
    GGSCI (primaryserver) > START EXTRACT PHREMD2
    ```

4. Start the the Replicat on the standby database as shown in the following example:

    ```
    GGSCI (standbyserver) > START REPLICAT RHREMD2
    ```

Now you have completed Part 5 of your replication switchover process and the databases are back to their original configuration. As a result, you have minimized the downtime for your application from four hours to the minimum required to switch your application to the standby database and back. Next let's cover a different scenario using our disaster recovery replication to perform an unplanned failover.

Performing an Unplanned Failover

In an unplanned failover scenario, you lose your entire primary database server to a disaster. After the disaster occurs, you can use GoldenGate to apply the last database transactions to bring the standby database current and then the applications can use the standby database until the primary database is repaired and brought back online. Once the primary is back online, you will need to go through some steps to resynchronize it with the standby.

In our example, let's assume that you've had a disaster and your primary database server is destroyed. A new primary database server is on its way from the vendor and will be delivered and operational within 24 hours. Until that time, you will use the standby server as the primary database server. Let's go through the steps using GoldenGate replication to failover from the primary database to the standby database. After that, you will go through the steps to fall back to the new primary database server after it gets installed and is operational. Once again, to keep it simple, we've divided the unplanned failover steps into five parts each with several steps. Let's begin with part 1, as shown in Figure 12-4.

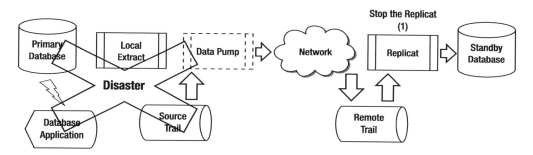

Figure 12-9. Disaster recovery unplanned failover, part 1

Following is a description of the steps in part 1 as shown in Figure 12-9.

1. After verifying there is no lag, stop the Replicat as shown in the following example:

```
GGSCI (standbyserver) > LAG REPLICAT RHREMD2
Sending GETLAG request to REPLICAT RHREMD2 ...
Last record lag: 7 seconds.
At EOF, no more records to process.
GGSCI (standbyserver) > STOP REPLICAT RHREMD2
```

Now you've completed part 1 of the failover process. The standby database has caught up with all the changes that are available from the primary database. Now you can proceed to part 2 and start the standby Extract and switch the application to use the standby database as shown in Figure 12-10.

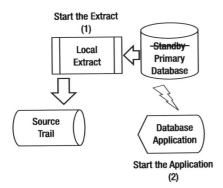

Figure 12-10. Disaster recovery unplanned failover, part 2

Let's review the steps in part 2 from Figure 12-10 next.

1. To begin capturing changes in preparation for the application switchover, alter the Local Extract for the standby database to begin capturing changes *now* and then start it as follows:

```
GGSCI (standbyserver) > ALTER EXTRACT LHREMD3, BEGIN NOW
GGSCI (standbyserver) > START EXTRACT LHREMD3
```

2. Prepare the standby database for the application and start the application connected to the standby database. In preparation, you may need to grant some SQL permissions to your application users. Also remember to enable any triggers or cascade delete constraints you may have stopped while the standby was the replication target.

After completing part 2, you are done with the failover to the standby database and the users can continue normal processing using the standby database. Any database DML changes made to the standby database will be accumulating in the GoldenGate source trail files on the standby server until the primary database is repaired or replaced and brought back online.

Once the primary database server is repaired or replaced and back online, you can begin part 3 of the process of moving the applications and users back to the primary database. The first steps of this process are shown in Figure 12-11.

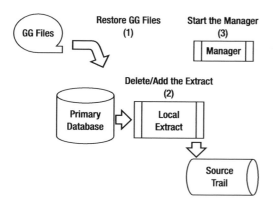

Figure 12-11. Disaster recovery unplanned failover, part 3

Following are descriptions of the part 3 steps in Figure 12-11.

1. Restore the GoldenGate software directories and files from your offline server backups.

2. Delete the Local Extract and the source trails and then add the Local Extract back as shown in the following example. Do not start the Local Extract until later.

```
GGSCI (primaryserver) > DELETE EXTRACT LHREMD2
GGSCI (primaryserver) > DELETE EXTTRAIL dirdat/l3

GGSCI (primaryserver) > ADD EXTRACT LHREMP2, TRANLOG, BEGIN NOW
GGSCI (primaryserver) > ADD EXTTRAIL dirdat/l3, EXTRACT LHREMP2, MEGABYTES 100
```

Deleting the Local Extract and trails reinitializes them so you can start over with extracting changes. The delete exttrail command only removes the GoldenGate checkpoints, so you may also want to remove any leftover trail files from the operating system directory using O/S commands to avoid any conflicts.

3. Start the GoldenGate Manager as shown in the following example:

```
GGSCI (primaryserver) > START MANAGER
```

Now that you have your GoldenGate files restored and the GoldenGate Local Extract ready on the primary database, you can begin part 4. The next steps are to resynchronize the primary database from the standby database as shown in Figure 12-12.

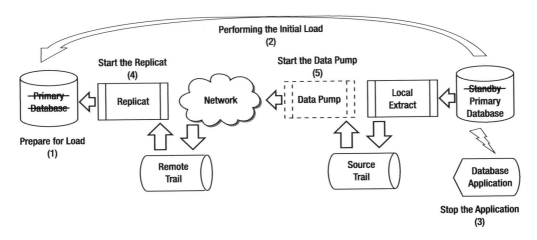

Figure 12-12. Disaster recovery unplanned failover, part 4

The part 4 steps for Figure 12-12 are described next.

1. Disable any triggers or cascade delete constraints on the primary database.

2. Perform the initial data load from the standby to the primary database. This step can be done in "hot" mode while the standby database is running, since the GoldenGate Extract will be capturing any DML changes made while the load is running.

3. Once the initial load is done from the standby to the primary database, stop the application running against the standby database. At this time be sure to leave the Local Extract running on the standby database so it can capture any remaining database transactions.

4. Start the Replicat on the primary database to prepare to process the changes that were made on the standby database as shown in the following example:

```
GGSCI (primaryserver) > START REPLICAT RHREMD3
```

5. Start the data-pump Extract to send database change transactions to be processed by the Replicat. Once the replication is complete and the lag is showing "At EOF, no more records to process", you can stop the Extracts and Replicats as shown in the following example:

```
GGSCI (standbyserver) > START EXTRACT PHREMD3
```

```
GGSCI (primaryserver) > LAG REPLICAT RHREMD3
Sending GETLAG request to REPLICAT RHREMD3 ...
Last record lag: 6 seconds.
At EOF, no more records to process.

GGSCI (primaryserver) > STOP REPLICAT RHREMD3
```

```
GGSCI (standbyserver) > STOP EXTRACT LHREMD3
GGSCI (standbyserver) > STOP EXTRACT PHREMD3
```

■ **Note** Once you have finished synchronizing the primary and standby databases, you should perform data validation. You can do this manually with sql queries for row counts and selected data values, or use an automated tool such as Oracle GoldenGate Veridata. Refer to Chapter 9 for more information on Veridata.

The last part is to move the users and the application back to the primary database and restart the original replication configuration from the primary to the secondary database. Let's review those steps in part 5, as shown in Figure 12-13.

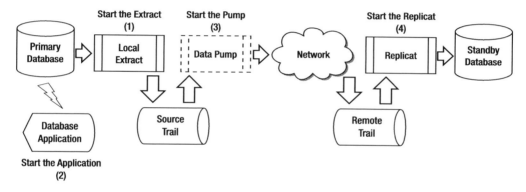

Figure 12-13. Disaster recovery unplanned failover, part 5

Following is a description of the steps in part 5 as shown in Figure 12-13.

1. To begin capturing changes in preparation for the application switchback to the primary database, alter the Local Extract for the primary database to begin capturing changes beginning *now* and then start the Extract as follows:

```
GGSCI (primaryserver) > ALTER EXTRACT LHREMD2, BEGIN NOW
GGSCI (primaryserver) > START EXTRACT LHREMD2
```

2. Prepare the primary database for the application and start the application connected to the primary database. In preparation, you may need to grant some SQL permissions to your application users. Also remember to enable any triggers or cascade delete constraints you may have stopped while the primary database was the replication target.

3. Start the data-pump Extract on the primary database as shown in the following example:

```
GGSCI (primaryserver) > START EXTRACT PHREMD2
```

4. Start the the Replicat on the standby database as shown in the following example:

```
GGSCI (standbyserver) > START REPLICAT RHREMD2
```

Now you have completed Part 5 of the unplanned failover process and the databases are back to their original configuration. The standby is now synchronized and ready for the next switchover or failover.

Summary

In this chapter we covered how to set up and configure GoldenGate replication for disaster recovery purposes. We showed how to configure GoldenGate to support a planned switchover scenario to minimize the application outage window during database maintenance. We also showed how to configure GoldenGate to failover to the standby database and back to the primary during unplanned disasters. If you want additional information on using GoldenGate to maintain a standby database, you can also refer to the *GoldenGate Windows and UNIX Administrator's Guide*. In the next chapter, we'll cover another specific use of GoldenGate for zero downtime migrations and upgrades.

CHAPTER 13

Zero-Downtime Migration Replication

Many IT organizations today are trapped for too long with old releases of software and old database hardware platforms because they can't tolerate the downtime involved with migrating to new software releases and hardware platforms. Even planned database outages for busy online websites can result in lost revenue and make customers angry. Oracle GoldenGate can help with these challenges by providing a way to implement the new, upgraded database platform ahead of time and have it ready and waiting for the application to cutover. The only downtime needed is the time for the application to cutover and reconnect to the new target database. Also, by replicating from the new upgraded target back to the old source database, Oracle GoldenGate can provide a way to easily fall back to the old database if there are problems with the migration. In addition, Oracle GoldenGate has the advantage of working across many different heterogeneous databases and hardware platforms. For example, you can use Oracle GoldenGate to migrate from NonStop SQL/MX to the latest release of an Oracle database on Red Hat Linux. Using Oracle GoldenGate, you can develop standard zero-downtime database migration processes and implement them across your organization, regardless of the specific DBMS or platform being used.

This chapter introduces another application of Oracle GoldenGate replication to implement a specific replication configuration for zero-downtime migration purposes. This chapter covers setting up and configuring Oracle GoldenGate replication for zero-downtime migrations. It covers how to handle both cutover to the new database and fallback from the new database to the old database if there are problems. This chapter refers to the database you're migrating from as the *old database* and the database you're migrating to as the *new database*.

Prerequisites

You need to have the following prerequisites in place before you can start setting up replication for zero-downtime migration:

- The Oracle GoldenGate software installed on the source and target servers as described in Chapter 2

- The Oracle GoldenGate database User ID created on the source and target databases

- The server name or IP address of the target database server

- The Oracle GoldenGate Manager process up and running on the source and the target

- TCP/IP network connectivity open from the source server to the target server's Oracle GoldenGate manager port and visa versa

- An understanding of the business and technical replication requirements of the planned migration

A few additional prerequisites are important for zero-downtime migration replication:

- Backups of your Oracle GoldenGate software and working directories on the source and target servers

- SQL scripts to grant any necessary object privileges required by your application during the cutover or fallback procedure

- Processes and scripts to move your application and users from the old to the new database and back again

Let's start by reviewing the requirements for zero-downtime migration replication.

Requirements

Before you begin to configure the replication, you must have a solid understanding of the specific requirements that drive the zero-downtime migration replication technical design. Here are some of the typical requirements. As a reminder, this section refers to the source database you're migrating from as the *old database* and the target database you're migrating to as the *new database*.

You need to ensure that you can meet these requirements using Oracle GoldenGate zero-downtime migration replication:

- Keep the old database you're migrating from synchronized with the new database. After the migration cutover, keep the old database synchronized for some period of time until you're certain there will be no fallback to the old database.

- The old database will actively process SQL changes until the migration cutover. Typically the cutover occurs during a scheduled weekend maintenance window or during a slow period for the website or application.

- During the interim period until the migration cutover, the new database can be used for read-only queries as needed. Although supported by Oracle GoldenGate's bidirectional replication feature, typically the data in the new database isn't being updated until after the cutover. If updating data in the new database before the cutover is a requirement for your project, you need to configure bidirectional replication to keep both databases synchronized.

- Database data and structures in the old database can be different than the new database. This depends on the type and complexity of migration. For example, specific data types or structures may need to change if you're migrating from a SQL Server database to an Oracle database. If you're simply migrating from an Oracle 10g to an Oracle 11g database, you may have the exact same application data and data structures. You may also be using Oracle GoldenGate to migrate other types of applications from old to new releases, and the data structures in those cases may be different.

- Data in the old database must be kept current with the new database, and there should be no replication lag at the time of cutover or fallback. Before the cutover or fallback some lag can be tolerated, but the lag must be eventually eliminated prior to the application cutover or fallback. Any replication lag present at the time of cutover could cause a delay.

- Cutover to the new database and fallback from the new database to the old database must happen quickly to minimize any downtime. Keep in mind that Oracle GoldenGate is only one piece the greater migration project, and you need tested procedures in place for all parts of your migration project, such as switching your application connections.

- After cutover to the new database, the database roles are reversed and the new database becomes the replication source and the old database becomes the target. This allows for migration fallback to the old database if needed.

- The time period permitted for the cutover and fallback procedures should be well understood. For example, a two-hour window for cutover and fallback has much different requirements than if an entire weekend is allowed for the cutover.

Now that you have an understanding of the replication requirements, let's review the zero-downtime migration topology.

Zero-Downtime Migration Topology

The underlying topology for zero-downtime migration is one-way replication, with a few changes for zero-downtime migration, as shown in Figure 13-1. Chapter 3, "Architecture," covered the concepts of one-way replication. One-way replication is the simplest topology and is often used for reporting or query offloading purposes. In this chapter, one-way replication topology is used for zero-downtime migration purposes. Data is replicated from a single source database to a single target database in only one direction at a time. Changes to database data are only made at the source database and then replicated to the target database. The source database is the old database you're migrating from prior to the migration. After the migration cutover to the new database, the replication is reversed and data is replicated back from the new database to the old database to allow for migration fallback. This backward replication can stay in place for as long as needed. Once you're sure you'll stay on the new database and fallback isn't needed, you can turn off the backward replication. Usually this period is a few days to a few weeks, but it can be longer if needed.

In order to meet the zero-downtime migration requirements covered in the last section, you have to ensure that you can quickly and accurately switch the application activity from the old database to the new database and back again. Also, you must be able to replicate back from the new database to the old database in case a fallback is needed from the migration due to problems. Figure 13-1 indicates that with a dotted arrow.

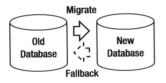

Figure 13-1. Zero-downtime migration replication topology

Now let's look at how to implement the replication requirements and topology using Oracle GoldenGate.

Setup

Once the prerequisites are complete, setting up zero-downtime migration replication can be accomplished in two parts and seven total steps, as shown in Figured 13-2 and 13-3. The steps are similar to setting up basic one-way replication, as covered in Chapter 4. Part 1 includes the first four steps for setting up replication from the old database to the new database. These steps include initially loading the data and then keeping the data synchronized after the initial load. Part 2 includes the last three steps for configuring replication back from the new database to the old should it be needed for fallback. Because Chapter 4 covered the Oracle GoldenGate parameter files, this section only explains new concepts as needed.

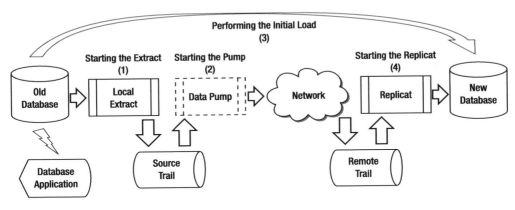

Figure 13-2. Zero-downtime migration replication setup, part 1

The example migrates the PAYROLL database to a new database software release. In the Oracle GoldenGate parameter files, you can use the PR abbreviation to indicate the payroll application. In addition, there are two tables that contain data that doesn't need to be migrated, so you exclude those tables from the replication. The example could apply in many different specific migration scenarios, such as migrating from an Oracle 9i database on a Sun Solaris platform to an Oracle 11g database on a Red Hat Linux platform. Keep in mind that whatever database or application you happen to be migrating, the concepts and steps are similar to this example. It can get more complicated if, for example, you're migrating heterogeneous databases or doing complex application migrations. In that case, you may have more complex Oracle GoldenGate mapping or transformation filters and parameters, but the overall process is still the same. Oracle GoldenGate can handle those mappings and transformations as demonstrated in the previous chapters. Because Chapter 4 covered steps 1-4 in detail, let's move on to the detailed steps for part 2.

In part 2 of the initial setup, you configure, but don't start, the replication back from the new database to the old database, as shown in Figure 13-3. These steps are necessary to set up the replication for migration fallback if needed. The three steps include setting up and configuring the Local Extract, data-pump Extract, and Replicat. These Extracts and Replicats are used later for the fallback scenario.

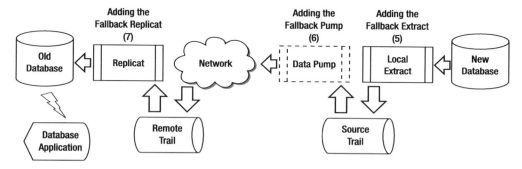

Figure 13-3. Zero-downtime migration replication setup, part 2

Following are descriptions for steps 5-7, as shown in Figure 13-3:

1. Configure and add the fallback Extract. The fallback Extract is started later to capture changes after the migration cutover and used for fallback if needed.

2. Configure and add the fallback data-pump Extract, which is started later after the migration cutover and used for fallback if needed.

3. Add the fallback Replicat, which is started later after the migration cutover and used for fallback if needed.

Let's look at each of the zero-downtime migration replication steps in the next section, beginning with setting up and starting the Local Extract.

Configuring the Local Extract for Zero-Downtime Migration

After you've verified that the prerequisites are complete, the first step in setting up zero-downtime migration replication is to configure, add, and start the Local Extract. Remember that you should start the Extract first to begin capturing changes made while the initial data load is running. If you can afford to take an application outage and stop all change activity on the source database while the initial load is running, then you can start the Extract after the initial load.

Refer to Chapter 4 for detailed steps for starting the Extract. This section covers only the specific configuration for the zero-downtime migration Extract.

Let's begin by configuring the Local Extract. In order to do this, you first need to create a parameter file for the Extract. Remember, you're configuring the Local Extract to capture all the SQL DML changes from the example PAYROLL schema.

Let's look at the parameters for the Local Extract as shown in the following example:

```
GGSCI (oldserver) 1> edit params LPREMP1

Extract LPREMP1

-------------------------------------------------------------------
-- Local extract for PAYROLL database
-------------------------------------------------------------------

USERID GGER, PASSWORD userpw

ExtTrail dirdat/p1

ReportCount Every 10000 Records, Rate
Report at 00:30

DiscardFile dirrpt/LPREMP1.dsc, Append
DiscardRollover at 02:00

Table PAYROLL.*;
TableExclude PAYROLL.EXCLUDETABLE1;
TableExclude PAYROLL.EXCLUDETABLE2;
```

Remember from the Oracle GoldenGate naming conventions for the Local Extract group name that the *L* is used to designate the Local Extract. Because you're replicating the PAYROLL database, you can use PR as the abbreviation for PAYROLL in the Local Extract name. You can use EM to indicate that the PAYROLL database is part of the employee application. You exclude the two tables that don't need to be replicated, EXCLUDETABLE1 and EXCLUDETABLE2, with the TableExclude parameter. Notice that you're replicating all of the tables in the PAYROLL database using the asterisk as a wildcard and then excluding *only* the two tables you don't want to replicate.

Now that you've set up the Extract configuration parameters on the old server, the next step is to add the Extract group. You can do that using the following commands from the GoldenGate Software Command Interface (GGSCI):

```
GGSCI (oldserver) > ADD EXTRACT LPREMP1, TRANLOG, BEGIN NOW
GGSCI (oldserver) > ADD EXTTRAIL dirdat/p1, EXTRACT LPREMP1, MEGABYTES 500
```

You can use p1 as the Local Extract trail file name. Because the payroll application has a high volume of data changes, you make the trail file size 500MB.

After adding the Extract, you need to start it to actually begin capturing changes as shown in the following example:

```
GGSCI (oldserver) > START EXTRACT LPREMP1
```

Next, let's check to make sure the Extract is running properly, using the INFO command:

```
GGSCI (oldserver) 2> INFO EXTRACT LPREMP1
```

If the Extract isn't running, you can review the Oracle GoldenGate error log and report file and try to resolve the problem.

You should also run the STATS command on your Extract. This shows if the Extract has processed any DML changes:

```
GGSCI (oldserver) 2> STATS EXT LPREMP1
```

You're now finished adding, starting, and verifying the Local Extract, so let's move on to the next step: starting the data-pump Extract.

Configuring the Data Pump for Zero-Downtime Migration

When the Local Extract is started, you can proceed with configuring, adding, and starting the data pump. In this example, you configure the data pump to read the p1 trail file written out by the Local Extract named LPREMP1 on the old server and pump it over the TCP/IP network to the target server to be processed by the Replicat on the new server.

From GGSCI, you can edit the parameters for the data pump as shown in this example:

```
GGSCI (oldserver) 1> edit params PPREMP1

Extract PPREMP1


--------------------------------------------------------------------
-- Data-pump Extract for PAYROLL database
--------------------------------------------------------------------

PassThru

ReportCount Every 10000 Records, Rate
Report at 00:30

DiscardFile dirrpt/PPREMP1.dsc, Append
DiscardRollover at 02:00

RmtHost newserver, MgrPort 7809
RmtTrail dirdat/p2

Table PAYROLL.*;
TableExclude PAYROLL.EXCLUDETABLE1;
TableExclude PAYROLL.EXCLUDETABLE2;
```

Now that you've set up your data-pump Extract configuration parameters, the next step is to add the data-pump Extract group on the old server. You can do that using the commands shown in the following example:

```
GGSCI (oldserver) > ADD EXTRACT PPREMP1, EXTTRAILSOURCE dirdat/p1
GGSCI (oldserver) > ADD RMTTRAIL dirdat/p2, EXTRACT PPREMP1, MEGABYTES 500
```

After adding the data-pump Extract, you need to start it to begin processing records from the source trail file:

```
GGSCI (oldserver) > START EXTRACT PPREMP1
```

Next, you can verify that the data-pump Extract has started using the INFO EXTRACT command:

```
GGSCI (oldserver) 2> INFO EXTRACT PPREMP1
```

You should see a Status of RUNNING. If you see a Status of STOPPED or ABENDED, there may be a problem.

You should also run the STATS command on the data-pump Extract to confirm it's processing data:

```
GGSCI (oldserver) 2> STATS EXT PPREMP1
```

Now that the Local Extract and Data-pump Extract are started, you can begin the initial data load.

You learned about the different methods for initially loading data in Chapter 4. These methods also work for the initial data load for the zero-downtime migration replication. Remember that the initial load process is happening during the period *prior* to the actual application migration cutover. This period can be a few days, weeks, or even months before the actual cutover. You can perform the initial load and have the data synchronized, waiting for the scheduled cutover window. You can use either Oracle GoldenGate itself or the DBMS vendor load utilities to do the initial data load. Refer to Chapter 4 for more details on the initial load process.

Configuring the Replicat for Zero-Downtime Migration

After you've loaded your data, you can start the Replicat to apply the changes that have been captured by the Extract while the initial data load was running. These changes have been queued up in the trail files while the load was running and are waiting to be applied by the Replicat. After you've configured, added, and successfully started the Replicat, the changes from the trail are applied to the target tables.

When the initial changes have been applied and there is no Oracle GoldenGate lag left, the databases are fully synchronized. At this point, the Local and data-pump Extracts and Replicat can continue to run and keep the old and new databases synchronized in real time with the ongoing changes. The new database is ready and waiting for the application to cutover for the migration.

This section covers the various ongoing change Replicat configuration settings and options. After that, it discusses how to start the Replicat and verify that it's properly applying changes to the target. Let's begin with configuring the Replicat.

Before you start to configure the Replicat, you should go back and double check the Oracle GoldenGate prerequisites on the target server, as covered in the earlier section "Prerequisites." Then you can begin configuring the Replicat. In order to do this, you first need to create a parameter file for the Replicat. Remember, you're configuring the Replicat to apply all the SQL DML changes from the PAYROLL database, except for the two tables you're excluding.

Let's look at the Replicat parameters for RPREMP1 on the new server, as shown in the following example:

```
GGSCI (newserver) 1> edit params RPREMP1

Replicat RPREMP1

-------------------------------------------------------------------
-- Replicat for PAYROLL database
-------------------------------------------------------------------

USERID GGER, PASSWORD userpw

ReportCount Every 10000 Records, Rate
Report at 00:30
```

```
DiscardFile dirrpt/RPREMP1.dsc, Append
DiscardRollover at 02:00

-- HandleCollisions should be turned off after the initial load synchronization.
HandleCollisions

AssumeTargetDefs

Map PAYROLL.*, Target PAYROLL.* ;
```

You may wonder why you don't exclude the two tables that you excluded in the Extracts. The reason is that the tables were already excluded in the Extracts, so the data isn't included in the trail files being processed by the Replicat. You can simply tell Oracle GoldenGate to apply all the data in the trail file for the PAYROLL database, which doesn't include the two excluded tables.

Now that you've set up the Replicat configuration parameters, the next step is to add the Replicat group. The following example adds the RPREMP1 Replicat to the Oracle GoldenGate configuration:

```
GGSCI (newserver) > ADD REPLICAT RPREMP1, EXTTRAIL dirdat/p2
```

■ **Tip** When adding your Replicat, you can use a specific checkpoint table name in the database or use the default database checkpoint table specified in the GLOBALS file, as discussed in Chapter 5. You can also specify NODBCHECKPOINT to indicate that the Replicat will only write checkpoints to a file on disk.

After adding the Replicat, you need to start it to actually begin applying changes to the target database. The following example starts the Replicat RPREMP1 on the new server:

```
GGSCI (newserver) > START REPLICAT RPREMP1
```

You can verify that the Replicat is running using the INFO REPLICAT command. You should see a Status of RUNNING. If you see a Status of STOPPED or ABENDED, there may be a problem.

Let's do an INFO command on the Replicat RPREMP1 to check the status:

```
GGSCI (newserver) 2> INFO REPLICAT RPREMP1
```

After verifying that the Replicat is running, you should also confirm that the Replicat is processing data using the STATS command.

■ **Note** When you're finished synchronizing the old and the new databases, you should perform data validation. There may be cases where the data isn't replicated properly, or perhaps there is an error in the configuration. You can do data validation manually with SQL queries for row counts and some selected data values, or use an automated tool such as Oracle GoldenGate Veridata. Refer to Chapter 9 for more information on Veridata.

Next, let's add the Oracle GoldenGate processes for the replication from the new database back to the old database.

Configuring the Fallback Local Extract for Zero-Downtime Migration

When you're successfully replicating from the old database to the new database, the next part is to add the fallback Extract. For now, you're only *adding* the Extract. Later, you *start* it after the application cutover activities.

Let's begin by configuring the fallback Local Extract. In the example, you're configuring the Local Extract to capture all the SQL DML changes from the PAYROLL database on the new database, except two tables that are being excluded. Because you've already used trail files **p1** and **p2**, you can use trail files **p3** and **p4** for replication from the new database back to the old database.

Begin by reviewing the parameters for the Local Extract on the new server, as shown in the following example:

```
GGSCI (newserver) 1> edit params LPREMP2

Extract LPREMP2

------------------------------------------------------------------
-- Local extract for PAYROLL database
------------------------------------------------------------------

USERID GGER, PASSWORD userpw

ExtTrail dirdat/p3

ReportCount Every 10000 Records, Rate
Report at 00:30

DiscardFile dirrpt/LPREMP2.dsc, Append
DiscardRollover at 02:00

Table PAYROLL.*;
TableExclude PAYROLL.EXCLUDETABLE1;
TableExclude PAYROLL.EXCLUDETABLE2;
```

Next, add the fallback Extract to the Oracle GoldenGate configuration so you're ready to start it after the application migration cutover. You can do that using the following commands from GGSCI:

```
GGSCI (newserver) > ADD EXTRACT LPREMP2, TRANLOG, BEGIN NOW
GGSCI (newserver) > ADD EXTTRAIL dirdat/p3, EXTRACT LPREMP2, MEGABYTES 500
```

You start the fallback Local Extract later after the application cutover. Next, let's add the fallback data pump.

Configuring the Fallback Data-Pump for Zero-Downtime Migration

With the fallback Local Extract added, you can configure and add the fallback data pump. In this example, you configure the data pump to read the **p3** trail file written out by the fallback Local Extract named LPREMP2 and pump it over the TCP/IP network to the old server to be processed by the Replicat.

From GGSCI, you can edit and review the parameters for the data pump as shown here:

```
GGSCI (newserver) 1> edit params PPREMP2

Extract PPREMP2

----------------------------------------------------------------------
-- Data-pump Extract for PAYROLL database
----------------------------------------------------------------------

PassThru

ReportCount Every 10000 Records, Rate
Report at 00:30

DiscardFile dirrpt/PPREMP2.dsc, Append
DiscardRollover at 02:00

RmtHost oldserver, MgrPort 7809
RmtTrail dirdat/p4

Table PAYROLL.*;
TableExclude PAYROLL.EXCLUDETABLE1;
TableExclude PAYROLL.EXCLUDETABLE2;
```

The next step is to add the data-pump Extract group. You can do that using the following commands:

```
GGSCI (newserver) > ADD EXTRACT PPREMP2, EXTTRAILSOURCE dirdat/p3
GGSCI (newserver) > ADD RMTTRAIL dirdat/p4, EXTRACT PPREMP2, MEGABYTES 500
```

You don't start the data pump until later, so let's move on to adding the fallback Replicat.

Configuring the Fallback Replicat for Zero-Downtime Migration

Next you should add a fallback Replicat that will be ready to apply any changes to your old database after the application migration cutover. By adding it now, before it's needed, you're ready to start it when needed.

First create a parameter file for the Replicat. You're configuring the Replicat to apply all the DML changes from the newly migrated PAYROLL database back to the old database in case of fallback. Notice that you removed the HANDLECOLLISIONS parameter from the fallback Replicat. You shouldn't have any collisions at this point because the databases are already synchronized.

Let's look at the Replicat parameters for RPREMP2, as shown in the following example:

```
GGSCI (newserver) 1> edit params RPREMP2

Replicat RPREMP2

----------------------------------------------------------------------
-- Replicat for PAYROLL database
----------------------------------------------------------------------
```

```
USERID GGER, PASSWORD userpw

ReportCount Every 10000 Records, Rate
Report at 00:30

DiscardFile dirrpt/RPREMP2.dsc, Append
DiscardRollover at 02:00

AssumeTargetDefs

Map PAYROLL.*, Target PAYROLL.* ;
```

The next step is to add the Replicat group. Here's you're adding the RPREMP2 Replicat to the Oracle GoldenGate configuration:

```
GGSCI (oldserver) > ADD REPLICAT RPREMP2, EXTTRAIL dirdat/p4
```

Remember, you won't start the fallback Replicat until after the application migration cutover to the new database.

You're now finished with the initial setup for the zero-downtime migration replication. All the steps you've completed so far are in preparation for the application cutover. With old and the new databases synchronized, you're prepared for the cutover to the new database during your migration window.

Performing the Migration Cutover

During the migration cutover, you switch your database application from the old database to the new database. After the application is cutover to the new database, replication is reversed back to the old database to allow for fallback.

This section goes through the steps using Oracle GoldenGate replication to cutover to the new database. To keep it simple, the migration cutover is divided into two parts, each with several steps (see Figure 13-4). Let's begin with part 1.

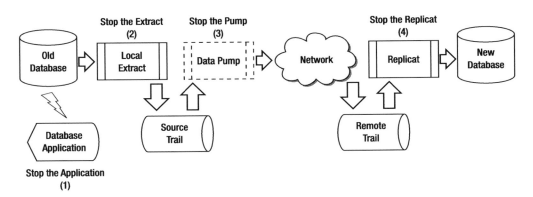

Figure 13-4. Zero-downtime migration cutover, part 1

Following are descriptions for steps 1-4 as shown in Figure 13-4:

1. Stop the application connected to the old database.

2. After verifying that there is no lag, stop the Local Extract as shown in the following example:

```
GGSCI (oldserver) > LAG EXTRACT LPREMP1
Sending GETLAG request to EXTRACT LPREMP1 ...
Last record lag: 10 seconds.
At EOF, no more records to process.
GGSCI (oldserver) > STOP EXTRACT LPREMP1
```

3. After verifying that there is no lag, stop the data-pump Extract as shown here:

```
GGSCI (oldserver) > LAG EXTRACT PPREMP1
Sending GETLAG request to EXTRACT PPREMP1 ...
Last record lag: 6 seconds.
At EOF, no more records to process.
GGSCI (oldserver) > STOP EXTRACT PPREMP1
```

4. After verifying that there are no more records to process, stop the Replicat as shown here:

```
GGSCI (newserver) > LAG REPLICAT RPREMP1
Sending GETLAG request to REPLICAT RPREMP1 ...
Last record lag: 7 seconds.
At EOF, no more records to process.
GGSCI (newserver) > STOP REPLICAT RPREMP1
```

Now the old database is no longer being used by the application, and the replication from the old database to the new database is stopped. You can proceed to part 2 (see Figure 13-5) and start the fallback Extract and switch the application to use the new database.

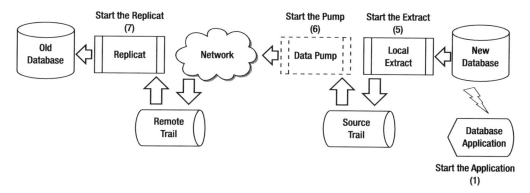

Figure 13-5. Zero-downtime migration cutover, part 2

Following are descriptions for steps 1-4 as shown in Figure 13-5:

1. To begin capturing changes made to the new database in preparation for the application cutover, alter the Local Extract for the new database to begin capturing changes and then start it as follows:

   GGSCI (newserver) > ALTER EXTRACT LPREMP2. BEGIN NOW

   GGSCI (newserver) > START EXTRACT LPREMP2

2. Prepare the new database for the application, and start the application connected to the new database. In preparation, you may need to grant some SQL permissions to your application users on the new database. Also remember to enable any triggers or cascade-delete constraints you may have stopped while the new database was the replication target.

3. Start the data-pump Extract on the new database as shown in the following example:

   GGSCI (oldserver) > START EXTRACT PPREMP2

4. Start the Replicat on the old database as shown next. Make sure to disable any triggers or cascade-delete constraints on the old database before processing the Oracle GoldenGate changes from the new database:

   GGSCI (newserver) > START REPLICAT RPREMP2

Performing the Migration Fallback

After completing the migration, you may decide you need to revert back to your original database due to problems or for other reasons. This section covers the steps necessary to fall back. These steps are divided into two parts: in part 1, you stop the replication from the new database back to the old database (see Figure 13-6); and in part 2, you start the replication back up again from the old database to the new database in preparation for the next cutover attempt.

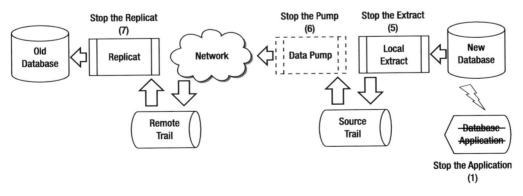

Figure 13-6. Zero-downtime migration fallback, part 1

Following are descriptions for steps 1-4 as shown in Figure 13-6:

1. Stop the application running against the new database. At this time, be sure to leave the Local Extract running so it can capture any remaining database transactions.

2. After verifying that there is no lag, stop the Local Extract on the new database as shown in the following example:

```
GGSCI (newserver) > LAG EXTRACT LPREMP2
Sending GETLAG request to EXTRACT LPREMP2 ...
Last record lag: 5 seconds.
At EOF, no more records to process.
GGSCI (newserver) > STOP EXTRACT LPREMP2
```

3. After verifying that there is no lag, stop the data-pump Extract on the new database:

```
GGSCI (newserver) > LAG EXTRACT PHREMD2
Sending GETLAG request to EXTRACT PHREMD2 ...
Last record lag: 4 seconds.
At EOF, no more records to process.
GGSCI (newserver) > STOP EXTRACT PHREMD2
```

4. After verifying that there are no more records to process, stop the Replicat on the old database:

```
GGSCI (oldserver) > LAG REPLICAT RHREMD2
Sending GETLAG request to REPLICAT RHREMD2 ...
Last record lag: 6 seconds.
At EOF, no more records to process.
GGSCI (oldserver) > STOP REPLICAT RHREMD2
```

Now that the replication from the new database to the old database is complete and stopped, you can proceed with restarting the original replication from the old database to the new database in part 2, as shown in Figure 13-7.

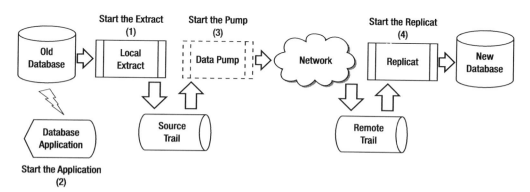

Figure 13-7. Zero-downtime migration fallback, part 2

Following are descriptions for steps 1-4 as shown in Figure 13-7:

1. To begin capturing changes in preparation for the application switchover back to the old database, alter the Local Extract for the old database to begin capturing changes and then start the Extract as follows:

   GGSCI (oldserver) > ALTER EXTRACT LPREMP1, BEGIN NOW

   GGSCI (oldserver) > START EXTRACT LPREMP1

2. Prepare the old database for the application, and start the application connected to the old database. In preparation, you may need to grant some SQL permissions to your application users. Also remember to enable any triggers or cascade-delete constraints you may have stopped while the old database was the replication target.

3. Start the data-pump Extract on the old database, as shown in the following example:

   GGSCI (oldserver) > START EXTRACT PPREMP1

4. Start the the Replicat on the new database. Make sure to disable any triggers or cascade-delete constraints on the new database before processing the Oracle GoldenGate changes from the old database:

   GGSCI (newserver) > START REPLICAT RPREMP1

The databases are back to their original configuration and ready for the next cutover attempt after any issues are resolved.

Summary

This chapter covered how to set up and configure Oracle GoldenGate replication to support a zero-downtime database migration scenario. First you set up the basic Oracle GoldenGate processes for forward and reverse replication from the old to the new databases. Then, you saw how to configure Oracle GoldenGate to support the migration cutover to the new database and also fall back to the old database if needed. For an additional reference on zero-downtime migrations, Oracle has a whitepaper titled *Zero-Downtime Database Upgrades Using Oracle GoldenGate* available on the Oracle Technology Network website, `www.oracle.com/technetwork/middleware/goldengate/overview/ggzerodowntimedatabaseupgrades-174928.pdf`.

The next chapter covers some Oracle GoldenGate tips and tricks to help you set up and manage your Oracle GoldenGate replication environment in the best possible manner.

CHAPTER 14

Tips and Tricks

Over the years of using GoldenGate, we've learned a number of helpful tips and tricks. This chapter looks at some that you can use when you're setting up and managing GoldenGate replication. These suggestions should save you time in getting your environment up and running in the best possible fashion. Keep in mind that these tips are based on many different experiences, and they will generally give the best results. However, systems have different needs and requirements, so these shortcuts may not be applicable in your case. Also keep in mind that the tips and tricks will change over time as GoldenGate and the technology evolve. You should always consult the standard Oracle GoldenGate product documentation, which is the official guide for using the product.

Requirements and Planning

This section is focused on preparing for your GoldenGate replication setup. This process is often shortchanged or skipped altogether, which later results in mistakes that end up costing more in the long run. You should ensure that your project devotes proper time and focus to gathering and understanding requirements and that all the stakeholders approve of the requirements. As with all projects, carefully planning the replication project helps ensure its success.

Knowing the Business Objectives

It's important for you to have a clear understanding of the business objectives for setting up GoldenGate. The business objectives drive many of the technical decisions around the replication setup. For example, if the business objectives can be achieved with one-way replication instead of bidirectional replication, the technical complexity is greatly reduced.

You can start by having an informal whiteboard session with the key team members and review the proposed scope and objectives for the replication. You can even begin to sketch out the high-level replication scenarios and flow so everyone understands what's involved. After that, you can formalize the rough-draft business objectives, share them with the team members, and ask for feedback. Finally, the project scope and objectives should be reviewed and approved by the major stakeholders.

Here are just a few examples of business objectives you can achieve with GoldenGate:

- Minimize downtime while migrating from Oracle database 10g to Oracle 11g.

- Create an integrated database made up of sales, customer, and product data into a new, read-only database for analysis and reporting.

- Offload intensive query and reporting activity from the primary OLTP database.

- Keep a copy of the primary database synchronized at an offsite location for disaster-recovery purposes.

- Create an enterprise data warehouse for business users with near real time data integrated from multiple heterogeneous source databases.

- Minimize downtime while moving to a new platform and ensuring that a backout plan is available.

Understanding the Requirements

You need to gain a solid understanding of the specific requirements that will drive the replication technical design. Here are some of the factors that impact the replication design:

- *Source and target configurations:* Describe the existing or planned source and target databases. What are the software releases for the database and operating system? Are the servers stand-alone or clustered? How is the data storage configured? What are the character sets for the source and target databases?

- *Data currency:* How quickly and how often does the data need to be updated? Can any lag in the data replication be tolerated? If no lag can be tolerated and there is a high volume of changes, you may need to devote more time in the project to designing and tuning the replication to avoid any lag. Keep in mind that often, reporting systems can tolerate lag, and the target data doesn't need to be completely up-to-date with the source.

- *Data volume:* How much data needs to be replicated? How often is it updated? You may be able to examine the existing database-transaction log files to determine the amount of data change that is occurring in the source database. The data-change volume impacts the network bandwidth requirements between the source and target and the amount of disk space required for trail files.

- *Data requirements:* You should understand any unique or special data requirements so they can be handled properly in GoldenGate. For example, if there are triggers, they may need to be disabled in the target database. Sequences need special parameters added if they need to be replicated. Certain data types may need special handling or may not be supported. For example, in GoldenGate 11, data types such as BFILE and ANYDATA aren't supported. Other data types may be supported but with certain limitations. *(Be sure to check the Oracle GoldenGate product documentation for a list of data types supported.)*

- *Security requirements:* How much security is required? For example, is it necessary to encrypt the data GoldenGate is replicating? GoldenGate can encrypt both the data stored in trail files as well as the data being sent from the source to the target. Also, is the data in the database encrypted? For example, Oracle can encrypt database data using a feature called Transparent Data Encryption (TDE). If the database is using TDE, GoldenGate needs special parameters to unencrypt the data for replication. Finally, GoldenGate itself requires security to install and own the GoldenGate software and execute the replication inside the database. You need to plan for this and ensure that your organization allows the new users and security access required for GoldenGate.

- *Network requirements:* Describe the network between the source and the target. Are there any firewalls that need to be opened for the replication? What is the distance? How much bandwidth is required for the replication, and how much is available?

Determining the Topology

As discussed in Chapter 3, "Architecture," GoldenGate supports many different topologies. Each topology has its own unique requirements and complexities. Determining the topology as soon as possible can help drive the technical requirements and design. For example, a one-way replication topology is much simpler to set up than bidirectional replication. Replication involving a single source and target database is easier to set up than a single source and multiple target databases.

Installation and Setup

Now, let's look at some tips and tricks related to GoldenGate installation and setup. These include suggestions for setting up users, specifying Extract and Replicat parameters, and naming standards.

Creating Dedicated Users

You may be tempted to simply use the existing database and operating-system users for GoldenGate. Instead, you should create dedicated operating-system and database users only for use with GoldenGate. Doing so ensures that any activity from GoldenGate users can be tracked separately. If there is a database performance issue, for example, you can isolate activity from the GoldenGate database user to determine if it's causing a problem. Some example user names are *gger, gguser, ggate,* and so on.

Depending on your platform, GoldenGate users may require some elevated privileges that often are reserved for the DBA team. For example, with Microsoft SQL Server, a user with the System Administrators role is required for the Extract process. You need to determine, based on your organization's security requirements, whether the GoldenGate user should belong to the DBA team or a separate team. If the GoldenGate user ID isn't owned by the DBA team, then the GoldenGate responsibilities need to be divided between the DBA team and the GoldenGate team based on security required.

Encrypting Passwords

You should encrypt the GoldenGate database user passwords in any secured environment. The following example shows how to use GoldenGate to encrypt the password *abc* and specify it in the parameter file. The example uses a default encryption key, but you can use a specific key if needed.

```
GGSCI (server) 1> encrypt password abc
No key specified, using default key...

Encrypted password:  AACAAAAAAAAAAAADAVHTDKHHCSCPIKAFB
```

After you determine the encrypted value for the key, you can specify it in the Extract or Replicat parameter file as shown in the following example.

```
USERID "GGER", PASSWORD "AACAAAAAAAAAAAADAVHTDKHHCSCPIKAFB", ENCRYPTKEY default
```

Next let's review using a dedicated GoldenGate installation directory.

Creating a Dedicated Installation Directory

You should install the GoldenGate software in its own separate directory, which is owned by the dedicated GoldenGate operating-system user. This keeps the GoldenGate software and other files separate and allows them to be located and monitored quickly and easily. Because the GoldenGate software is specific to a DMBS vendor release, you may want to qualify the subdirectory by the DBMS release. Example installation directories are /gger/ggs/ora10 for an Oracle 10 GoldenGate installation and c:\ggate\sql2008 for a SQL Server 2008 installation.

Using a Checkpoint Table

You should add a checkpoint table in your target database to keep track of checkpoints for your Replicats. By default, GoldenGate keeps track of checkpoints in a file on disk. If you add a checkpoint file to the database, GoldenGate makes the checkpoint part of the Replicat transaction, which permits better recoverability in some situations. The following example creates the checkpoint table:

```
GGSCI (targetserver) 1> dblogin userid gger password abc
Successfully logged into database.

GGSCI (targetserver) 2> add checkpointtable gger.chkpt

Successfully created checkpoint table GGER.CHKPT.
```

You should add the CHECKPOINTTABLE parameter to your GLOBALS file in the GoldenGate software installation directory (for example /gger/ggs) so the checkpoint table is used for all of your Replicats as shown here:

```
CHECKPOINTTABLE gger.chkpt
```

Verifying the Character Sets

Sometimes you replicate between databases with different database character sets. It's always a good idea to explicitly set the database character set inside the parameter file using the **SETENV** command. This way, you won't accidentally pick up a default character set from your environment settings that may be incorrect.

The following example shows how to set the database character set in the GoldenGate Extract or Replicat parameter file.

```
SETENV (NLS_LANG = AMERICAN_AMERICA.AL32UTF8)
```

Next we'll cover using naming standards for your GoldenGate components.

Developing Naming Standards

Develop naming standards for your Extract and Replicat groups. Doing so helps you identify at a glance what the Extract or Replicat is used for and where it's running. Naming standards are especially important in problem-solving situations where you need to get downed replication up and running again quickly. The current limitation for Extract and Replicat group names is eight characters.

Here are some items you should include in the patterns you create for your naming standard:

- The type of process, such as Extract, Data Pump, or Replicat

- The application that is using the process, such as payroll, sales, or billing

- The environment context where the process is running, such as development or production

- An indicator to show if there are multiple Extract or Replicat groups

For example, a Replicat group named RPAYRP1 is the *first Replicat* for the *payroll* application (PAYR) running in *production*. You can easily tell RPAYRP1 is a Replicat, because the first character is an *R*. The *P1* at the end indicates the first Replicat running in the production environment.

Naming standards can also be developed for trail files, although you're limited to only two characters. You can use the first character to indicate whether a trail was created by the local Extract or by the data-pump Extract. The second character can be any valid letter or number. For example, trail P1 can be used for a data-pump trail.

Using a Data Pump

Although technically a data-pump Extract isn't necessary, you should almost always use a data pump. The local Extract can be configured to send changes directly from the source server to the remote target without a data pump. Adding a data pump to the configuration, however, introduces another protective layer to insulate the local Extract from any disruptions caused by the network connection to the target or from a problem with the target itself.

For example, if there was a network issue between the source and the target, this could cause the local Extract to fail. By having a data pump between the source and the target, the local Extract can continue to extract changes, and only the data pump is impacted. This way, when the network issue is resolved, you can restart the data pump and quickly process the queued changes that the local Extract has already captured in the trail. Keep in mind that the data pump requires an extra trail file, so you should make sure to allow some extra disk space in your configuration.

Management and Monitoring

This section covers some tips and tricks that make it easier to manage and monitor your GoldenGate environment. By utilizing these suggestions, you can simplify the day-to-day management of your GoldenGate setup and ensure that it stays up and running smoothly.

Using GGSCI Command Shortcuts

By now you should be familiar with the GoldenGate Software Command Interface (GGSCI) and many of the basic GGSCI commands. Let's look at some shortcuts that may not be as familiar. These can save you a lot of time (and typing!).

You can use common abbreviations in your commands, such as *ext* for *Extract*, *rep* for *Replicat*, *mgr* for *Manager*, and *er* to refer to both Extracts and Replicats. Let's look at a few examples using the INFO command on Extracts, Replicats, and, in the third example, both Extracts and Replicats.

```
GGSCI (server) 1> info ext *
GGSCI (server) 2> info rep *
GGSCI (server) 3> info er *
```

Now, let's use the exclamation point (!) command to reexecute the last INFO command.

```
GGSCI (server) 4> !
info er *
```

Notice that the ! command reexecuted the info er * command. Next, let's reexecute the second command info rep * by adding the specific command number 2 to the ! as shown here.

```
GGSCI (server) 5> ! 2
info rep *
```

Suppose you want to execute an operating-system command to display your current directory contents while you're inside GGSCI. You can do this with the SHELL command, as shown in the following example.

```
GGSCI (server) 6> shell dir
```

You can quickly see information about your GoldenGate environment using the SHOW command. SHOW is especially helpful to get a quick listing of your GoldenGate directories.

```
GGSCI (server) 7> show

Parameter settings:

SET SUBDIRS     ON
SET DEBUG       OFF

Current directory: /gger/ggs

Using subdirectories for all process files

Editor:  vi

Reports (.rpt)                    /gger/ggs/dirrpt
```

```
Parameters (.prm)              /gger/ggs/dirprm
Stdout (.out)                  /gger/ggs/dirout
Replicat Checkpoints (.cpr)    /gger/ggs/dirchk
Extract Checkpoints (.cpe)     /gger/ggs/dirchk
Process Status (.pcs)          /gger/ggs/dirpcs
SQL Scripts (.sql)             /gger/ggs/dirsql
Database Definitions (.def)    /gger/ggs/dirdef
```

Now, let's display the history of the commands you've executed by using the HISTORY command as shown in the following example.

```
GGSCI (server) 8> history

GGSCI Command History

    1: info ext *
    2: info rep *
    3: info er *
    4: info er *
    5: info rep *
    6: shell dir
    7: show
    8: history
```

By using HISTORY combined with the ! command, you can really save time. You can use the ! # command to reexecute any command number contained in your history. For example, ! 7 reexecutes command number 7, which in this case is the SHOW command.

Finally, you can use HELP to get help on any of the GoldenGate commands as shown here.

```
GGSCI (server) 9> help
```

Next, let's look at OBEY files, which are another tool to make it even easier to manage GoldenGate.

Using OBEY Files

You should store your frequently used commands in GoldenGate OBEY files. OBEY files are command files (similar to .bat files in Windows or shell scripts in UNIX) that you OBEY files in the /diroby directory under your GoldenGate installation. You can name the OBEY files anything; but it's a good idea to have a naming standard, such as using a standard filename extension like .obey.

Let's look at an example OBEY file. Assume you want to add an Extract for your production payroll data named LPAYRP1 along with the corresponding trail file. You can create an OBEY file to add the Extract as shown in the following example.

```
$ cat diroby/LPAYRP1.obey

ADD EXTRACT LPAYRP1, TRANLOG, BEGIN NOW
ADD EXTTRAIL /gger/dirdat/l1,  EXTRACT LPAYRP1,  MEGABYTES 25

GGSCI (sourceserver) 1> obey ./dirdat/LPAYRP1.obey
```

Using OBEY files gives the added advantage that your files are stored centrally as a good reference and can be reused. You can create a standard set of OBEY files and ensure a consistent, reusable, scripted process for your GoldenGate setup and maintenance. Anyone supporting the replication can easily find the files you used to set up the replication. In addition, if something goes wrong, you always have your scripts to use as a reference point.

Generating Interim Statistics

By default, GoldenGate generates a report each time an Extract or Replicat process is started. In addition, you should include the `REPORT` parameter to generate interim runtime statistics at least on a daily basis. This information can be invaluable when you're debugging or evaluating performance. You should also include the `REPORTCOUNT` parameter with the `RATE` argument to display the number of records being processed and the processing rate.

In the following example, Extract or Replicat parameters are configured to report the number of records processed every 15 minutes, report the processing rate, and generate interim runtime statistics every day at 12:00.

```
ReportCount Every 15 Minutes, Rate
Report at 12:00
```

Now let's look at using a discard file for records GoldenGate can't process.

Using a Discard File

You should specify a discard file in the Extract and Replicat parameter files. GoldenGate uses this file to write any records that it can't process along with the error code. You can use this file for debugging purposes in the event of failure. You should check the discard file for changes periodically and resolve any discards as soon as possible.

Here is an example of using the discard file parameters in the Extract parameter. We reviewed this in Chapter 5, "Advanced and Bi-Directional Features".

```
DiscardFile dirrpt/LHREMD1.dsc, Append
DiscardRollover at 02:00 ON SUNDAY
```

Next let's review reporting on the health of your GoldenGate processes.

Reporting Regularly on Process Health

You can use the GoldenGate Manager process to report on the health of the Extract and Replicat processes. At a minimum, you should consider including the following parameters in your Manager parameter file:

- `DOWNREPORT`: Reports on down processes every user-specified number of hours or minutes.

- `DOWNCRITICAL`: Writes a critical message if the Extract or Replicat fails.

- `LAGCRITICAL`: Writes a warning message when the user-specified time period is exceeded.

- `LAGINFO`: Tells Manager to report lag info every user-specified time period.

Purging Old Trail Files Regularly

Old trail files can accumulate and cause disk-space issues. Trail files can usually be purged after a couple days, but they can be kept for more or less time depending on your requirements and the amount of available disk space. You can specify automatic purge criteria in the Manager parameter file, as shown in the next example. Keep in mind that specifying the purge criteria using Manager applies to any Extracts and Replicats running under the Manager. This allows you to manage the purging criteria centrally.

The following example tells Manager to purge any trail files older than two days. The `UseCheckPoints` option tells Manager not to purge the files until *after* they have been processed, as shown in the following example.

```
PurgeOldExtracts dirdat/*, UseCheckPoints, MinKeepDays 2
```

Next let's look at some tips for automatically starting your GoldenGate processes.

Automatically Starting Processes

Use the `AUTOSTART` Manager parameter to have the GoldenGate Manager automatically start your Extract and Replicat processes when Manager starts. Another parameter, AUTORESTART, is also available but should be used with caution. Sometimes a process fails due to a temporary resource issue or network problem and simply needs to be restarted. `AUTORESTART` automatically *attempts* to restart any failed processes. To be sure you are not unknowingly overlooking any problems, you may prefer to have an Extract or Replicat process fail and then resolve the issue manually instead of using AUTORESTART.

Performance

This section covers some tips and tricks for making your GoldenGate setup achieve the best possible performance. Following these suggestions early in your project will help ensure that you don't experience performance issues down the road.

Running Performance Tests

You should always test the performance of your GoldenGate setup by running tests that execute or simulate the execution of your actual production-processing workload. This is the single best insurance against future problems. Ideally, the tests should be run on a system with hardware and software identical to the production system. In addition, you should use a copy of the actual production data or at least a realistic subset of the production data for testing against a typical production workload.

During the tests, you can capture statistics about GoldenGate performance and measure the lag to determine if the configuration can handle the load. You can also gather server, network, and database statistics and review them for potential performance problems.

You can examine the lag and determine if it's too high to meet the business requirements. For example, suppose that during testing you experience a peak lag of 15 minutes on a critical Replicat. Your business requirement says that any lag over ten minutes for this Replicat is a serious problem. In this case, additional tuning, hardware, or design changes are required to bring down the lag.

Limiting the Number of Extracts

You should try to extract as much data as possible with a single Local Extract. The Extract processes usually aren't a performance bottleneck because they're reading the data. Performance lag usually occurs in the Replicats that are processing changes, and not the Extracts. In addition, if the data needs to be filtered, use the data pump to create separate streams to send to the Replicat.

For example, let's assume you're extracting data from the CUSTOMER table and replicating to two different databases: one for reporting and the second for high availability. The CUSTOMER table should be extracted from the source database *only once*, and you can use two data pumps to filter and send the data to each of the different target databases.

Using Passthru Mode for Data Pumps

If the data pump is only passing the data on to the target system and not doing any filtering, use the data pump Extract PASSTHRU parameter. This causes the data pump to skip reading any data definitions from the database or a definitions file and improves performance. Keep in mind the tables being replicated need to be identical to use PASSTHRU.

Using Parallel Replicats

To improve performance, you can split the Replicats into parallel processing groups. Here are some considerations for splitting your Replicats:

- You shouldn't split tables involved in referential integrity into different Replicats.

- One approach is to use a different Replicat for each schema. If the schema is large, split it into multiple Replicats.

- High-volume tables can be split into their own Replicats. If further separation is needed, you can split these high-volume tables into separate Replicats based on a key range within the table using the GoldenGate RANGE function. For example, the Orders table can be split into two Replicats based on the ORDERID key column, as shown in the following example.

  ```
  -- In the first Replicat parameter file
  MAP SCHEMA_OWNER.ORDERS, TARGET SCHEMA_OWNER.ORDERS_AVAILABILITY, COLMAP
  (USEDEFAULTS), FILTER (@RANGE (1,2));

  -- In the second Replicat parameter file
  MAP SCHEMA_OWNER.ORDERS, TARGET SCHEMA_OWNER.ORDERS_AVAILABILITY, COLMAP
  (USEDEFAULTS), FILTER (@RANGE (2,2));
  ```

Using the Fastest Available Storage

Where performance is a concern, you should always use the fastest available storage for GoldenGate trail files. For best performance, store the trail files on dedicated disk in separate mount points. Trail files should be sized appropriately, based on the amount of data captured. Refer to Chapter 2, "Installation', for disk requirements and sizing formulas based on your transaction-log activity.

Tuning the Database

Often, GoldenGate performance issues aren't really caused by GoldenGate but instead by problems in the underlying DBMS. Before starting replication, you should make sure the performance of your database is adequate. Then, while your replication is running, execute DBMS performance-monitoring reports (such as AWR for Oracle) and verify that there are no outstanding performance issues. If possible, make sure your database tables have updated performance statistics and appropriate indexing on key columns used by GoldenGate.

Summary

You can use the following checklist of questions to verify that you're taking advantage of the tips and tricks presented in this chapter:

- Requirements and planning

    - Do you have a clear understanding of the business objectives, and have they been approved by your stakeholders?

    - Do you have a solid understanding of the requirements?

    - Did you determine the appropriate replication topology?

- Installation and setup

    - Did you create dedicated GoldenGate database and operating-system users?

    - Did you encrypt the passwords in the GoldenGate parameter files?

    - Did you create a dedicated GoldenGate installation directory?

    - Are you using a database checkpoint table?

    - Did you verify the source and target database character sets?

    - Are you following naming standards for your GoldenGate components?

    - Did you use a data pump?

- Management and monitoring

    - Have you learned the GGSCI command shortcuts?

    - Did you use OBEY files for your commands?

    - Are you generating interim reporting statistics for your Extracts and Replicats?

    - Are you using a discard file?

    - Are you reporting on the health of the Extracts and Replicats?

    - Are you purging the old trail files to keep the disk from filling up?

    - Do you have the Extracts and Replicats set up to start automatically?

- Performance
    - Did you run adequate performance tests?
    - Did you limit the number of local Extracts?
    - Are you using passthru mode for the data pumps?
    - Did you set up parallel Replicats if needed?
    - Did you use the fastest storage possible for your trail files?
    - Did you tune the underlying source and target databases?

You should review the checklist during your GoldenGate project. Let your answers guide you to implement best practices that you may be missing out on. Implementing those practices generally leads to an efficiently running GoldenGate environment.

Additional Technical Resources for the Oracle GoldenGate Administrator

Now that you have read the book, we hope that you now have a solid foundation in your quest to master Oracle GoldenGate. To aid you in your journeys, we have provided you with a list of technical resources and command tips to use as a reference guide as you work with the product. The appendix consists of the following three sections:

- The first section provides you with a list of references to consult for further reading and investigation of Oracle GoldenGate topics discussed in the book.

- The second section provides you with a list of commonly used Oracle GoldenGate commands with syntax and an example of how to use each.

- The third section contains a listing of useful Logdump commands and syntax to use for troubleshooting Oracle GoldenGate environments.

References for Further Reading

The Oracle GoldenGate documentation set encompasses thousands of pages of documentation. This section serves as a reference guide to the frequently used documents and support notes, to help you delve deeper into the content.

The following installation and configuration guides for Oracle GoldenGate are available online via the Oracle Technology Network (OTN) site located at `http://otn.oracle.com`:

Oracle GoldenGate SQL Server Installation and Setup Guide 11g Release 1 (11.1.1) August 2010

Oracle GoldenGate MySQL Installation and Setup Guide 11g Release 1 (11.1.1) October 2010

Oracle GoldenGate Teradata Installation and Setup Guide 11g Release 1 (11.1.1) October 2010

Oracle GoldenGate Sybase Installation and Setup Guide 11g Release 1 (11.1.1) September 2010

Oracle GoldenGate DB2 LUW Installation and Setup Guide 11g Release 1 (11.1.1) August 2010

Oracle GoldenGate Windows and UNIX Administrator's Guide 11g Release 1 (11.1.1) August 2010

Oracle GoldenGate Windows and UNIX Reference Guide 11g Release 1 (11.1.1) August 2010

Oracle GoldenGate Windows and UNIX Troubleshooting and Tuning Guide 11g Release 1 (11.1.1) August 2010

Oracle GoldenGate Oracle Installation and Setup Guide 11g Release 1 (11.1.1)

Oracle GoldenGate Director Administrator's Guide 11g Release 1 (11.1.1)

Oracle GoldenGate Veridata Administrator's Guide version 3.0Teradata Replication Services Using Oracle GoldenGate Release 13.0 August 2010, Teradata (`www.info.teradata.com/`).

In addition to the Oracle documentation, it's recommend that you review the following support notes for Oracle GoldenGate, available online with a valid Customer Support Identifier (CSI) account at `http://support.oracle.com`:

Note 1063374.1: "Why Do I See ERROR: Failed To Open Data Source"

Note 1290427.1: "GoldenGate 11 Doesn't Parse"

Note 966106.1: "Considerations for Choosing to Use a Datapump"

Note 965703.1: "My Checkpoint Table Is Corrupted"

The book also references the following articles, available online via the OTN site at `http://otn.oracle.com`:

"Zero-Downtime Database Upgrades Using Oracle GoldenGate," February 2010

"Oracle GoldenGate high availability using Oracle Clusterware," March 2010

The next section provides a quick guide at frequently used Oracle GoldenGate commands.

Quick Guide to Oracle GoldenGate Commands

For the beginner who's new to Oracle GoldenGate as well as the experienced practitioner, Oracle GoldenGate commands present a complex jungle to master. This section shows you the commonly used commands to aid you in your quest to perform tasks in Oracle GoldenGate. It will also serve as a reference if you need to look up the syntax for a command.

ADD

Syntax: `ADD EXTRACT|REPLICAT`

The **ADD** command performed in the GoldenGate Software Command Interface (GGSCI) is the method for adding new configurations to Oracle GoldenGate. You can use it to add new Extract, Replicat, or data-pump groups as well as to add local or remote trail files on the source or target system for an Oracle GoldenGate configuration.

Examples:

```
ADD EXTRACT extora, RMTHOST prod, MGRPORT 7800, RMTNAME prodfin
ADD REPLICAT repora, EXTTRAIL d:\ggs\dirdat\rt
```

GGSCI

GGSCI is the command to enter the command-line interface used to perform most administrative tasks for Oracle GoldenGate. In the simplest form, you open a shell prompt and type GGSCI from the Oracle GoldenGate base installation directory. You can also set the **path** variable for Windows or UNIX/Linux as a direct link or alias to simplify use of the GGSCI command.

Example:

```
C:\ggs\mssqlserver>ggsci

Oracle GoldenGate Command Interpreter for ODBC
Version 11.1.1.0.0 Build 078
Windows (optimized), Microsoft SQL Server on Jul 28 2010 18:55:52

Copyright (C) 1995, 2010, Oracle and/or its affiliates. All rights reserved.
```

HELP

The HELP command provides syntax assistance to look up the parameters and details for a specific Oracle GoldenGate command. In its most basic form, after logging into the GGSCI interface, type the HELP command from a GGSCI command shell prompt as shown in the following example:

```
GGSCI (oracledba) 1> help

GGSCI Command Summary:

Object:         Command:
SUBDIRS         CREATE
ER              INFO, KILL, LAG, SEND, STATUS, START, STATS, STOP
EXTRACT         ADD, ALTER, CLEANUP, DELETE, INFO, KILL,
                LAG, SEND, START, STATS, STATUS, STOP
EXTTRAIL        ADD, ALTER, DELETE, INFO
GGSEVT          VIEW
MANAGER         INFO, SEND, START, STOP, STATUS
MARKER          INFO
PARAMS          EDIT, VIEW
REPLICAT        ADD, ALTER, CLEANUP, DELETE, INFO, KILL, LAG, SEND,
                START, STATS, STATUS, STOP
REPORT          VIEW
RMTTRAIL        ADD, ALTER, DELETE, INFO
TRACETABLE      ADD, DELETE, INFO
```

```
TRANDATA        ADD, DELETE, INFO
CHECKPOINTTABLE ADD, DELETE, CLEANUP, INFO

Commands without an object:
(Database)      DBLOGIN, LIST TABLES, ENCRYPT PASSWORD
(DDL)           DUMPDDL
(Miscellaneous) FC, HELP, HISTORY, INFO ALL, OBEY, SET EDITOR, SHELL,
                SHOW, VERSIONS, ! (note: you must type the word
                COMMAND after the ! to display the ! help topic.)
                i.e.: GGSCI (sys1)> help ! command
For help on a specific command, type HELP <command> <object>.
```

    Example: HELP ADD REPLICAT
    In the following example, you need to find the syntax and description for the ADD EXTRACT command:

```
GGSCI (oracledba) 2> help add extract
```

```
ADD EXTRACT

Use ADD EXTRACT to create an Extract group. Unless a SOURCEISTABLE task
or an alias Extract is specified, ADD EXTRACT creates checkpoints so
that processing continuity is maintained from run to run. Review the
Oracle GoldenGate Windows and UNIX Administrator s Guide before
creating an Extract group.
```

INFO

The INFO command provides status information for the current Oracle GoldenGate configuration. Some examples follow.
    INFO ALL shows a complete overview of GoldenGate processing:

```
GGSCI (oracledba) 11> info all allprocesses
```

Program	Status	Group	Lag	Time Since Chkpt
MANAGER	RUNNING			
EXTRACT	STOPPED	EATAA	00:00:00	1435:43:49

```
GGSCI (oracledba) 12> info all
```

Program	Status	Group	Lag	Time Since Chkpt
MANAGER	RUNNING			
EXTRACT	STOPPED	EATAA	00:00:00	1435:43:52

INFO EXTRACT {extract process group name} displays a status report for Extracts, as shown in the following example:

```
GGSCI (oracledba) 15> info extract eataa
```

```
EXTRACT     EATAA      Initialized   2011-03-15 21:50    Status STOPPED
Checkpoint Lag         00:00:00 (updated 1435:45:44 ago)
Log Read Checkpoint    Oracle Redo Logs
                       2011-03-15 21:50:47  Seqno 0, RBA 0
```

You can also use the * wildcard to show all Extracts:

```
GGSCI (oracledba) 14> info extract *
```

```
EXTRACT     EATAA      Initialized   2011-03-15 21:50    Status STOPPED
Checkpoint Lag         00:00:00 (updated 1435:45:09 ago)
Log Read Checkpoint    Oracle Redo Logs
                       2011-03-15 21:50:47  Seqno 0, RBA 0
```

To view status and details for local and remote trail files, you can enter the INFO EXTTRAIL * command:

```
GGSCI (oracledba) 16> info exttrail *
```

```
        Extract Trail: AA
              Extract: EATAA
                Seqno: 0
                  RBA: 0
            File Size: 10M
```

SEND

The GGSCI command SEND is used to update the messaging facility to refresh the status-reporting utilities. In addition, you can use it to send processing directives to an Oracle GoldenGate process group—for example, to instruct an Extract or a Replicat to perform a specific task.

Example:

```
GGSCI (oracledba) 37> send mgr, getlag
```

STATUS

The STATUS command allows you to check the current status for process groups such as Replicat and Manager in the current Oracle GoldenGate environment.

Example:

```
GGSCI (oracledba) 40> status mgr
```

```
Manager is running (IP port oracledba.50001).
```

You can find a complete list of commands in the Reference Guide available online as part of the Oracle GoldenGate documentation.

Logdump Commands and Syntax for Troubleshooting

The Oracle GoldenGate Logdump utility is the Swiss Army knife of analysis and troubleshooting. You should understand and learn to use it, because it's a potent tool in your arsenal. By using Logdump, you can view data in transactions present for a trail file, identify missing transactions, and troubleshoot replication issues (such as duplicate and lost data transactions). Let's look at some common techniques and commands to use with Logdump.

Accessing the Logdump Utility

Logdump is an operating system utility that is accessed from outside the GGSCI interface. To start a new Logdump session, navigate to the Oracle GoldenGate base installation directory, and type the command logdump as shown here:

```
C:\ggs\mssqlserver>logdump

Oracle GoldenGate Log File Dump Utility
Version 11.1.1.0.0 Build 078

Copyright (C) 1995, 2010, Oracle and/or its affiliates. All rights reserved.

Logdump 8 >
```

By default, Logdump doesn't execute anything in and of itself. It opens a unique prompt session that waits for your commands to perform tasks.

Getting Help with Logdump Syntax

Logdump contains dozens of commands that present a challenge to new and even experienced Oracle GoldenGate administrators. To obtain help with its cryptic syntax, you can enter the help command as shown here:

```
Logdump 7 >help

FC [<num> | <string>]    - Edit previous command
HISTORY                  - List previous commands
OPEN | FROM  <filename>  - Open a Log file
RECORD | REC             - Display audit record
NEXT [ <count> ]         - Display next data record
SKIP [ <count> ] [FILTER] - Skip down <count> records
     FILTER              - Apply filter during skip
COUNT                    - Count the records in the file
     [START[time] <timestr>,]
     [END[time] <timestr>,]
     [INT[erval] <minutes>,]
     [LOG[trail] <wildcard-template>,]
     [FILE <wildcard-template>,]
     [DETAIL ]
      <timestr> format is
        [[yy]yy-mm-dd] [hh[:mm][:ss]]
```

```
POSITION [ <rba> | FIRST | LAST | EOF ] - Set position in file
         REVerse | FORward           - Set read direction
RECLEN [ <size> ]   - Sets max output length
EXIT | QUIT         - Exit the program
FILES | FI | DIR    - Display filenames
ENV                 - Show current settings
VOLUME | VOL | V    - Change default volume
DEBUG               - Enter the debugger
GHDR  ON | OFF      - Toggle GHDR display
DETAIL ON | OFF | DATA - Toggle detailed data display
RECLEN <nnn>          - Set data display length
SCANFORHEADER (SFH)  [PREV]  - Search for the start of a header
SCANFORTYPE   (SFT) - Find the next record of <TYPE>
      <typename> | <typenumber>
      [,<filename-template>]
SCANFORRBA    (SFR) - Find the next record with <SYSKEY>
      <syskey>                - syskey = -1 scans for next record
      ,<filename-template>
SCANFORTIME  (SFTS) - Find the next record with timestamp
      <date-time string>
      [,<filename-template>]
         <date-time string> format is
            [[yy]yy-mm-dd] [hh[:mm][:ss]]
SCANFORENDTRANS (SFET) - Find the end of the current transaction
SCANFORNEXTTRANS (SFNT) - Find start of the next transaction
SHOW <option>       - Display internal information
     [OPEN]         - list open files
     [TIME]         - print current time in various formats
     [ENV]          - show current environment
     [RECTYPE]      - show list of record types
     [FILTER]       - show active filter items
BIO  <option>       - Set LargeBlock I/O info
     [ON]           - Enable LargeBlock I/O (default)
     [OFF]          - Disable LargeBlock I/O
     [BLOCK <nnnn>]- Set LargeBlock I/O size
TIMEOFFSET <option> - Set the time offset from GMT
     [LOCAL]           - Use local time
     [GMT]             - Use GMT time
     [GMT +/- hh[:mm]] - Offset +/- from GMT
FILTER SHOW
FILTER ENABLE | ON   - Enable filtering
FILTER DISABLE | OFF - Disable filtering
FILTER CLEAR [ <filterid> | <ALL> ]
FILTER MATCH     ANY | ALL
FILTER [INClude | EXCLude] <filter options>
   <filter options> are
      RECTYPE  <type number | type name>
      STRING [BOTH] /<text>/ [<column range>]
      HEX      <hex string>  [<column range>]
      TRANSID  <TMF transaction identifier>
      FILENAME <filename template>
      PROCESS  <processname template>
```

```
        INT16    <16-bit integer>
        INT32    <32-bit integer>
        INT64    <64-bit integer>
        STARTTIME <date-time string>
        ENDTIME   <date-time string>
        SYSKEY   [<comparison>] <32/64-bit syskey>
        SYSKEYLEN [<comparison>] [<value>]
        TRANSIND [<comparison>] <nn>
        UNDOFLAG [<comparison>] <nn>
        RECLEN   [<comparison>] <nn>
        AUDITRBA [<comparison>] <nnnnnnnn>
        ANSINAME <ansi table name>
        GGSTOKEN <tokenname> [<comparison>] [<tokenvalue>]
        USERTOKEN <tokenname> [<comparison>] [<tokenvalue>]
        CSN | LogCSN [<comparison>] [<value>]
    <column range>
        <start column>:<end column>, ie  0:231
    <comparison>
        =, ==, !=, <>, <, >, <=, >=  EQ, GT, LE, GE, LE, NE
X <program> [string]  - Execute <program>
TRANSHIST nnnn          - Set size of transaction history
TRANSRECLIMIT nnnn      - Set low record count threshold
TRANSBYTELIMIT nnnn     - Set low byte count threshold
LOG {STOP} | { [TO] <filename> } - Write a session log
BEGIN <date-time>       - Set next read position using a timestamp
SAVEFILECOMMENT on | OFF  - Toggle comment records in a savefile
SAVE <savefilename> [!] <options>  - Write data to a savefile
    <options> are
    nnn RECORDS | nnn BYTES
    [NOCOMMENT]  - Suppress the Comment header/trailer recs, Default
    [COMMENT]    - Insert Comment header/trailer recs
    [OLDFORMAT]  - Force oldformat records
    [NEWFORMAT]  - Force newformat records
    [TRUNCATE ]  - purgedata an existing savefile
    [EXT ( <pri>, <sec> [,<max>])] - Savefile Extent sizes on NSK
    [MEGabytes <nnnn>]          - For extent size calculation
    [TRANSIND <nnn>]            - Set the transind field
    [COMMITTS <nnn>]            - Set the committs field
USERTOKEN       on | OFF | detail  - Show user token info
HEADERTOKEN     on | OFF | detail  - Show header token info
GGSTOKEN        on | OFF | detail  - Show GGS token info
FILEHEADER      on | OFF | detail  - Display file header contents
ASCIIHEADER     ON | off      - Toggle header charset
EBCDICHEADER    on | OFF      - Toggle header charset
ASCIIDATA       ON | on       - Toggle user data charset
EBCDICDATA      on | OFF      - Toggle user data charset
ASCIIDUMP       ON | off      - Toggle charset for hex/ascii display
EBCDICDUMP      on | OFF      - Toggle charset for hex/ascii display
TRAILFORMAT     old | new     - Force trail type
PRINTMXCOLUMNINFO  on | OFF   - Toggle SQL/MX columninfo display
```

```
TMFBEFOREIMAGE      on | OFF        - Toggle display of TMF before images
FLOAT  <value>                      - Interpret a floating point number
       [FORMAT <specifier>]         - sprintf format default %f

Logdump 8 >
```

HISTORY

The Logdump HISTORY command shows all recent activity performed in a Logdump session, as shown in the following example:

```
Logdump 8 >history
1> ghr on
2> help
3> open dirdata/aa
4> open aa
5> open c:\ggs_src\trails\aa
6> host
7> help
8> history
```

Opening GoldenGate Trail Files with Logdump

The most common use for Logdump in Oracle GoldenGate is to open trail files for analysis and troubleshooting. After starting a Logdump session, you need to issue the OPEN command as shown here, specifying the path name and trail file name:

```
Logdump 1>open ./dirdat/aa00001
Current LogTrail is /ggs/orasrc/dirdat/aa00001
```

After you open the trail file, you need to turn on some useful features to make full use of the Logdump utility. The first command is GHDR ON. It enables display of the record header for the transactions in the trail file for Oracle GoldenGate:

```
Logdump 2 >ghdr on
```

Next, you need to toggle the option for viewing the hex and ASCII values for trailfile data. To do so, execute the detail data command:

```
Logdump 3 >detail data
```

Now you can move to the next record in the trail file by using the next command in Logdump. When you issue the next command, Logdump moves forward one record:

```
Logdump 5>next
```

```
Hdr-Ind    :     E  (x45)     Partition  :     .  (x00)
UndoFlag   :     .  (x00)     BeforeAfter:     A  (x41)
RecLength  :     0  (x0000)   IO Time    : 2011/05/04 21:22:17.611.797
IOType     :   151  (x97)     OrigNode   :     0  (x00)
TransInd   :     .  (x03)     FormatType :     R  (x52)
SyskeyLen  :     0  (x00)     Incomplete :     .  (x00)
```

```
AuditRBA   :          0      AuditPos  : 0
Continued  :    N  (x00)     RecCount  :    0  (x00)

2010/08/04 21:22:17.611.797 RestartOK           Len       0 RBA 936
Name:
After  Image:                                   Partition 0   G  s
```

Here you can examine the before and after image of the transactions contained in the trail file as displayed by Logdump.

For additional details on using the Logdump utility with Oracle GoldenGate, consult the Oracle GoldenGate Troubleshooting Guide, which contains a list of all Logdump commands, syntax, and usage. It's available online at http://download.oracle.com/docs/cd/E15881_01/doc.104/ gg_troubleshooting_v104.pdf for release 10.x and at http://download.oracle.com/docs/cd/E18101_01/ doc.1111/e17792.pdf for release 11.1.

Index

▓ D

▓ G

H

I

■J

■K

■L

▓ P

▓S